My Ashes - Memoirs of a misbehaving woman

Jenna Avery

Copyright © 2017 by Jenna M. Avery
All rights reserved. This book or any portion thereof may not be reproduced or used in any manner whatsoever without the express written permission of the publisher except for the use of brief quotations in a book review.

Printed in the United States of America

First Printing, 2017

ISBN 0-9984862-0-5

www.Jennaaverys.life

Table of Contents

Prologue 1
A Letter to My Grandfather 3
A letter to my first crush 4
A letter to a younger self 5
A letter to my first internet weirdo 8
A Letter to my little brother 10
A letter to my first kiss 13
A letter to my father 16
A letter to my first teenage boyfriend 26
A letter to my second teenage boyfriend 31
A letter to a shitty human 34
A letter to my first narcissistic boyfriend 37
A letter to a lazy partner-in-crime 46
A letter to ex-husband #1 53
A letter to a best friend 61
A letter to a life changing person 67
A letter to a random hookup 72
A letter to a southern gentleman 74
A letter to ex-husband #2 78
A letter to a nerdy virgin 94
A letter to a man-child 109
Coo-Coo-Ca-Chu Part Two 126
A brief respite from the crazy men 135
A letter to my past addiction 136
A Letter to Ex-Husband #3 138
A continuation of the insanity saga 163
When will I learn my lesson: part three 186
Departing from it all: I finally learn my lesson, once and for all 194
A letter to a fellow traveler 208
A letter to a womanizer 211

A letter to the men that didn't choose me 223
A letter to a man that changed it up 225
A Letter to Present-Day Me 236
A letter to my future 238
Epilogue 242
Acknowledgements 244

PROLOGUE

You're going to read this novel. Occasionally, you might put down the book, look at the person beside you, and say, "What the fuck was this girl thinking?!"

I won't blame you. I've spent my entire life picking shitty men. My worth came from their approval, their demands, their opinions. It seldom mattered how hard I tried; I was rarely good enough for the men in my life. Since puberty, I've picked men that enforced this idea, sometimes without even realizing it.

As a woman, I feel as if I'm constantly being pulled in a thousand different directions: my sexuality is inappropriate, but if I don't put out, I'm a prude; I'm supposed to love myself, but fuck all if I can't fit into size-four jeans; my Prince Charming exists, but damn it, I better cling to my independence when I find him.

Society can be so goddamn confusing.

I beg of you, dear reader, to take my words with a grain of salt. I've been incredibly selfish throughout my life. For a long time, it was the only way I knew how to be to protect my heart. I've used men in the same ways they've used me—as pawns for my sexuality. I've treated significant others as if they were less than dirt. I've thrown hissy fits just so I can get my way.

I'm imperfect in the most perfect sense of the word.

The following letters were written to share a story—*mostly* not for revenge and certainly not for gossip—and to show others that it is possible to rise above of all the icky shit and transform into the person you were meant to be. It's my hope that these letters resonate with readers, if only a few. The journey of life can be lonely as hell and every kernel of support is helpful. I've changed certain details to protect the dick heads and the certifiably insane. In some instances, I've been forced to recreate some conversations to the best of my memory while also pulling emails and texts when possible. There are triggers ahead, so guard yourself well. Our abusers only gain power from our silence. Speak up. Speak out. You are not alone.

A Letter to My Grandfather

Dear Gampa,

Everyone tells me I'm loud and I am; I'm the loudest laugher I know. People come up to me and say, "I knew it was you because I heard you all the way over yonder." All right, they don't say "yonder," but you get the gist. Every time they say something to that effect, I smile and say, "My grandfather is a loud man. I get it from him." I say it with pride, knowing that there is *something* from my lineage that I am proud of. Your voice reminds me of wonderful things. My childhood was anything but a run through the park, but you were the fleeting sunshine one week every year

I remember lying in bed at the beach house in Avalon, falling asleep to your booming voice. It comforted me to hear you, to know that you were there right above my head talking with the family.

The same voice would sing Johnny Cash songs on long road trips through the East Coast. It took me over a decade to realize why "Sixteen Tons" resonated with me when I first heard it sung by Johnny. You introduced me to the classics without me even realizing it.

You were patient with me, even when my sass was exasperating. Gamma would lose her cool before you did, but when she was fed up, you would point your crooked pointer finger at me and loudly demand that I behave. I adored you; I almost usually sometimes listened.

The last time I saw you, I asked if you would mind making me pancakes like you used to. Mickey Mouse pancakes used to be all the rage with my cousins and I at the beach house. Your favorite story to tell was of one particular Sunday when I begged you to continue making pancakes, coming back for third and fourth servings. You knew I had to be doing something with them, as I couldn't possibly be eating them all. You laughed so hard when you found the tower I had created behind the TV. Because of this, pancakes are practically my spirit food. So when I asked you for pancakes on a slow Sunday morning, I was just silently asking for some untainted nostalgia from my childhood.

"I haven't made those in years," you said thoughtfully. I thought you might say no, but you seemed unable to deny your twenty-something granddaughter pancakes. We woke up early that Sunday, while Gamma slept in, and I watched you make pancakes. We sat in silence, munching on the gooey delicious breakfast, just chatting about this and that. It was such a special moment for me. I knew that you hadn't made them in years and probably wouldn't again. I appreciate that. I haven't had a lot of positive male role models, and while I don't see you often and we barely talk, please know that I love you.

I dread the day you're gone from this Earth. I feel like I've made so many mistakes, some of them being impatient with my own family. I'm grateful for your voice though, it's deep rumble filled with quiet patience—a baritone I'll never forget. I hope that once, just once, you'll be able to hold my children in your big, firm hands and sing them some Johnny Cash. And I hope they're loud like me. And like you.

A letter to my first crush

Dear Kindergarten Boyfriend,

I still have a single photo of you, so I know what a cutie you were. Toe-headed little cutie, a hint of a tan. We did a lot of arts and crafts together, pasting and gluing shit to pass the time—macaroni necklaces, finger paintings. Our parents thought our love was adorable, but they didn't know how *legit* it was.

You gave me my first peck on the cheek—at least that's what my mom says. I don't remember it. However, our two-year relationship was filled with the simplicity that only young, delusional love can bring. The majority of our time spent together was in class, passing notes and holding hands.

You taught me some things about myself, even at that tender age. In first grade, you wanted to hold hands with this brunette. She was pretty, *I guess*. I didn't want to give you up, so she and I spent most of second grade pretending to be okay with sharing a boyfriend. We both blew you kisses after recess, giggling at how cute you were.

You broke up with me at the start of third grade for a girl named Lauren. I have no idea how or why I remember her name. I even remember her long, curly blonde hair and how you would chase her in tag instead of me. My young instincts told me we were over, but when you noticed me watching, you sauntered over to break the news.

"I don't want to see you anymore, I want this bitch Lauren."

I'm paraphrasing, of course.

I have to admit, I'm over you now. I moved on and after a three-year hiatus, found a new boyfriend who brought me used teddy bears and stolen jewelry. I wish I could say I never again shared a man's affection with another woman, but that would be a lie. You were simply the beginning of my boy-crazy life.

Sincerely,

The kindergarten girlfriend you barely remember

A letter to a younger self

When I look back on my life, I spend time contemplating when it was I was at my most hurt, most afraid, most lost. One could argue it was when I was in rehab, and then jail, or broke, or enduring abusive boyfriends. Through it all I was a warrior—I had a raging inferno inside me that refused to quit.

Thirteen-year-old me, however, was lost, bullied almost daily, desperate to fit in. If ever a child needed a hug, it was her. This is thirty-year-old me taking a moment to write a letter to the social reject I used to be.

Dear Thirteen-Year-Old Me:

This is going to be the most awkward phase of your life. You're a weirdo, a social outcast with a penchant for reading four books a week. Almost sixteen years separate us now, but I assure you, you're only going to become more eclectic in your lifestyle. That obsession with horses will never die. And just wait until you get to Ecuador! You're going to be able to tell people all about the Titanic. So keep reading that intensive Titanic encyclopedia, because it's going to come in handy some day.

Admittedly, life has sucked for you . . . a lot. You're still flat chested, and those blasted baby hairs crowning your forehead look awful. But fret not, my ugly duckling: your knobby knees will transform into a pair of gams considered long, lean, and skinny in a way that makes those middle school bitches jealous.

And oh my, your crushes these days. Right now, it's a gorgeous kid in algebra. Turns out he's gay—just a heads-up. And yes, that means he is never going to choose you (by no fault of your own, I might add), so seriously, on to the next!

Look, kiddo (yes, I'm being condescending to myself), it's okay to be fucking weird. So go ahead and keep your hairy legs, fake stick-on earrings, and classical music collection.

But take out the butterfly hair clips—they're hideous.

And no, you don't need a Furby. Trust me.

I know you haven't had your first kiss yet. Try not to worry about it—it's going to be awful. Absolutely awful. I'm sorry. Don't worry—some men will make your fingers tingle and set your hair on fire with passion. It will come, just be patient. It gets better.

Your days are filled with stress brought on by your dad—our dad. Gosh, how many times this week alone has he screamed at you for your clothes being too revealing? You can't help it that your arms are octopus-long and that the school has a fucking stupid dress code regarding fingertip length. As a result, those stupid assholes you call friends will tell you your hair is greasy and sneer at your brand-less jeans. You'll come home crying at least twice a week, spending too long in front of the mirror wishing you were someone different. I promise, in a decade, you won't give a shit.

However, Ms. Metabolism will eventually catch up, so enjoy those frozen 3 Musketeers and Slim Jims. Ignorance is bliss.

Beware the cheerleaders. You joined just to feel popular, but you'll never quite fit in. You're only now discovering the depths of cruelty in cliques, and sleepovers will just make you feel more isolated so stop going to them. You're never going to connect with everyone, that's a promise. You're too authentic, too caring, too forgiving and more blunt than a hammer. You remind others of their shortcomings, their failings.

But you are worthy. It's going to take you decades to understand how worthy you are—of love, of friendship, of adventure. You're gonna find some of the best humans ever as you get older—people who will be your support, true cheerleaders to your success.

You're gonna be a badass, my little flat-chested drama queen.

This year, you're going to discover your love of horror novels and movies. Bentley Little is going to change your life. But don't watch The Blair Witch Project at night! You'll spend days being terrified of the dark.

Your fear of the dark will never go away, but by now I'm sure that terror is a subconscious manifestation of the abuse we endure at home almost every day. The dark is the evil that could appear without warning—like Dad's abuse, which would show up out of nowhere. Breathe easy, little bird. You'll journey to try and overcome deep scars that will never fully heal, but instead learn to wear them as badges of honor. Because that's what they are. You are not a victim; you're a survivor.

Never be ashamed of your empathy or your desire for love. Sometimes you'll feel an emptiness in your chest that you'll convince yourself can be filled by a man, when in fact a man created it. I'm not going to tell you to change your path, but I am going to tell you that one day you will find clarity. It will take going through three divorces before you're thirty, numerous other assholes, and several life altering experiences, but it will come.

You'll have regrets though, massive ones. Almost as large as what you'll feel after getting that ridiculous Superman tattoo when you're twenty. (On your stomach? Good lawd, what were we thinking?) But each regret will lead you to a new path, a redirection. You're sure as shit more careful about your tattoos now. Listen to your gut and you'll be fine.

I hurt for you. I mourn for you. You're going to feel like an outsider for the rest of you life, an observer of other people's lives. Just know it's okay to feel all the feelings. Revel in that pain, that hurt; it will fuel your success. You'll thirst for more.

Things will be okay. I honor your pain, your confusion, your tears. Just keep making your mixed tapes, little bird.

A letter to my first internet weirdo

I remember the first day my father installed the internet. I was fourteen, my fingers already itching to explore the online world. The first household edict was, "Do not stray from these pre-assigned websites <u>or else</u>!" Naturally, gurl.com quickly grew boring, my imagination drawn to the other corners of the interwebs.

The following letter describes my first chat room experience. Eventually, I became a chat room addict, "ASL" replacing "hello!" while "lol" gradually became mainstream. In fact, I just heard a teenager use it in replacement of an actual laugh. It made my head hurt.

Internet dating became a massive part of my life, with most of my relationships beginning on dating sites. This particular letter is for the guy who started it all.

Dear Creepy Internet Dude:

Let's be honest: you were probably a pedophile. Fourteen-year-old me had no way of knowing. I chose a random Texas-based chat room off the AOL list, excited to speak with strangers from around the world. Since it was around midnight, there were only four people in the room, typing out inane bullshit. It was 1999, the year of chat room popularity, a time when your experience wasn't yet inundated with "bots."

A/S/L?

You typed out my screen name beside the question, making sure I knew you were talking to me. I felt a thrill at the attention. A boy was talking to me! I thought about my response and decided to be older than the truth.

18/f/dallas. U?

22/m/dallas. What are you doing up so late?

n/m. Can't sleep.

I saw nothing wrong with our conversation, reveling in your attentions. You started talking about a dreamy date you wanted to take me on, suggesting we meet in person, which sounded so adventurous and exciting. You even sent me a rose emoticon, causing my skin to tingle with excitement. Someone actually wanted to pay attention to me!

That rose emoticon changed my life. After fourteen years of rejection from my father, you helped me realize that maybe a man would someday think I'm worthy. I felt butterflies swooping around in my stomach and my face broke out in a huge smile. I instantly began to plan our wedding, envisioning your good looks, big smile, kind eyes. What kind of kids would we have? Would you support my desire to become a marine biologist?

Then the worst thing in the world happened: the internet froze while we were talking about meeting IRL!

As it was close to midnight, and I wasn't supposed to be on the computer in the first place, my pleas with the computer gods were mere whispers. I frantically hit CTR-ALT-DEL. *Please, please let this work. This guy sent me a rose!* Tears sprang to my eyes as I restarted the blasted thing. Fifteen minutes later I was back in the chat room, hoping against hope that you were there waiting for me.

Please don't hate me! Where are you? I scanned the names, looking for my Prince Charming, king of dashing words and emoticons.

But you were gone. Poof! You probably found another prepubescent girl to give a flower emoticon to. The idea hurt my feelings, my thoughts filled with anguish. Would I ever find someone to love me? Would I be alone forever?

A Letter to my little brother

Dear Brother,

When Mom first told me that you were on the way, I poured over books of baby names, determined to give you the best that had ever existed.

"Jafar!" I joked, much to Mom's chagrin. I was on an *Aladdin* kick, due to only being eight years old, but I never wanted to name you after his sworn enemy. Not really.

I thumbed through the book, picking names like Josh, Trevor, etc.—normal boy names. That's when I came upon it, the name that lit a bulb in my tiny brain.

"HUNTER!"

I declared your new name with confidence, so positive our parents would agree. I mean, how could they not? I was devastated when they refused, choosing to instead name you after a different Disney character. I fought with them, insisting that you were a Hunter. Names give power, and I thought for sure Hunter would only boost yours. You would turn into a macho Tarzan, slaying deer and feeding your family.

Where that idea came from Lord only knows, since we never owned guns or went hunting.

After you were born, I gingerly held you, cooing over your soft, furry head. I declared my love for you instantly, secretly calling you Hunter for a good six months. I refused to call you by your given name, saying, "Is Hunter hungry?" or, "Mom, Hunter needs his diaper changed!" I took my job as older sister very seriously, giving into your chosen birth name, but sometimes, I still think you should have been born a Hunter.

You don't know this, but I feel like I've failed you. Since I'm the oldest and smartest and coolest sibling (just kidding, Sister!), I've always felt like I'm your protector. However, because of our eight-year age difference, I haven't really been there for you. The last time we lived together, I was a drug-addicted rage machine and left you terrified of me for years.

I tried to make it up to you whenever I visited Texas on vacation. One of the best days was when we went to Six Flags together, without anyone else. I bought both of us the fast pass, which let us ride as many rollercoasters as possible. You were so terrified at first, having never been on one, but by the end of the day you were on cloud nine, ready for more.

Remember when we went to that haunted house back in 2012? It was one of the longest haunted houses in the world, taking over an hour to get through. You literally guffawed with nervousness, letting me dig my claws into your forearm as I shrieked in terror. I think I almost peed myself when that one girl crept from below the bed, her paws reaching for flesh. I screamed myself hoarse. That was the most terrifying thing *ever*. Despite the knee-buckling fear, I'm grateful for that memory. I lived so far away for so long we made it a point to ensure all our time spent together was quality time.

I tried to be there for you, but how do you connect with someone so much younger? I've tried so hard to give you advice, but more often than not, it comes off as being condescending and you quickly lose patience with me.

I love you, little bro. You are such a kind and generous man, balancing your need to party with being an adult. Your passion for theatre is inspiring and I hope to be able to see you perform someday. For years Mom has been saying how good you are and I can't wait to finally see it for myself.

I hope that by moving away from Hawaii, you and I can have a better relationship. I'm excited to be spending holidays with the family for the first time in over a decade. When I saw you a few months ago, I thoroughly enjoyed sparring with you about politics and cultural sensitivity. You've gotten so damn smart! When the hell did that happen?

How did I miss all of this?

For the longest time, our family was incredibly broken, torn apart by Dad—or sperm donor, as I'm sure you prefer. You were caught in the crossfire, debris from a war that happened years prior. I don't know if you remember angrily blaming me for everything, but if you do, don't worry about it. I never held it against you. I just wish I could have been a better support system, rather than curling into myself, trying to find a haven of quiet.

So I feel a little inspired now to offer a little bit of sisterly advice, since I've been neglectful in that department. Take it all with a grain of salt—I've been divorced three times, you know.

1. Don't get married before you're thirty. Mom has probably tried to drill this into your head and the lady is right.
2. When a woman says things are "fine," buy her flowers. Or a puppy, if she screams the word.
3. All things come to an end. Even happiness. But don't worry—all things with an end also have a beginning.
4. No matter how much it hurts, revel in the pain. Feel it—all of it—because it's what is going to make you a better person down the road.
5. Money never has to hold you back. If you want to have something, stop eating out and buying movies. You'd be surprised what you can afford.
6. Do what makes you feel good. Just wrap it before you tap it.
7. Value experiences over things.

I hope you find a pretty girl to love you like you deserve. I want to be the one who photographs your wedding, your little babies, your growing family. Find yourself a girl that supports your acting, one who thinks you are the most talented man on Earth. I may have to slowly choke her if she doesn't appreciate you, so choose well or my prison sentence will be on your head.

You know I'm there for you, always. I don't know any better way to end this letter. A part of me is sad, thinking maybe this is too short. Some other men got pages and pages of words; however, this shows that you haven't hurt me. I love you, and the only way you've affected me is positively.

Here's to the upcoming holidays, the inevitable heated debates, the future laughs.

You're the best of them.

A letter to my first kiss

Dear First Frog,

How often are girls told that they have to kiss a few frogs in order to find their Prince Charming?

Did you have to take that so seriously?

You received the honor of breaking my tongue-dancing cherry merely because you were the first boy that tried. I seriously wish I'd waited until First Boyfriend though. 'Cause dude, you sucked.

It was in the backseat of my mom's Suburban, on the way home after school. She loved giving my friends rides, so it was an easy setup.

"Mom, First Frog needs a ride but his mom doesn't come home for a little bit. Can we let him tag along while we pick up Bro and Sis?"

In retrospect, my mom isn't an idiot and most likely knew what was going to happen. Thanks Mom. I dedicate this letter to you, probably to your own mortification.

You were smooth, First Frog. You started with a tickle fight, but we both knew what you were trying to do: get a feel for the pubescent wonderland that was my fourteen-year-old body. I was a late bloomer, and quite proud of the little boobies that had FINALLY arrived. Your quick fingers made their way around my ribs, poking here and there, eliciting screams of glee.

Somehow my head landed in your lap, peering up at you, excited at the prospect of my very own first kiss. All mine, no one else's. Certainly not yours, First Frog. You were older and more experienced, and known in school for being a bit of a "girlizer," you devil. I laid there in a semi-sleeping pose, my glossed lips puckered, ready to be swept away like Disney promised me.

Your face inched closer, your breath heavy with mint. You licked your lips, and when they touched mine, my mind began to race. THIS IS IT! THIS IS THE MOMENT. THIS IS WHEN . . . WAIT . . . WHAT THE FUCK?

WHAT THE FUCK ARE YOU DOING? IS YOUR TONGUE ON MY CHIN?

Good god. My heart stopped, my mind now scrambling for an escape plan. I tried to let my tongue dance around yours, but you refused, preferring to roam the real estate of my nose and chin. I mean have you seen James Bond suck the chin of his chosen flavor du jour? No. You haven't. Do you know why?

Because that's not how you fucking kiss.

I pushed up, trying to find a gentle way to reject your exploration of my pores. I gave a shy smile and scooted over the other side of the car, hoping that my terror didn't show. You looked away for a moment, talking about something boyish, and I wiped my chin and mouth with my sleeve. It came away damp.

You were undeterred, ready for a second round of tickling. I felt dread building, hoping you weren't planning another assault.

I was to be sorely disappointed.

The second time you kissed me was just as bad, only this time you left flecks of saliva coating my nose.

This time, I didn't wait so long, pushing you away almost instantly.

"Let's go find my mom."

I scrambled to exit the car, still trying to hide my discomfort as I wiped my face *again*. I sensed your concern, but how do you tell someone they're a bad kisser? I was only fourteen!

My mom seemed surprised when she saw us, but she didn't question it. We took you home and I immediately ghosted you. As in, we never spoke again. When I saw you in the hallways I avoided you, turning in the other direction.

Did you ever wonder what happened? Did anyone ever show you the light? Did you ever find a romantic spirit guide to show you the proper way to suck face? There is a mathematical ratio of tongue/lip work. While it isn't an exact science, I've since learned you're either a good kisser or you aren't. Some are born with the talent for kissing . . . others are meant to be the frogs girls have to kiss before they can find their prince. Or in my case, a lot of imposter princes.

A letter to my father

This chapter was incredibly hard to write. I remember sitting on a ratty couch in a hostel in South America, on a divorce vacation, trying not to let anyone see my tears. I paused repeatedly, struggling, some of these words at times too difficult to even consider baring to the world. I have daddy issues—deep ones, some of which will never heal. These issues have influenced a lot of my decisions in the last decade, hoping to find absolution, reasoning, and forgiveness. Some of us spend our whole lives demanding apologies from our parents. I've come to understand, you won't always receive one.

Dear Dad,

You know, you're the whole reason this book is even happening. This year—actually for the past two years—I vowed to enter my thirties clean and free of you. Considering the fact that you abused me in one shape or form for sixteen years, this is no easy feat. I haven't spoken to you in a year and the guilt, the unexplainable and confusing guilt, is finally easing. I used to feel bad when I didn't write you back, but now . . . I don't. I don't feel anything. I owe you abso-fucking-lutely nothing.

My very first memory is of you being an asshole. There was this little doll, Ariel from *The Little Mermaid*, which I really loved. You were in bed, in our small plastic home in New Jersey, and you snatched it out of my tiny hands. You taunted me with it, working me into a frothy three-year-old fervor as I begged for the toy. Instead of just teasing me and giving it back, you tossed it behind the bed where I couldn't get it.

Then there was the time the two of us built a snowman in the barely-there snowfall. Our snowman was probably the size of a small dog, but there's a photo of us, with you clutching me closely, grinning at the camera.

My third memory is of you in a moving truck, our old Dobermans Duchess and Argo snapping a jelly donut out of your hands as you laughed.

But my most prominent memory of you, the one that makes my palms sweat and head hurt, is the first time you raped me.

I was only seven. I had white-blonde hair and bangs that Mom never let me grow out. I was maybe thirty-five pounds soaking wet—always the scrawny kid, nicknamed "chicken legs" by everyone I met. Even at that age I was a handful, challenging any type of authority at every possible moment. I was diagnosed as having ADHD, but I believe much of my behavior was symptomatic of the abuse I endured at home. I was spanked regularly, usually five slamming hits on my bare behind, sometimes leaving bruises. Before you started raping me, you were already skilled at taunting me, abusing me, causing terror. Pouring water over my face repeatedly in the tub, pseudo water-boarding me at the age of six. Beating me black and blue over some random offense. I still struggle with triggers of having a pillow or blanket put over my face. If ever a significant other teases me by covering my face, I try to patiently explain that they can't do that. This is an improvement; I used to panic and scream before I learned to control my triggers.

Triggers. They're the *worst*. The memories of what you've done are sometimes easily avoided, like pushing away a plate of food that disgusts me. The triggers, however, are what sneak up like the boogeyman. More than twenty years later, I still have trouble processing everything, despite over a dozen therapists, years of drugs, and thousands of hours spent "fixing." Hell, even you and I have spent hours talking about this in person, but I'm realizing one does not simply ever overcome sexual abuse. Ever. We deal, we mourn, we rage. Sometimes we accept and adjust. But for me, if fate hadn't intervened, I would definitely be dead by now.

I was seven years old when you first raped me. While other little girls my age got new Barbies, Lisa Frank paraphernalia, or even puppies, I got my first lesson in life: when Mom's away, Dad wants to play.

Your favorite reasoning was that I had "poor personal hygiene," or as you liked to say, "you don't wipe enough, Jenna." It didn't even make sense, but as a seven-year-old, who am I to question my father? There was that other time when I had a high fever and woke up in the middle of the night to you already behind me, claiming you were just "taking my temperature." Whatever excuse you used the first time, it doesn't actually matter. It almost always started the same way:

You would call me to the bedroom. "Help me with something in here!" you'd holler from across the house. I was clueless the first time to the soon-to-be frequent pretense and did as asked.

"What do you need, Daddy?"

"Come over here to the bed and take your panties off."

"But why?"

"Just do as I ask."

You closed the door and hastily turned the lock, turning your sights back to me to ensure my underwear quickly removed. You instructed me to get on the bed, get on all fours, expose myself and place a towel over my head. Yes, you refused to look at me, reinforcing the initial feeling that what we were doing was incredibly shameful. That first experience, and those that followed, left me feeling humiliated, my backside in agony, but thankfully the physical pain subsided after a few days, leaving only emotional wounds that would soon scar over.

I learned that screaming made it worse, even though it felt like I was being split in half. My sub-conscious took pity on what my body endured and helped me mentally separate myself from those awful moments. I can't describe what it took to survive this experience; I just hope I never need that kind of strength again.

This went on for years, my childhood punctuated with memories of intense fear. Every time my mother left to run errands or attend a meeting, you were there, waiting. Sometimes, we'd drive up to the house and you'd say, "Meet me in the bedroom, Jenna." Dread isn't a strong enough word for how I felt in those moments. It was as if a squirrel lived in my belly and was trying to claw its way out. I tried to come up with excuses—chores that needed my immediate attention—but you were rarely distracted from your urges. The earliest parts of my life were spent in terror.

I still mourn the loss of my childhood, wiped out because of your sick desire to satisfy your own needs and pander to your demons. I champion the brave girl who sat across you in a courtroom. My diaries were the documented evidence needed to convict you. You're serving twenty years for each documented account of "aggravated abuse of a minor," culminating in what was a hundred year sentence and you will spend the rest of your life there far away from me. You're destined to die in prison and to be honest, I don't care; I too am serving a lifetime sentence of triggers and memories, so it's only fair.

Your public persona was a cliché right out of a Lifetime movie. You had everyone fooled, playing the role of a good man and doting father, spirited entrepreneur with your own home improvement company, and a steadfast Christian. You went to soccer games and school plays, always ready to help me with my science projects. And your ruse worked. Who would've known that you beat your children and raped your eldest daughter almost as often as you attended church?

Because of you, my idea of what love is has been completely fucked. I mean *completely*. I spent the majority of my twenties trying to prove to you my worth, and to so many men, my inherent worth.

I've punished myself because I feel like I should have stopped you. That moment when I was twelve, crying underneath you once more, you paused and asked me if I wanted you to stop. You could've been asking if I wanted ice cream for dessert, for all your nonchalance. *I was allowed to ask you to stop?* This had been an option? I punished myself for most of my adulthood because I thought I deserved to be miserable. I've picked men who could never really love me like I deserved to be loved because I didn't believe I deserved it. Why would I? You criticized me, my looks, my kindness, my energy, my fierceness, always.

My fierceness is the reason I'm here. It's why I'm alive.

The few times I tried to reach out to other adults, to ask for help, I was ignored. My obvious bruises were met with averted eyes, whispers. I will *never* be that person who ignores another's pain because I don't want to be uncomfortable.

Did you know that I tried to kill myself when I was seventeen? My mother had already forced me into rehab once, but I fought against it the entire time. One night, after a particularly shitty day with a now ex-boyfriend, I swallowed all of my anti-depressants hoping I would just fucking die. What about life was worth living?

The pills didn't kill me—thank the gods. Instead I hallucinated through the night. When I was lucid enough to function, I crawled to my mother's room, woke her up around three in the morning, and cried into her chest, begging to go back to rehab. This wasn't me; I was a fighter deep down. It isn't in my nature to give up. For years, the terror of you is what had kept my inner demons in check. But when you left I began to crumple up, enough that the wind could have swept me away, into oblivion. I had to learn how to drive myself back to success.

Through the years, people have asked me why I never said anything. Honestly? For a time I thought I'd made it all up. When forced to endure close quarters with one's rapist, what must one do to survive? I didn't think my mother was strong enough to survive without you. I knew that if I told anyone things would only get harder. I can't say it was the best logic. You never threatened to kill anyone if I told. Maybe this is the root of my survivor's guilt. You spent years manipulating me before you ever began raping me, but it has taken me decades to arrive at this conclusion.

My life immediately after your arrest is fuzzy, my memories clouded from the constant sleep my body demanded. I passed junior year by the skin of my teeth, but by the time I entered senior year, my self-destructive phase was in full swing. Three months into the fall semester of 2003, I gave up on high school. I just withdrew, refusing to attend classes. It became even more stressful when I was called to the stand as a witness against you, since you consistently denied the abuse, calling me a liar. I had to sit on the witness stand, watch you sitting at the table across the room, and discuss everything that had happened. Luckily, my diaries did a lot of the heavy lifting, but taking the stand was the only way we could solidify a case against you.

It took months for the sentencing to come to fruition, but finally, the evening before your fate was decided, you called me on the phone, begging for just a moment of my time to explain yourself. It was late at night and raining outside. I sat in my boyfriend's truck, rain pelting the windows, as you pleaded for forgiveness.

"I'm so sorry, Jenna. I know it doesn't change anything, but I wish I could take it back. I'll plead guilty, for you. I'm so sorry."

It's possible you received a plea deal, though I can't imagine that being the case since you were sentenced to a hundred years. Nevertheless, that apology meant a lot to me, even if I didn't recognize it at the moment. To finally admit what you'd done, after denying it even when you were arrested, was a pretty big deal. Suddenly everything I'd been through was validated. It felt like a relief to know that the years of forced silence didn't have to continue any longer.

I'm not angry with you anymore; I'm just frustrated at the loss of my childhood. I sit and wonder sometimes what kind of person I might have been had I been blessed with a functional father. I doubt I would be three-times divorced. I never would have tolerated some of the treatment I've endured throughout the years from other men.

I imagine what it would have been like to graduate high school, to go to college, maybe even pledge a sorority. What if I'd had a father that cherished me, protected me, and helped to guide me toward the right spouse? Hell, I might even have been religious, or pursued my dream of being a marine biologist.

Do you remember that first time I came to see you in prison? You'd been in jail for almost ten years by then, adjusting to life inside fences and bars. I was so nervous, but I knew it would be a good experience for me. I was brought into a white room, with tables placed all over. It was an open-contact room, with vending machines, although I didn't know I could bring quarters. There was enough distance between tables to give an air of privacy, even though we were watched with scrutiny. We sat there talking for four hours, dancing around what I really wanted to ask but didn't have the guts to say. Mom had driven me three hours for this and I'd gone through all that frisking, so why the hell couldn't I just spit it out? I gathered my courage, the question boiling in my gut before clawing its way up my throat, demanding to be spit out.

"I have a question," I finally said.

"I promise, I'll never lie to you."

"Why did you do it?"

Tears threatened to spill down my cheeks as my lower lip quivered. I didn't want to cry in a room filled with convicts—men who probably ate tears as snackies.

Sadness rimmed your eyes. I'd like to think you were legitimately remorseful.

"I don't know. I tried to stop myself. You know, my father did it to me, and I think his father did it to him. I didn't want to, I just didn't know how to not do it. I wish I could take it back."

I left the prison that day feeling a little lighter, enough to begin the arduous journey of finally letting go and moving on. I didn't share with anyone what we spoke about, carefully placing the memory into a little cubby within my brain.

I wrote you two to three letters a year, sometimes sending you books and pictures. A part of me couldn't separate my dad from the man who destroyed my ability to truly trust another human being. However, as the years passed, I began to resent the guilt I felt when I took longer than a couple months to write you back. Sometimes you'd write and say things like, "Haven't heard back in a while, you okay?" or "Hope all is well. Love to hear from you!"

Then around 2012, I came to see you again. I showed up unannounced. Your face lit up with surprise when you saw me sitting in the same room as before, but at a different table this time. I came with a purpose though, and jumped right to it, intending to make the visit brief.

"Did you touch my brother or sister?"

You immediately leaned forward, furiously shaking your head. "No, never. I didn't touch anyone else, I swear!"

Once again, I felt despair at being singled out. "Then why me?!" The question tumbled out before I could stop it. I saw shame in your eyes, paired with an impulsive shrug. You knew that you didn't have a sufficient answer. I began tearing you apart.

"Do you have any idea what you've done to me? I trigger; I have nightmares. I stay with men I shouldn't. My boyfriend thinks my abuse is a *red flag*. What am I supposed to do about that?" By this point tears were pouring down my face and I was trying to hide them as people cast curious glances our way. I didn't want them to think you had the power to make me cry. You gently slid a hand forward, extending comfort as a peace offering. I stared at it with revulsion.

"Jenna," you began, "I don't know what to say. I'm sorry, so sorry, for what I did. I wish I could take it back."

"Then *why*!" I demanded, refraining from slamming down my fist, attempting to avoid a scene.

The rage that had settled into a swirling mass in my heart burned brighter, years of repression bubbling up to the surface. I wasn't going to leave until I felt better, suddenly realizing that fifteen minutes of absolution wasn't enough. I wasn't going to share any more of my life until I got the answers I deserved. I sat there silently, waiting expectantly.

"I . . ." You paused, glancing around the room. "I asked myself that for years, Jenna. I don't know why I started, and every time it happened I felt so guilty. It's why we went to church more and more. I asked for forgiveness in confession, and for a while it stopped. Do you remember how it stopped for a year or so?"

I nodded, wiping my nose angrily.

"I had tried so hard to stop. I knew I was hurting you but I couldn't make myself end it. I felt so ashamed when it started again. Then one day I asked why you were crying and you said it hurt. I vowed never to do it again."

I listened, processing the words. Everything rang as truth—the timeline was right. "Is that why you were so mean to me after?"

You nodded solemnly. "I had a really hard time processing what I did. I wanted to apologize to you then, to beg for forgiveness, but I didn't know how. You became an unruly teenager and it was easier to just be angry. I took my shame and turned it into hatred, taking it out on you."

"What about when I confronted you?" I asked, thinking of that dark night years earlier, when I threatened to tell. It happened, ironically, only about a month prior to my mother finding out. We'd been screaming over ridiculous things like my clothing, my attitude, etc. I had finally built up the courage to threaten to tell someone about what you'd done. I hadn't mentioned outright what I was referring to, but I could see the fear in your eyes. You point-blank told me no one would believe me, and my courage swiftly abandoned me.

You paused for a moment. "Oh yes, you scared the shit out of me that night. I knew my time was coming to an end."

I left that day feeling lighter. The following year was filled with massive growing pains. I always joke that 2013 was the epitome of a "train wreck" as I was busy processing everything, even subconsciously. I began to drink heavily, embarrassing myself thoroughly in the photography industry. Surprisingly, my promiscuous behavior from my early twenties came to a close but I still somehow got myself into debt, ruined friendships, and found myself phenomenally lost.

When I turned twenty-seven, I began to resent how I felt tied to you. I knew I wasn't truly dealing with everything I'd been through, though I was better off than some survivors. Every activity, goal, and response I made was tinged with the need to tell you, "You didn't break me." When I jumped out of a plane for the first time, when I traveled abroad, when I started my business, I somehow thought it would make me more worthy, for the father that had always rejected me. Why did I think I needed your approval? I can't even buy a milkshake with that. So why did it matter so much?

Once I realized this, I stopped cold turkey. Instead, I started asking myself, "Is this important to me? Why?" It was an arduous process, but eventually I stopped living my life for you. This isn't to say my life got better or worse, it just meant my choices were all my own.

I look at all that's happened to me and you are the root of everything. I'm ready and willing to change that though. I want to move forward with the rest of my life. I want my choices to not be influenced by insecurities about my worthiness. Because

I am worthy of love—I am worthy of a man better than you by tenfold. It may take me a long time, but eventually I will be severed from you and what you've done. I will raise children without fear in my heart and, if the gods are good, without extreme paranoia. I will love a man who'll treat me like I'm worthy, every single day.

I can't keep you in my life. Not if I want to learn what it means to be loved, what it means to live a life void of triggers and fears. It's impossible to erase what you did, and without these painful life experiences, this particular novel wouldn't exist. I will make these lemons into frothy, spiked lemonade. I will acknowledge the gifts received from the pain inflicted and move the fuck on. I am a phoenix.

A letter to my first teenage boyfriend

By the time I met my first boyfriend, I had become known for two things: horseback riding and reading books. I volunteered over twelve hours a week at an equine riding center, earning riding lessons for myself. I greeted the hard work with a smile; horses helped me deal with all of the abuse I'd kept hidden in my subconscious. When everything that happened with my father came to light, horses were my refuge, my saving grace. My first boyfriend was incredibly supportive of this, providing transportation to the different barns I eventually found myself working at. I could never really fully delve into the hardships of my fifteenth and sixteenth years of life, because that would require a book all its own. But my first boyfriend was there from the start, trying his best.

Dear First Boyfriend,

Rumor has it you're in prison now and this brings forth some sadness, as I remember the sweet boy you used to be, connected at such a young age by our brokenness, looking for refuge in one another. Since our relationship ended well over fifteen years ago, please forgive me if I muck up the details or maybe skip a few things because they're fuzzy. I just want to pay homage to you and how you affected the rest of my life, and then I want to put this to rest.

With being such a shy boy, it took a couple months for you to even ask me out. You were the brother of Rabbit, my best friend at the time, but always the older broody guy that would watch me shine but say nothing. When we finally decided to try this out, I was so nervous I thought I was going to pass out.

Our first date was Italian for dinner followed by a movie, the title long forgotten. This became our normal dating routine, sitting in a darkened theatre, with me holding my hand out, palm up, hoping you would finally take it, which you did after a month, your fingers shaky and sweaty. Our first kiss happened after almost two months of dating, on the way back from yet another movie. You stopped the car a block away from my home and leaned over. Your lips were full, soft, and gentle, and an explosion consumed my brain. Somehow fifteen minutes passed in a second. I stumbled out of your truck, my knees weak, twenty minutes past curfew. I walked in the house, on cloud nine, hoping that my father's anger at me being late wouldn't ruin my buzz.

Soon after our first kiss, we started staying up past our bedtimes so you could sneak over and hang out with me outside of my window. We'd press ourselves against the hard wooden frame, ignoring the pain so we could use our mouths and hands to explore. Weeks passed and my parents didn't suspect anything, so you slowly made your way into my room, first by the window and eventually into my bed. By the time we'd been dating for four months, you would sleep in my twin-sized bed until early morning, holding me tight. Twice my mother walked in to check on me and thank the heavens she never saw you through the draping above my bed, which I'd insisted on years earlier. I think both our hearts froze when she walked in. Could you imagine if it had been my dad that walked in? We'd both be dead, I think.

On dates, we were unable to keep our hands to ourselves, like the wanton virgin teenagers we were. Everything was new and exciting; neither of us could do wrong. We once spent four hours in a parking garage, nonstop kissing and canoodling. I think we both had raw lips for days after, but the teenage memory still makes me smile. Adults don't make out—not like teenagers, not like virgins. It's a lost art, for sure.

I ponder sometimes what would have happened to us if my father hadn't been arrested. His arrest transformed me, his absence finally allowing me to release years of pent-up rage. I went down a self-destructive path that you gleefully followed me down due to your own thin line of self-hate. My mother, dealing with her own grief and confusion, lost control of me, barely noticing when I stayed at your house for days. Since Rabbit was my best friend at the time, I pretended to spend the night with her instead of you. The band of us, her and another friend included, we were a bunch of hoodlums, playing *Dance*

Dance Revolution like it was going out of style and terrorizing poor people as we drove around.

Do you remember what a damn control freak I was when I decided I wanted to lose my virginity? God . . . I planned some bed-and-breakfast for us, remember? I wanted everything to be perfect, because that's what society says losing our virginity should be. I even had a checklist:

√ soft sexy nightgown from Walmart

√ condoms for my pleasure

√ lube (what was this for?)

√ sex position list (a minimum of five)

√ candles (vanilla scented, duh)

√ music

√ overnight bag

√ snacks (for energy)

√ water (to stay hydrated of course)

Intensity was my middle name. I began obsessively researching sex, pouring over my *Cosmo* like it was the Bible. I was determined to be good at sex, even though I was a virgin. I swear some of this neurosis has disappeared over the years . . . I think. Maybe.

Finally, after nine months together, we decided after a half-naked make-out session to do the deed. It was random, impulsive and still somehow perfect in the grand scheme of virginity-losing. I use the word "perfect" rather loosely though. The mattress was on the floor for whatever reason, the room sweltering, smelling of rat cages. Sublime's "Jailhouse" played in the background. Rabbit was next door, somehow already knowing what we were doing. I decided I didn't care about all the fancy ideas I'd planned; I just wanted to get this whole virginity thing over with. As any teenage boy would, you just simply asked, "Are you sure?" while simultaneously rolling on the condom.

It was brief, virgin boys rarely known for their staying power, but I'll never forget how you stopped to look at me after it was done. Your eyes were big, filled with surprise, as you said, "I love you." I loved you very much then, as much as a damaged sixteen-year-old can love another human.

I really did enjoy your company. I learned about all sorts of nerdy things, getting my introduction to both computer programming and cars. We would fall asleep wrapped up in one another's limbs, holding each other as we cried over the hurts our families inflicted on us. The pain of my own family falling apart helped me slip into a deep depression. My senior year was fucked from the beginning for various reasons and I just *gave up*. You would drive me to the school parking lot and let me sleep in the back of your car for hours. I couldn't deal with school or even real life; reality was too painful once my father's trial began. Everyone made it about himself or herself, claiming they could have been my saviors if I had *just said something* . . . You never guilted me though, never twisted the situation to focus on yourself. You gave and gave to me, but I couldn't do the same. I just took and took and . . . I'm sorry for that. I didn't have the capacity to really love or empathize with any situation at that point in time.

My selfishness was reaching a peak, especially after my father was convicted and given a lifetime sentence. I became a disgusting martyr, convinced the world owed me a *lot* of shit. You were trying so hard and were met with my rejection and continued disdain. We began to fight and scream at one another over petty things. I turned to soft drugs, which became an escape, creating a bubble of apathy for anything else. We became angry friends more than lovers, the relationship dwindling into a mockery of what it had been.

Our breakup is incredibly fuzzy. I know our relationship diminished into something phenomenally unhealthy. Prior to ending things, we had a nasty fight over our mutually owned parakeet. We were sitting on the ground by the cage and I had irrationally come to the conclusion you were going to hurt the bird as you reached for it. I slapped you, hard, on the face. We both sat there, wide-eyed and shocked. You responded swiftly by standing up and violently trying to crush my sternum with your foot. You attempted to plow into my chest with all of your weight, breath escaping from my lungs in a loud *whoosh*. I screamed and clawed at your torso as you picked me up and threw me against a wall, infuriated and frustrated with our situation. You opened the bedroom door and threw me against the hallway wall, right in front of your mother, who was vacuuming. She stared at me, apathetic and continued cleaning.

I do accept some of the blame for how violent and cruel we had become. The boy who months earlier had loved me was trapped with a girl who was incapable of managing any kind of extreme emotions. Everything was a trigger for my rage, which would pop up in any situation. That happy, soft girl you fell in love with smacked you because it felt good to hurt others.

We broke up soon after the beating. I dove right into dating again, trying to mask my pain and fill the empty void that had sat in my chest since I was a child. We didn't see one another for years after that. During that time, you became addicted to meth and were unable to keep a job.

The last time I saw you, you were a recovering addict, your eyes huge and twitchy. Your soft, thin brown hair hadn't been washed, the anxiety palpable in your fidgety limbs. You were kind and bought me dinner, but the sight of what you'd become left me feeling so sad. Those soft and tender teenagers who once shook with excitement at the thought of holding hands . . . they were gone. Your behavior left me feeling alarmed and bewildered. I also pitied you a little, because despite similar childhoods, you weren't able to pull yourself out of the trenches. Our childhoods were gone, but the ghosts remained.

So, First Boyfriend, know that I think of you fondly. I honestly wouldn't take any of it back . . . though I wish I could've stopped you from trying drugs. I won't be surprised if I find out you've died sometime in the next five years. But I'll hold a torch for the young boy you were.

A letter to my second teenage boyfriend

*I had never been taught sexual boundaries, mainly because when you're raised Catholic, you're just told to "save yourself," not learn the general importance of consent. My own father had gifted me a "True Love Waits" necklace, making me vow to save myself for marriage, when I didn't even understand what any of it meant. I wish I'd been taught that it's okay to say no to men—like **really** taught. Society had raised me to believe that all boys want sex, and that to be loved I had to put out. At sixteen years of age, how was I to know society's expectations were based on lies? Even before my father was kicked out, I had never had a proper father figure, one to teach me how I should be treated. After he was put into prison, my mother tried to keep her sanity and care for my siblings as well. I had become a violent, aggressive handful better handled with a ten-foot pole. I took advantage of this free reign and got myself into trouble a lot.*

Dear Mr. Coke Can,

Sometimes I'll catch a whiff of your scent, usually from a stranger walking by. It's bizarre, since I don't recall how most of my exes smell. Somehow, the memory of yours still lingers in my olfactory.

The smell is unique, reminding me of a mix between sweet musk and weed, with a hint of leather. You had this black leather jacket that you always wore, wrapping it around me the first night we met. That was my very first concert ever, at some grungy bar where a band called Mindless Self Indulgence was playing. I met you and your friend at a bar, with Rabbit and her flavor-of-the-week in tow. I was only sixteen at the time, and though you were only fifteen, I thought you were the bee's knees.

We snuggled in the bed of a pickup on our way back from the concert, fighting the chilly air, probably talking about teenage things like weed, music, and school. Suddenly you kissed me, and while I didn't feel a flare of anything in my gut I let you continue kissing me. We made a game of it, kissing every time we went under a bridge. I breathed in your smell, basking in the maleness of it.

We decided almost immediately to start dating, even though you told me you weren't over your ex yet. Who cared? I was just beginning to start my journey dating unavailable men and you were more than happy to fill the role.

You invited me over to your house, nonchalantly informing me that your parents wouldn't be home for hours. Kind of like Netflix and chill . . . only before the invention of Netflix. When I arrived, you led me to the garage, which was filled to the brim with boxes of shit. In among the chaos was a lone, ratty couch, a hideous tan-plaid pattern with holes in the seats.

We cuddled up under a blanket talking about movies, weed, and school. We started kissing again and something inside me shifted. I can't really explain it, but suddenly I felt like we were supposed to have sex. It just felt expected, despite zero pressure from you.

I was sixteen and no one had ever taught me boundaries. Why don't we teach our children boundaries anymore? We either throw condoms at them or tell them to wait for marriage, but so often children are not told it's okay to wait even after you've lost your virginity. Adults are expected to wait only three dates, which is also silly. Why the hell is penetration expected after maybe just fifteen hours of knowing someone?

I remember pulling back from you then and offering to have sex. You were shocked. Hell, I surprised myself. Being a teenage boy, you didn't turn me down and eagerly yanked down your pants. You pulled out a condom from your wallet, excited at the prospect of unexpected sex. I laid back on that ratty couch, trying to get in the mood.

Perhaps not being in the mood is what made it this way, but sex with you was excruciating. You were phenomenally well endowed, earning your nickname and then some. I grit my teeth through the experience for a solid five minutes before tapping out. I made promises to try again in a couple days, forcing you to cuddle with me in that cold garage, trying to stave off my doubt and insecurities.

Imagine the shock and surprise when you suddenly dumped me, six days after we had sex. "I'm getting back with my ex," you said, flippant with your words, not caring how I felt. I suddenly felt an understanding: sex with boys did not mean you earned their loyalty. I was strangely willing to compromise my self-worth to have sex with someone, anyone. To feel wanted, needed, desired. I just had to come to terms that it meant a loss of something inside me.

Before never speaking again, I went over to your house one more time and had my first experience with marijuana. I'd tried to use the opportunity to convince you to get back with me, but while that failed, I found a new best friend in "the Pot." I loved the relief marijuana brought, clearing my mind of anything, especially thoughts. I felt free from all of my burdens, hooking me on the sweet, mindless embrace. The same reason I loved pot as a teenager is the reason I still occasionally imbibe as an adult. Who doesn't love getting high and watching mindless TV while binging on chips.

A letter to a shitty human

I know I keep saying it, but the first year after my father was removed from the household, I went off the deep end of dating. I suddenly didn't have someone to fear, someone to drive the hammer when it came to rules. I did whatever I wanted, whenever I wanted, which led to some nasty decisions. I met a lot of guys from online, some of them I vaguely remember. Most of them I never even kissed, some barely making it through a whole date before I grew bored. Most I don't even recall enough to write a paragraph about. The vast majority didn't have an impact on me—except Guilter. He epitomized, then as now, what's wrong with a society that teaches young boys to expect sex in return for being nice to a girl. This boy unfortunately taught me to fear rejection from men, making me an eager plaything for future relationships.

Dear Guilter,

I remember your practiced words, your promises of a good time. You drove a red Cadillac, picking me up at my home, passing me a bag of donuts as I got in in the passenger seat. I saw it as a sweet gesture; you most likely saw it as a down payment. I greedily gobbled up the sweet morsels while chatting about things all seventeen year olds chat about. My first thought—after "damn, this is a good donut"—was how you definitely didn't look the way you'd described yourself online. You were at least a hundred pounds more than you said you were.

I had already become a "seasoned veteran" to online dating, and was a staple in Dallas dating chat rooms. I searched for that elusive spark that would lead me to my "soul mate." By the time we began to talk in earnest, your name had popped up multiple times among my new online friends. This was back in 2003, when prolific internet use wasn't a thing yet. Looks, age, and personality were easy as hell things to fake. People were catfishing before the term was even coined. I was all about the risk and honestly didn't give two fucks. Back then I even reasoned, "I've been raped before, it's okay if it happens again."

Yeah, I was a hot mess.

Which you probably preferred.

We arrived at a house where you rented a room from your parents. I shyly smiled at your dad before we headed to your room. He didn't seem too impressed, resting on his throne-like La-Z-Boy. I mentally shrugged and walked to your bedroom, where the TV was already on, your full-sized bed shoved into a corner.

Without delay, you activated your half-hearted seduction, starting by pulling down my pants and attempting to elicit interest with your tongue. "You taste like strawberries," you murmured from down there, making me wonder what the hell you were smoking—and could I have some?

You were fumbling for a condom within the amount of time it takes to warm up a microwave meal. You slid it on, eager to get to your own end. However, within a minute of penetration, I triggered.

See, I hadn't yet started the years of therapy I had coming to me. Anything could set me off—a shirt, a smell, even a yoga pose. My only reasonable response was panic. I began to hyperventilate as I shoved you away from me, all of your bulky weight heaving off in protest. I slid back to the edge of the bed, trapped in my own mind, flashbacks hammering my psyche in waves. I tried so hard not to cry but couldn't help myself. Tears poured down my face, humiliation burning my cheeks. I wasn't able to speak coherently but you didn't ask too many questions.

Instead of comforting me, you became belligerent and angry, especially when I made it clear that we were definitely not picking up where we left off. You muttered insults at me, telling me what a tease I was, how it was unfair for me to start something and not finish it.

Your words stung but I held my ground, asking to be taken back home. That turned into one of the most awkward drives of my life. The whole way you muttered about how selfish I was, saying I wouldn't get anywhere in life with that kind of behavior. I felt almost as if I should have let you bend me over in the car, just to get you to calm down. Your anger trapped me, setting the tone in my life for a long while.

I went home and took a long, hot shower, anxious to scrub your words from my soul. Is this the reaction I could expect every time I freaked out? Should I never deny another man? We never spoke again but I struggled for years to set boundaries for other men, fearful of their anger.

In other words, you're a fucking dick, you entitled piece of crap.

A letter to my first narcissistic boyfriend

The following letter is to a boy who found me when I was completely shattered. I was no longer riding horses; I had quit school, was using drugs, popping pills and looking for a new father figure. In a nutshell, I had lost myself. Right before I met Hockey Freak, I had spent a day in jail for refusing to attend school. Texas has a law where kids are fined for truancy, but at the time the fine was two hundred dollars and my mother refused to pay it, letting it turn into a warrant. When we attended court for my second truancy offence, they saw I hadn't paid for the first fine and sent me to jail. This is an incredibly sore point, to this day, between my mother and I. We don't speak about anything that happened before 2005. It just leads to arguments.

I ended up only spending a day in jail, despite owing about twenty days worth of time, because I faked being sick. The officers must have taken pity of the teenager "vomiting" in the toilet and called the EMTs to let me go. They said, right before I was released, "Don't forget to pay your fine. You have ten days to take care of it." But I didn't have a job. I moved on with the train wreck that was my life and forgot about it all.

I haven't spoke to Hockey Freak since 2005 and have zero desire to reconnect. Rumor has it that he's in Austin, but I doubt he'd recognize my face.

Dear Hockey Freak,

It was lust at first sight. We met on the website Hot or Not—the original Tinder. One of the only photos I shared was a grainy cell phone selfie in a bikini—the last time I ever had a flat stomach, thanks to my teenage metabolism. I was some hot little seventeen-year-old, desperate and filled with daddy issues. My father had only just been sentenced to prison. I'd recently dropped out of school and my all around self-inflicted abuse was just beginning to ramp up.

I remember your thick dark hair, your tall, loping swagger, the slightly misaligned teeth that gave you a charming, boyish grin. Our first date was a movie, followed by sex in the bucket seats of your gray pickup. You didn't even kiss me, but I found worth in my soreness and the way you wanted me. Now, at thirty, I cringe at the idea of car sex. Everyone just walks away with bruises and injuries. At seventeen I saw those as "battle wounds."

I've re-read my LiveJournal a few times in recent months and I want to hug seventeen-year-old me. I just really wanted and needed love, confusing your abusive attentions for the real thing. We'd get high everywhere, have sex anywhere, and I even thought I loved you. Can we just take a moment to chuckle?

You knew I just needed to be loved and used it to your advantage. I wanted nothing more than to please you, and was incapable of setting sexual boundaries. On one particular day, after dating for a month or so, we were in your bedroom, about to have sex. You gave me a sly grin and suggested we do something different this time. When I asked what you had in mind, terrified you were going to suggest anal, your response of, "Let's take pictures of us doing it," seemed easy enough. I was uncomfortable with the idea but didn't want to upset you by refusing, so I agreed, letting you take photos of us as you pumped away in different positions. You promised to keep the photos safe and hidden, swearing that you'd be the only one to ever look at them.

You met me at such a rough time of my life. I had no direction. I had anger and repressed issues large enough that they made Everest look like a hill. The tension between my remaining family and I had begun to mount, with my aggression terrifying everyone involved. I would blow up at the smallest things, like not having control of the remote control to watch Xena or MTV music videos. I threw fit if people were too loud in the morning, or if my sister borrowed my shirt, again, without asking. One particular instance, when I hadn't showered in four days and had threatened to kill myself multiple times, I started raging around my house, intimidating all of my family members.

It was around eight in the morning and, locking herself in the bathroom, my mother called the cops. I had just physically attacked her and she was terrified of further escalation. They showed up, already familiar with our household, but I'd calmed down, greeting them with a smile when they knocked on the door.

My mother, terrified not only of me but that I might just kill myself that night, informed them of my warrant. The cop asked me if it was true and I nodded in the affirmative. That was one of the most humiliating moments of my life, being driven to jail in the back of a cop car. I sobbed on the way to the jail and the officer stared at me in the rearview mirror, looking sad.

"Sorry, kid. We don't get to pick who our parents are."

My mother and I argue this point. I could have sworn I was left in jail for four days—she argues only two—but to her credit, she came to see me twenty-four hours into that time and had an officer ask me if I was ready to live under the rules of her house.

I basically told her to go fuck herself.

I quickly regretted that decision, finding the confines of jail suffocating. Being in jail drove me up the wall, with freezing temperatures, a single blanket, and lights that never turned off. I must have called you every chance I got, during the three times we were allowed out of our cells each day. Your mother thought I was insane. I can't blame her. What mother would be thrilled to hear "This is a collect call from the Carrollton City Jail with a call for Hockey Freak. Do you accept these charges?" The first couple days of conversation were filled with anger and dismay towards my mother, but it quickly unraveled into edginess. After much begging on my part, you resigned yourself to visiting me in jail. You came to visit me on the third day, trying to hide your shock at my appearance: my hair was unwashed and stringy, my eyes were bruised from not sleeping, my fingers twitched with anxiety. I'd spent hours pacing my cell, singing to myself, even doing push ups to stave off the monotony. I felt like a caged lion, ready to snap at her handler.

There was nothing you could do. I saw the aversion in your face as you left the visiting box. When my mother's boyfriend finally bailed me out, we met up that night and screwed in your car. Even four days in jail couldn't slow down my ruinous behavior.

After begging and pleading from my mother, as well as stern encouragement from you, I resigned myself to taking the GED. I didn't study for any of it and instead just walked in, filled it out, and left. I ended up scoring in the top percentile for the state for in reading and writing, and average scores for math. This single act set me up for plenty of success later in life, but at the time, I resented the interruption of my daily TV binge watching.

I think all we ever did was smoke pot and engage in unfulfilling coitus. We were normal teenagers, so I don't really apologize for it; however, I don't think you quite understood the responsibility you had to me. You didn't have a solid father figure in your life teaching you how to respect women, which became apparent in the months that followed. In one specific instance, when I told you for the third time that evening that I wasn't in the mood to have sex, you kept cajoling me, knowing full well I didn't know how to say no.

It was in the cab of your stupid truck, on the side of the road, where there were no streetlights to shine down on us. I cried silently, cringing in pain while you did whatever you wanted on top of me. I don't think you even noticed my tears, though I didn't exactly make an effort to hide them. I was relieved when it was over, gingerly sitting up, trying not to put any weight on my hips.

Things began to go downhill from there.

You showed up one day at my house, slightly distracted and sad. I anxiously greeted you and brought you back to my bedroom, motioning for you to sit on the bed. "What's wrong, baby?" I asked, trying to crawl into your lap, hoping some physical affection would cheer you up.

"Jenna, we need to break up."

My eyes bugged out of my head, recoiling as if I had just been slapped.

"Br-br-break up?" my lip quivered, threatening tears. "What do you mean break up?"

You sighed and shifted away from me. "I've met someone."

Someone had dared to cheat on me? How was this possible?

"Who is she?" I demanded, almost screaming the words. You didn't even flinch, clearly expecting a volatile response.

"Her name is Jesus Freak, I met her on LiveJournal. She is my age, has a car, goes to church, and I think I'm in love with her."

"LOVE? YOU'RE IN LOVE? BUT I THOUGHT YOU LOVED ME?!" At this point, my voice became a shriek.

"Jenna, I'm sorry but I just can't. I have to go now."

All I know is that I refused to let it happen, even when you admitted to cheating on me, saying you wanted to be in a relationship with the other girl. She was a better version of me, or so I thought. A soft-spoken red headed bible thumper, she was even more dedicated to you than I was.

After only two weeks, you called and told me you missed me, but still couldn't break it off with Jesus Freak. "She'll kill herself if I leave," you said, regret plain in your voice. I felt so bad for you, a good man trapped by an insecure girl!

"Don't worry, it's okay. We can keep seeing one another." I said, wanting to be the hero of the situation.

While I juggled this love triangle, I was also enrolled in group art therapy that specialized in helping abused children to recover from sexual abuse. It had become a safe haven, every Wednesday filled with paints, canvas I could destroy, and the occasional pizza. I divulged to the group all of the details of our relationship, swearing you planned to leave Jesus Freak when it was safe to do so. When you promised that you had finally broken it off a few weeks later, I went to Wednesday therapy, elated, so sure that I had become worthy of the love of this boy. My therapist must have laughed internally, but instead tried to build me up with painting and pizza.

Things were great between us, until Jesus Freak emailed me and told me you *hadn't* broken up. After being shown proof with emails and texts, I took my rage out onto my online journal, which had quickly become my venting grounds. We had created this weird community on LiveJournal, some of who are still wonderful friends today. As a *completely and totally* sensible teenager, I would use my online outlets as a weapon, to stir up drama.

"IS THAT HOW'S ITS GOING TO BE? WELL, INTERNET, HOCKEY FREAK IS A LIAR. HE NEVER EVEN MADE ME ORGASM, THE ONE-BALLED MOTHERFUCKER."

In all fairness, it wasn't your fault you were born with only one testicle and needed to makeup for your perceived shortcomings.

In true narcissist form, you couldn't quietly tolerate my insults toward your manhood, lashing out in the only way you thought made sense: posting all the naked photos you'd taken of us fucking in your bed. My face, tits, everything . . . everywhere. On multiple websites. Some were downright cruel. You even pasted the head of the Chihuahua from Taco Bell on my face, saying that my tits made up for my ugly face.

I am super grateful that revenge porn is a felony now in most states, but back then, even the cops couldn't do anything. Seventeen was the age of consent, and since I knew you were taking the photos at the time, you were free to do with them whatever you wanted. Everyone I knew saw them, including my mother, who was mortified for me.

I vowed to cut you off, the humiliation too great to continue to see you. I demanded you remove the photos and you countered that you wanted back a T-shirt that you had left at my house. After your stupid shirt was returned, you took down all of the photos. Thank god it was back when "going viral" wasn't a thing, and neither were caches. I feel awful for young girls nowadays who are just as trusting and end up on porn sites.

I poured myself into my journal, finally discovering writing as a creative outlet. I wasn't the best writer, mind you, but it was a wonderful place to vent frustrations and sadness. Writing helped me focus my emotions and work through how I felt, beginning my ability to be introspective. I still have that journal and it's heartrending to see the severe mood swings I used to have, especially when I decided to take you back for a short period of time, despite the horrific way you treated me.

April 11, 2004

its days like these i doubt my beauty, my life, my choices, my morals . . . i doubt myself . . . i feel like i've pulled every bit of strength out of my soul, and i'm so tired now . . . i just feel like . . . killing myself? no . . . not that. too stupid . . . i feel like, just disappearing into nothing. i don't wanna be remembered, i don't wanna be thought of . . . i wanna be forgotten. i don't wanna exist anymore . . .

someone . . . kill me? and make sure its painful. so i can finish my life like it started.

full of pain.

April 14, 2004

i went to therapy and i am so glad i did. My therapist and i decided the reason i went to Hockey Freak was because Hockey Freak is so much like my dad. see my dad took pleasure in my pain, loved to see me cry, and loved to piss me off. all of which Hockey Freak does. plus, Hockey Freak's personality is like my dad's. sometimes Hockey Freak, when we went out, would hurt me in minor ways, or would insult me, and then other times was so freakin' sweet. my dad was the same way. it was like there was two different personalities inside him. makes me wonder what else Hockey Freak has done . . . i mean, i'm only attracted to guys like my dad, and Hockey Freak is so similar. maybe Hockey Freak has a lot more secrets then we'd like to know. i mean, last night he told me he could freak me out, and i was like, i doubt it. ooo and both of them used me for sex. lol my therapist broke down what i was doing and said i was basically saying "single white female receptacle."

April 15, 2004

JESUS FUCKING CHRIST. what the hell is so great about Hockey Freak that EVERYONE HAS TO FUCKING TALK ABOUT HIM? he's some hot shot who isn't good in bed. GET THE FUCK OVER HIM. jesus.

April 19, 2004

question. lol and this is prolly gonna be my last entry for today, but do you guys think my life is interesting enough to start writing my autobiography? lol i really think my life would sell. i'm 17 and i've gone through so much shit. lol Hockey Freak alone would take up a fuckin' chapter (for now).

<u>April 21, 2004</u>

i think i'm gettin back to normal. i feel like the whole past drama is way in the past, not just two days ago. i'm ready to move on.

<u>April 25, 2004.</u>

*I JUST FOUND OUT THAT BECAUSE OF HOCKEY FREAK MY PICTURES WERE BEING HANDED OUT AT A **PARTY** AND EVERYONE I KNOW AND THEN SOME HAS SEEN ME NAKED. I SWEAR TO GOD, IF I EVER SEE THAT FUCKING FAGGOT AGAIN, HE DOESN'T HAVE A FUCKING CHANCE IN HELL. I HAVE NEVER BEEN SO HUMILIATED IN MY ENTIRE FUCKING LIFE.*

◆

Because I wasn't entirely sane at the time, I still went back to you after the revenge-porn debacle. You had apologized profusely for all of it, promising to never do it again. We dated again for a few weeks, me knowing full well you were still with Jesus Freak. You even began to rub the relationship in my face, comparing the two of us, telling me how I could improve myself to be more competitive. On a particular day lounging in bed, I picked at the half inch of flab on my belly, asking if I should lose weight. You grimaced and said, "I didn't want to mention it, but I *do* like my women to be fit." Thus started a brutal regimen of a thousand crunches every day. I also essentially avoided eating full meals and the infinitesimal fat melted off my body. I felt that I had zero power in my relationship with you, but the rumble in my stomach made me feel a sense of control I hadn't had in a long time.

Eventually, curiosity got the better of me and I reached out to Jesus Freak to see if we could find common ground. Imagine my surprise when I realized she had no idea you were cheating on her and hailed me as the hero, letting her know what a shitty human you were.

Much to your dismay, we decided to band together one day and ruin your prized pickup truck. Three bottles of glitter spray paint did the trick as we cackled and flitted around your truck, enjoying how it glinted in the sunlight. After a few moments, you must have heard our mirth, because after cautiously poking your head out the door to see the ruckus, you rushed outside with your mom, threatening to call the cops. Jesus Freak and I stood our ground, our anger washed away and replaced with amusement at your rage. Finally. Payback for all the times you made me feel like shit. Not understanding our motivations, your mother scolded us by trying to tell us what terrible people we were. I sneered, informing her of what kind of son she raised—a son who cheated on women, who plastered naked photos of them online. Who lied as much as he breathed. She grew quiet as the transgressions were listed and eventually stepped out of the conversation. Did you actually get into trouble for that? Was she ashamed for raising a son that exploited women?

The cops arrived ready to arrest us, until we proved the glitter was washable. They told us that we would have to wash the truck, but I countered with loudly explaining that it was payback for cheating on us and disseminating revenge porn. Jesus Freak and I left in her car, laughing so hard we were crying. We had a sleepover the night, promising over a bucket of ice cream that we would never go back to you.

Alas, she eventually went back to you, a glutton for abuse, but I had my cathartic release from you. I walked away and never saw you again. And while I resented her for being too weak, she had her own demons to slay.

I eventually moved on from what you did. You never apologized for the abuse and I never expect you to. The closure isn't required or even necessary. I just sincerely hope you learned *something* from washing off all of that glitter.

A letter to a lazy partner-in-crime

When I met Warcraft Addict, I was still getting over the abuse from Hockey Freak. I continued to attend art therapy in a serious attempt to try finding my center—to move on in my life. I finally quit my mental and emotional addiction to marijuana and didn't do drugs, hoping to find my own inner strength. Warcraft Addict was definitely a transitional period man, the type you date while trying to find yourself. I just happened to treat him like utter shit for most of it. Regardless, he was kind and patient to the best of his abilities. He also set a precedent of how I will never ever treat another human being ever again. For years, I never mentioned this period of my life, because it filled me with deep shame and remorse. Admittedly, I've omitted some of the worse behavior. Is this selfish? Yep. I simply don't want to be held accountable for what a very damaged seventeen-year-old did. This story is filled with mistakes, regrets, and most importantly of all, lifelong lessons that I take to heart almost every single day.

Dear *Warcraft Addict,*

First off, I'm glad we were able to talk last month for the first time in eleven years. I've been plagued with guilt, rarely discussing this particular time period of my life with friends or significant others, because I feel so dirty and awful with how everything went down. For the longest time I thought I had taken serious advantage of you, although now I think maybe it was mutual? Either way, thank you for taking the time to talk with me.

The beginning of our story started online, like most of my relationships. We met on LiveJournal and I swear, that website both changed and saved my life. Within the first few interactions you proved to be this beacon of kindness, someone who genuinely wanted to be my friend without the end goal of sex. This was a new sensation, almost freeing, and I was drawn to you because of it. Naturally, our relationship eventually turned sexual, but I think it was a solid two months before we even fooled around. You offered me a haven, a place to live away from my tumultuous life back home. Now, as a grown adult with experiences under my belt, I see your slow seduction for what it was. I mean, the first time we had sex was that evening you offered me a massage.

Massages *always* lead to sex.

I didn't resent you for it though. I knew there would be a price to pay if I was going to get rent and food paid for. It's science.

My mother wasn't entirely trusting of you, but I'd become such an emotional and mental burden that she didn't ask too many questions—like what a twenty-four-year-old was doing with a troubled seventeen-year-old?

Your home became a paradise, since I didn't have a job, an education, or a nickel to my name. You patiently drove forty-five minutes every Friday to pick me up, making sure I was fed food from my favorite fast food joints. You weren't much of a cook, but you spent oodles of cash on making me happy. I thought that if you spent your hard earned money on me, it meant that you wanted me for more than sex.

I kind of want to pat younger Jenna on the head; so lost, literally and figuratively.

I moved in with you when I turned eighteen, staying home to watch *Will & Grace*, and stuffing my gut with cheesecake and ramen. You adopted a pit bull puppy named Al, whose sweetness made me fall in love with a breed I didn't even know most people hated. You never asked for money for bills, which was a relief, but I was also such a bad cook I burned water, so I'm genuinely unsure why you kept me around. Was it pity? Was it that I was a hot, damaged eighteen-year-old willing to put out for room and board?

After the lease ended on that apartment, we became vagabonds, trying to find a place to live that we could afford. We tried to live with one of your coworkers, but moved out after a couple months when we realized they never picked up the poop their dog left around the house. We then moved into your parents' trailer for a couple months, in an attempt to save up enough money for a deposit on an apartment. We slept in a room filled with belongings that weren't ours, trying to find ways to eke out a living. You informed me it was time for me to get a job, especially since I now had my first car, a 1989 maroon Volvo.

Always trying to find the easiest answer, I first tried to sell my body, walking into a local strip joint called Baby Dolls and applying to be a waitress. I remember how we had talked for weeks about me working at a strip club, and had agreed I should wait on becoming a dancer. I was accepted as a waitress, which had me thrilled . . . until they told me I had to purchase eighty dollars worth of clothing for the uniform. We used our last bit of money to afford it all and I showed up to work, eager to earn back the money and then some. But there were hiccups:

- I am terrible at math. I left that day with less money than I brought in.
- Men can be creepy pigs.
- Some of the women took cruel pleasure in breaking someone as naive as me.

I also remember a few humiliating moments in the seven hours I pranced around that club. I didn't give a guy back his change because for some reason, since he didn't ask for it right away, I thought he was tipping me. I remember stuttering in embarrassment when he finally, condescendingly, asked where his change was. I walked away feeling the size of a squashed pea.

Then there was the old man who sat at a cocktail table surrounded by three or four women who leaned in close, cooing softly and tittering at his lame jokes. I wandered over and sat down, flashing him my best smile. He gave me a careful once over and asked me if I wanted to play a game. I nodded, thinking I had nothing better to do.

"You have a choice: either get a tip from me now or wait until later."

I contemplated his words and asked for the tip immediately. He handed me five dollars, which I greedily snatched up as a sly smirk spread across his face.

"You should have waited. I would have tipped you more."

His words were like a slap, his condescending manipulations crawling atop my skin, making me feel dirty. I got up and walked away while the other girls giggled, knowing the game better than I ever would.

I left after only seven hours in the strip club. I couldn't handle it anymore, realizing I just wasn't cut out for it. I knew deep down if I stayed, I would adjust like a chameleon and never recover. You didn't even pressure me to return, accepting that I was just too uncomfortable to continue.

We still needed money, especially after the loss of purchasing a leotard and heels I'd never use again, so I applied to a few places. Victoria's Secret gave the call, accepting my application, which left me feeling exhilarated. I romanticized the job, imagining being surrounded by soft materials and beautiful lingerie. However, upon showing up for my first day, I was informed that my hours would reflect how many credit cards I peddled to shoppers. More credit cards applied for meant more hours to work. At first, I rocked it, excited at succeeding and making some real money for the first time. However, the hard selling tactics quickly became difficult, and customers were occasionally cruel in their responses. I quickly went from getting twelve signups in a week, to seven, to three. Perhaps I would eventually have been let go for poor performance if not for a tiny detail.

I stole the shit out of everything.

It began when I was a small child as a way to rebel against my father. I would steal York Peppermint Patties from the 7-Eleven he worked at, to punish him. I then became frustrated when I looked at the people around me and realized I couldn't have this doll or that shirt—I had serious lifestyle envy. So I began stealing things.

This infuriated my mother. I remember she once tried to get a cop at Walmart to terrify me for trying to steal a fake flower, but instead I just rolled my eyes at his big, hulking frame. *I was seven*; I've always had problem with authority, but you know that.

When I was fourteen, I was caught with Rabbit stealing over three hundred dollars worth of clothing from JC Penney. I sat shaking and terrified in the security office, knowing my father would beat the shit out of me. Rabbit just rolled her eyes when her mother came and picked her up, zero consequences coming her way. Which is why she's now been to prison three times for theft. However, when Mom came to save me from the security officers, I sobbed in fear of my own father, threatening to accept jail time rather than go home to him.

My surprise fifteenth birthday party was subsequently cancelled.

I still hadn't learned my lesson though, and when I was eighteen I got a job as a dog trainer at PetSmart. Do you remember how exciting that was? We'd finally moved out of the trailer we shared with your parents and found ourselves a townhome only five minutes from work. Your loveable pit bull doggy needed a friend, so I went to the pet store and found Kai, an adorable German shepherd mix.

Thus began my pet addiction, which expanded quickly and in a very unhealthy manner. You began playing *World of Warcraft* every waking hour you weren't at work. Our relationship was already beginning to fade, sex being few and far between. We didn't fight; we just didn't have sex. I knew deep down I didn't even feel the façade of love any longer, but I strung you along, terrified you'd kick me out. I'm really sorry for that.

With my sex life cutoff, I began to fill my need for affection with my growing animal obsession. Within three or four months I'd amassed an insane collection of animals, topping out at thirty-six cats, dogs, fish, reptiles, and rodents. I even brought home an iguana, although he had to be re-homed for being too aggressive. To support my awful pet addiction I started leeching hundreds of dollars worth of things from PetSmart. I'd been demoted from being a dog trainer to a cashier, then to a stocker. It bothered me at first, the demotion stinging my pride, but honestly, working as a stocker was my favorite job. I loved the organizing, knowing where everything was.

Yet working occasionally as a cashier, I began faking customer returns to earn money to feed my menagerie of pets.

You let me do pretty much whatever I wanted, preferring to dive into *World of Warcraft*, ignoring me for hours while I went about my day. You paid the rent, and for some time that was all I cared about. Neither of us cleaned, the filth in the house reaching true hoarder status. I cringe now at admitting how awful I behaved back then, not cleaning out the litter boxes for weeks, buying animals and not being able to properly care for them.

Eventually we broke up, both of us realizing that we weren't happy together. You let me continue to live with you, possibly hoping I would change my mind, but I began dating again immediately. We continued on this uneasy path, not sure where to truly end our awkward living situation.

It was a Sunday night the day you changed my life forever. We were in your old blue truck, the one I'd almost totaled six months prior, sitting in almost silence as I sobbed. We'd been broken up for a couple months, and despite my fears you'd promised to continue supporting me while I figured something out. Multiple times you had suggested joining the military and I'd always shrugged off your suggestions. Tonight was different though.

"I'm never going to be able to afford college," I cried while you sat beside me, trying to comfort me. You know, we weren't a very good fit romantically, but you were always a super nice guy.

"Why don't you join the military?" I almost rejected the idea once again, but this time, for some reason, I paused. I'd recently explored the idea of becoming a cop and needed college to do so, but had no way to make the money I needed. Maybe the military was the answer?

My life has been filled with impulsive moments, grand gestures of change always punctuated with little forethought. Within five days of our conversation, I was sworn into the Navy, scheduled to leave shortly after my nineteenth birthday. Signing the paperwork alleviated some of the pressure I felt in my chest. I really want to thank you for that push, for supporting me in chasing after the rest of my life.

Soon after, my PetSmart tenure came to an end, a moment still vivid in my mind. Getting pulled into the dark manager's office, the proof of my theft across numerous receipts. The managers were kind and didn't call the cops, only forcing me to pay it all back. It was still humiliating, having to call my mother and admit what I had done, since I didn't have the hundreds of dollars owed. I was so ashamed of myself. I haven't stolen anything since—not even a hairpin.

I left for the military a couple months later. I'd become so selfish, and you'd given up so completely that the kitchen hadn't been cleaned in over a month. My hoarding was so out of control that I couldn't even afford cat litter. The downstairs area—your lair—was filthy and disgusting, reeking of fecal matter and dog hair. I cringe with deep shame at these memories. I never really told anyone about this period of my life.

By the time I left we weren't even on speaking terms. I spent my days on the internet, dating guys online, pretending you weren't downstairs playing *WoW*. I walked out the door, glancing into the dark cavern of your lair, feeling nothing but fear and the need to run far away from everything.

For years, while admittedly I didn't miss you at all, I felt awful about how I treated you. I sent you a friend request on Facebook ages ago, which you ignored. It sat there, pending, for seven years. Once a year or so, I would look up your profile to see if anything had changed. Finally, this year, while writing this book of letters, I felt inspired to suit up and try to contact you. Imagine my relief when you seemed confused as I professed my guilt. I felt a weight release inside, to know that I wasn't such a horrific human, that you hadn't held a grudge against me for the past decade.

You were such a pivotal part of my life. The biggest takeaway was realizing that I needed to change how I treated men. I needed to stop manipulating them, because they weren't all out to get me and, sometimes, people can get really hurt. You also encouraged me to join the military, which was a game changer. I thank you for that.

I hope life treats you well. Even if you never do accept my friend request..

A letter to ex-husband #1

Ah, the first husband. Nowadays, when I talk about marriage, sometimes I pretend I've only been married once, especially when talking to clients. I always mention I'm divorced, but rarely mention how many times. The shock on a person's face when I state that I'm well on my way to emulating Elizabeth Taylor makes my heart hurt. Every time.

I've been an impulsive woman. My mother claims I was diagnosed with impulsivity disorder as a child (her attempt to try and explain why I stole so much shit from TJ Maxx) but this is just an excuse. I had a deep void that needed filling for most of my twenties. This again is not a suitable excuse, but it's the reason nonetheless. I wish I could erase this marriage, but alas, it's now a chapter in the long story that is my life.

Dear Skeletor,

It wasn't necessarily my idea to call you Skeletor, but we haven't spoken in almost a decade, and really, it's what Mr. Chef called you from the start.

I've started this letter multiple times, trying to make it so my dislike of you doesn't muddy my words, but I can't help it: I dislike the fuck out of you. The last time we spoke, years ago, you'd once again "accidentally" used my bank account and were somehow attached to my social security number. No matter how many times I log a complaint about having never resided in Washington, Experian doesn't believe me.

To be completely frank, I wasn't remotely attracted to you. Your slightly balding head resembled a pallid rectangle. Your mouth turned purple when you drank too much wine. Your touch made me cringe. Right now, readers are wondering how the hell I even dated a man I found so unattractive.

I was twenty. I didn't even know my favorite liquor, let alone know what kind of man I liked.

With a decade now separating me from the self-centered bitch I was in my early twenties, I can honestly say you were taken for a ride on the Selfish Jenna Train. However, you aren't entirely faultless.

The first time we met was in a class for sailors who couldn't get their shit together. I had only been in the military for six months and already I needed remedial training. You sat across the room, arms slung across the table and chair, eyes watching me like a snake watches a mouse.

I was powerless when faced with your direct attention. Lacking confidence, I was naturally drawn to those who exuded it. I never stopped to ask myself why you were so cocky, since you were also in the "troubled sailor" class. I wasn't even available for courtship when we first met; I was still entwined with Mr. Chef, still crazy about him. Over ten years later, I can recall how you causally lounged in that hard plastic chair, confident in our future.

I gave you my number after chatting with you for two weeks, knowing you were interested but not willing to move on from my ex. I could feel the pressure of him leaving but couldn't let go. It was only a matter of time though, the idea of being alone terrifying enough to push me toward you.

The agony of losing the boyfriend that came before you caused me to react impulsively. I broke up with him two months prior to him actually leaving. Alas, you'd gotten yourself into trouble *again* and were restricted to the ship for thirty days. If I'm not mistaken, it was for messing up the one simple job you had. Jeez, dude, you just couldn't help yourself. Younger me didn't care, so long as I didn't have to be alone. I brought you meals, hung out with you until curfew. Everyone knows all successful, budding relationships begin when you can't even go on dates, right?

One thing that still sticks out in my brain is the build-up to our first time having sex. Due to you being on restriction, we weren't able to actually get naked anywhere that didn't involve non-slip flooring and pewter gray walls. For forty-five days we kissed in stairwells, hiding in the shadows, sharing secrets. I love secrets. Our excitement for you getting off the boat was mounting, intensifying, until I was positive that our first time was going to be mind-blowing.

Yet that first time, in your barracks, I was left feeling bewildered. Was that it? Three minutes? No foreplay? I think you apologized, as most men do, but I thought for sure it was something we could work on. I didn't realize at the time that many men merely see it as a bonus if the girl is happy afterwards.

Mr. Chef left to pursue his dreams in Washington, DC, a short time after and I was feeling lost. I wanted him, more than anyone, but you were all that was available. Our dating began in earnest, quickly moving through the courtship phase. We had only known one another for four months, but by November 2006, we were engaged. You didn't get down on one knee, but to be fair, I didn't give you the chance. I just wanted that bling on my finger, to let it glitter in the sunlight. The idea of being someone's wife was incredibly appealing; it didn't matter who it was.

Christmas Eve was the best date we could choose, since both our families were visiting Hawaii at the time. I bought a white dress from Victoria's Secret, because I was classy like that. We booked a cheap minister and got married at sunset, because we were classy like that. The biggest detail of the day that I can recall is what a bitch I was, freaking out about every detail, pissing off your sister, who hated me from the start. After we said our vows, we went to a hotel restaurant where I got so drunk, despite not being legal drinking age. After hours of drinking, you carried me up to our hotel room, where I drunkenly poured myself into the bed, only able to lie there when you insisted on consummating our marriage.

"It's my wedding night," you said. "I'm getting laid." It's probably the only time in my life I starfished, but I could barely walk, let alone move my hips. Such a good omen.

Married life was created quickly, thanks to the military. We got ourselves a house, moving in right before you were deployed for six months. We weren't able to talk a lot while you were gone, technology being very different back then. I tried to keep busy during that time, starting to train dogs professionally, drinking a lot, trying to ignore how much I hated being in the Navy.

For the majority of my enlistment, the Navy was NOT for me. Those who've met me know how anti-authority I am, even just visually. I'm usually dying my hair, getting tattoos and piercings, smoking pot occasionally. The Navy is not the place for someone to explore their individuality. Every day I felt suffocated. The only glimmer of relief I felt was the three months I spent working alongside the SEALS for on-the-job training as a computer technician. If I'd been able to continue doing that, maybe I would have stayed in the military. Leaving that job was incredibly devastating, especially when my only option was to return to an office where I was constantly treated like I had the intelligence of a snail.

You ended up missing my twenty-first birthday due to deployment, which was totally fine with me. My friend brought me out to the bars and strip clubs and I fell in love with a red head with a beautiful rack. I always fall in love with women when I've been drinking. The same friend bought me tickets to Thunder from Down Under, where I was brought up on stage and had an enormous schlong rubbed in my face. That evening, at the after-party, the dancers offered to fuck my friend and I, which I regretfully turned down. Reason #17456 I encourage people to not marry young!

You returned from deployment and we went to visit your family in Nebraska. My initial impression of the corn-fed state was positive. I fell in love with the wide-open fields and sunshine. I've always loved the quiet country, and in that sense Nebraska was perfect.

Let's be honest though: your family was fucking exhausting.

You and I fought constantly, about pretty much anything and everything. I accept a lot of it was my fault, as back then my hunger for perfection was insatiable. You were also a lazy husband in most endeavors, which probably had a lot to do with my impatience. During our ten-day trip to Nebraska, your family kept moving us between cities, shoving activities down our throat. I didn't get enough rest, which resulted in me falling asleep in the stadium at a Huskers game, my inner introvert weeping.

If I had to name a singular turning point for us, it would be a certain conversation we had one night in bed. Being on vacation had alleviated a lot of our real-world problems and we'd given ourselves a respite from fighting, attempting sex a few times, although never for longer than three minutes. After one such session, we cuddled in bed and talked about kids. You held deeply rooted fears regarding kids due to a degenerative muscle disease you had—something that honestly never bothered me.

Lying in bed, the house quiet around us, we talked about our future. You looked at me, moonlight streaming through the window, and asked me an important question.

"How would you feel if my father impregnated you?"

I realize that you worried about passing on your disease to our children, however, idea of impregnation by your father immediately sent me into hysterics.

"But our child would be your half sibling!" I wailed, completely inconsolable. You tried to comfort me by rubbing my back, but really, how the hell does one process such a proposition?

"I know," you said, "but at least we could keep my lineage intact."

This answer wasn't good enough. "I won't do it!" I said fiercely. I got up and padded to the bathroom to freshen up, wondering how the hell you even thought of such an idea. I ran into your older sister, the nicer one, who was brushing her teeth. My puffy eyes must have given me away because she asked what was wrong.

"You won't believe the conversation I just had with Skeletor," I said, feeling overwhelmed. She gave me a look of sympathy and nodded.

"Was it about my father impregnating you?" My eyes widened and my mouth made little fish motions, sound refusing to come out. The whole family had apparently sat down at the table one night and discussed this: *"How do we convince Jenna she needs to have Skeletor's half-sibling?"*

I was disgusted.

I didn't leave you though, like any sane woman would have. We tried to stay together and work on everything. My impatience with your premature ejaculation issues began to fray at the edges, resentment building as you flatly refused to see a doctor. I was so incredibly unsatisfied. We fought so much at home. Compounded with my emotionally abusive job in the Navy, I turned to alcohol to deal with my anger. I drank entire bottles of wine on the weekends, stumbling over to our neighbor's house, sick with drink. I decided to pursue schooling that would get me out of that office and elevate my career, and was accepted into a computer technician program based in Pensacola, Florida.

And right before I was scheduled to leave you got into trouble *again*, going on restriction for the second time, lasting another forty-five days. We didn't even get to spend time together before I left for three months, all because you were incapable of doing your job well. I remember being so angry with you for being incompetent.

To be honest, I left for Pensacola with a sinking feeling in my heart. I knew our marriage wouldn't last, especially with the distance. We couldn't stop fighting, whether it was over your dirtiness, your refusal to partake in chores, or your unwillingness to please me in bed. I couldn't wait to escape to school. Deep down, I knew we would fail, but I kept pushing on, like I always have.

Living in Pensacola for three months was the best and worst time of my life. It was so damn hot, with Pensacola being the armpit of America and all that. I focused on my schoolwork that first month, talking to you every day and enjoying living out of a hotel. I recall the long argument we had one day, with me begging for permission to have an open relationship while I was gone. I'm sure you were bewildered, but I reasoned that because you hadn't been pleasing me in bed, that I had the right to do whatever I wanted to do.

After much discussion, you gave me permission to kiss other people, but took sex right off the table. I agreed eagerly, even with the limitations, excited to explore my surroundings a bit more.

Let me take a moment to apologize. I didn't mean to cheat on you. That's not who I am. I mean yes, I was a very sexual twentysomething. However, I'm also an incredibly loyal person. Catalyst came out of nowhere, like a freight train, crashing through me and waking me up. I can definitively say that being sexually frustrated is what weakened my defenses. I was twenty-one and just wanted my ass slapped.

I broke down and did the deed with Catalyst. Less than twenty-four hours later, already knowing I couldn't sit on the secret for long, I told you what had happened. You were so angry with me, and you had every right to be. It was mighty big of you to agree to take me back. My most recent husband broke my heart into a million pieces, so I can now understand what it must have taken for you to agree to take me back after experiencing something similar. I thought it was what I wanted, but as time passed, I realized I didn't want to make it work with you. I didn't *want* you to take me back. I'd just experienced, up to that point, some of the best sex of my life and had zero desire to backtrack. I spent a week thinking about what I wanted, and in that moment I wanted to stay with Catalyst.

I didn't tell you this and I want to smack Past Jenna for that. Fuck, I am so sorry about that. I led you on for weeks, sometimes talking to you on the phone while I was in bed with Catalyst. I hated—loathed your beta personality. Back then I was still so filled with rage, destroying everything good in my life. You weren't a bad person, you didn't deserve the young little bitch I was. I don't like you, I never will, but you didn't deserve that.

After school was over, the plan was for me to meet you and your family in San Diego for a week, staying on the floor at your aunt's house. I was such a heavy cigarette smoker back then, up to a pack a day; I was a chimney with anxiety. I sent texts and phone calls to Catalyst while refusing to have sex with you.

I asked for a divorce one night as we sat on a chair by the pool. You kept pressuring me for sex and the thought made me sick to my stomach. I couldn't take it anymore, your arms wrapped around me, whispering promises and solutions.

"I can't do this anymore. I want a divorce." My voice was dull, void of emotion. I just wanted this lie I was living to be over and done with. You reacted with shock, never imagining that I would want to leave our oh-so-wonderful relationship.

You begged me to stay, promising to make it work. But I didn't want to be fought for; I just wanted to be allowed to leave and live my life. I left San Diego with your entire family pissed at me as you just couldn't wait to tell them. If we'd had any chance of recovery, it was lost the moment you ran to your mommy.

I got home to Hawaii before you, since you were in San Diego for school. Dude, you didn't even take the trash out before you left the week prior. Our dog hadn't been groomed the entire three months I was gone. You switched things around and took things down. I remember crying to Catalyst on the phone, hating you so much. The whole house smelled like rotten food.

Our divorce was quick and pretty painless, without any kids or real money to argue over. I remember our divorce decree came in on Halloween 2008. I cried in a friend's car, more sure than ever that I would die alone. I had dressed up as a "gangster," though I more closely resembled a disaster with long legs. I think there's a photo floating around on the internet with me lazily holding a beer cup, giving an inebriated smirk to the camera, my legs splayed in front of me. I was a hot soup sandwich in sexy heels.

We haven't really spoken since. I do know that as I was gearing up for my second divorce you were off marrying a pretty girl. I will probably speculate big time if she ever becomes pregnant. Is it your father's?

This letter is filled with a lot of our failures, cruel reminders how we weren't the right fit for one another. I'd like to close this letter by telling you what I'm grateful for, what I've taken away from our marriage.

First, if we hadn't divorced, I wouldn't have been inspired to leave the country for the first time. You also taught me how to appreciate wine—something for which my liver will be forever grateful. Finally, your resentment for me purchasing camera equipment pushed me to purchase more. And just look at me now.

A letter to a best friend

I met Mr. Chef right after I arrived in Hawaii following boot camp. I don't really touch base on my time in boot camp, or the military in general, mainly because I've blocked out most of the miserable shit show that was Great Lakes and beyond. I loved the Navy for the first six months, but it eventually wore me down. You grow tired of being told what to do, what to wear, who to talk to, who to avoid, etc. That is, if you're a rebel like I am. I always joke I got my nose piercing two years into my six year contract with the military. I would show up to work with Ronald McDonald red hair and expect to get away with it. I once snuck my dog into the office, trying to hide her under my desk, because she had separation anxiety. I tried to deny it when my boss asked, "Jenna, do you have a dog under there?" even as her wagging tail slapped against the metal desk. I talked back to everyone in charge of me, ever. Mr. Chef was a sailor that I technically shouldn't have been "fraternizing" with due to him being five pay grades above me, but neither him nor I cared about rules. We made our own rules. And he eventually became one of the best friends I've ever had.

Dear Mr. Chef,

Let me start off by saying you might have taught me how to make fried pork chops, but mine are better. The student has surpassed the teacher, bitch.

I think it was my sass that intrigued you and it was the sass that kept you on your toes, even when we were only friends. Even when you pissed me off so intensely I didn't speak to you for months. Your kindness, support, superb listening skills, and dirty jokes are sometimes what kept me treading water, preventing me from drowning in my own mistakes.

When I met you, I was the definition of the word "firecracker": I was impatient, fiery, angry, and sexually driven in almost all things, which to a twenty-five-year-old man was a blessing from the heavens. Because you were twenty-five, you were such a dick to me, a roaming alpha male hell bent on conquering as many chicks as possible. I made it my singular life goal to make you love me, confident that love could be attained by force. I started my intense courtship by throwing hissy fits when you talked to other women or didn't give me the time I felt I deserved. It didn't always work out as planned; the beginning of our relationship was mainly screwing and fighting, sometimes simultaneously.

Despite our dual Leo intensity, you were the only man that made me feel worthy. You'd tell me how beautiful I was, how stunning I looked in whatever short skirt I strutted around in. You would offer your arm to me, pride emanating in waves as we walked down the street. I think, were it socially appropriate, you would have told everyone, "She's mine." Something about being so proudly "owned" made me feel wanted, desired, appreciated. It was refreshing, after Hockey Freak and the various boys that came before you.

Remember that time I got so drunk I tried to fight a man wearing a cowboy hat? Or was it cowboy boots? Either way, I screamed at him that he wasn't really a cowboy, because he didn't have "cow shit on his boots" or something like that. You flung me over your shoulder as I screamed profanities, struggling to get out of your grasp, forgetting that it would have been an almost seven-foot fall if I had wriggled free but not giving a shit. You never put up with my attitude, did you?

You were the first man I ever truly loved; all that came before was a shell of what we had. In many ways, you've been the compass pointing North in my life. My love for you, even as it's changed throughout the years, has motivated me to do so many things. It all began with our breakup, which has affected my life in so many different ways. Back then, I struggled to deal with anything remotely hard, but you never held it against me. You had to leave so you could pursue your dream of cooking for the President while I stayed back in Hawaii, suddenly back in my emotional patterns of unworthiness and neediness. Back then, I would have married you if you had asked. God, could you imagine? We would have been awful together.

But you didn't ask me to marry you, and I dumped you two months before you left. The pain of losing you was intense, my self-worth demolished. I had the emotional maturity of a baby goldfish and felt that a premature breakup would help me find a new warm body that might distract me from the loss of you. Sensing weakness, my first husband slid into the void you left, gladly asking me to marry him in the amount of time it takes for a bottle of mascara to expire.

You left the island, undoubtedly hurting as well, bragging about how you were hell-bent on fucking your way through life. It all caught up to you when one of your temporary hookups became pregnant. You made the decision to make an "honest" woman out of her and marry her, making her wife #2. At the time I was refusing to speak to you and had to learn all this from mutual friends. Admittedly, each new facet of your life infuriated me, making me wish I could slap you for your stupidity.

It took almost a year for us to finally start speaking again. We settled into our unusual friendship, but for a solid two years I refused to hear about your kids or wife. I chose the selfish road and you respected that. Instead, we talked about cooking, the men I couldn't seem to stop diving into, how hard the Navy was, even movies that had just come out—anything but your family. When you bought your first minivan . . . how could you have sold that awesome truck of yours? The one we hung my panties from, to make my gate-guard ex-boyfriend jealous as we drove past? A minivan?! I mocked you mercilessly for that.

The moment I learned you had bought a house together, I felt myself tear in two. These were the life moments we were meant to have, not you and the woman who said she was straight but turned out to be a lesbian but you stayed married anyway. I'd held out hope that you would divorce her, especially when she finally, officially came out, but you stuck it out a few more years because of your job and the kids. It became increasingly clear to me that you're an "easy route" kind of guy, choosing to stay where the getting is good. As time passed, I realized how selfish I was being, how territorial, and over a man who couldn't be mine. I had to start letting go by changing the way I loved you. I began to ask more about your family, showing an interest in things I had steadfastly ignored.

We continued on a safe, platonic path, both of us comfortable in the ease of our relationship.

In 2011, I flew to DC after getting out of the military. I stayed with Schwasty, but was incredibly excited to see you for the first time in five years. You showed up with a fake mustache on your lip, leaning against your car with a mischievous smirk on your face. I don't think I ever told you this but I was so nervous. I felt intimidated, and for no real reason. I was still happily married to ex-husband #2 just as you were divorcing your crazy lesbian ex. Yet, you never pushed me for anything but conversation; we just enjoyed one another's company. That trip, I finally got to meet your kids, a little part of me falling in love with them because they were yours. You watched as I crawled through the grass with them, chasing geese in the park. That was the first time in my life I liked kids, and I think that was the shift I needed to want them.

Relationship-wise, we were always two ships passing in the night. When you were finally divorced from your second wife, I was in a relationship. I remember you being the first person I called when I thought any of my relationships were ending. You would sigh your normal big sigh and say, "I'm sorry, darlin'," and offer words of comfort. You were always the first person I turned to whenever anything happened. Deep down, I think I kept the flame of hope alive, silently wishing it would work out between the two of us. Wouldn't it be romantic to say "I married my best friend!" after years of friendship?

A few years ago, the stars almost aligned. You were with someone you weren't sure you liked and I had finally gotten divorced from my second husband. I can't remember how the conversation started, but suddenly . . . we realized that maybe we could try and make a go of it. There was only one obstacle: over three thousand miles separated us.

For over a month our conversations, the way we spoke to one another, began to shift. We were both apprehensive, not sure if things would work out. Have they ever though? We've led pretty messy lives, both of us now having been married three times and you with two kids. Yet we held to optimism as we talked about future possibilities.

Then the Universe threw us a curveball: you finally received time off . . . at the same time I was booked to photograph my first destination wedding in Seattle. It was a cruel joke the gods were playing, forcing me to choose between love and my business.

You never held it against me when I chose work.

You have always been my longest-standing cheerleader.

I think we both realized that the timing wasn't going to work. You told me that since we couldn't meet, to feel free to start dating. I think it was a sign when I didn't even hesitate to begin. I ended up meeting Nerd Boy, and when I called and told you, I cried. I was being forced to acknowledge that once again our attempts at being together had been laid to rest. It seemed to be the final nail in the relationship coffin; we haven't tried romantically connecting since.

What would've happened if I'd passed on that particular wedding? Those clients ended up being amazing friends, but really, do you think things would be different? I could be living on the East Coast right now, married my best friend . . . or we might have just plain killed one another. We're funny that way.

I don't regret taking that job and you've never once said I should have chosen differently. You know my personal success is incredibly important to me, and I think it's important to you, too. They're all "sniveling bitches," as you would say.

I still have that candle from my twentieth birthday, now broken in several places, the pinkness faded a bit. I picked it up out of my old jewelry box and held it, remembering how we'd gotten all fancy and you brought me to Ruth's Chris, determined to introduce me to a really good steak. I blame you for my love affair with filet mignon.

After dinner was done, you had a crème brûlée delivered with a lone pink candle in it. I blew it out and you got up to go to the bathroom . . . and I burst into tears, right there, overtop the expensive linen table. Up to that moment, no one in my entire life had done something so simple, so kind. You were the first man to make me feel worthy, and for that you have my undying loyalty.

To be honest, I should have measured every man I ever dated against you. Not as in "is he tall like Mr. Chef? Is he a good cook like Mr. Chef?" But instead I should ask, "Is he loyal like Mr. Chef? Does he make me feel worthy? Does he tell me

I'm beautiful like Mr. Chef? Does he support my successes like Mr. Chef?"

Admittedly, I'm super terrified to let you read this letter. I bet if I could block you from buying this book, I would, but we both know you'll be the first to do so, even after I ended the bulk of our friendship earlier this year. I can't believe that after ten years of friendship I had to put our communications on hiatus, but things had gotten too inappropriate. I'd made you a deal breaker with all of my exes, making it clear they had to accept you as a friend. I now realize how shady that was. Who am I to say, "if you want to be my boyfriend, you must tolerate my weird friendship with this married man."

I miss you, but I know you accept this as the best move. I found a man that taught me real relationships have openness and honesty . . . but I had always refused to be transparent about the two of us. Did I secretly hope that you would one day leave your current wife and sweep me out of my own misery? You bet. I've come to realize this will never happen and I'm only sabotaging myself by even considering it.

In the end, as we each fly closer to the sun, may we occasionally be the breeze lifting the other one up.

A letter to a life changing person

I met Catalyst when I was still married to Skeletor, having grown impatient with his shortcomings. I desperately wanted to be loyal, as loyalty is a factory default setting for me, but I was twenty, married to the wrong person, and just wanted to hook up with someone. In my mind, staying faithful for six months of deployment and then sticking it through another six months of bad sex meant I could have a "hall pass." I remember calling Skeletor from the hotel in Pensacola, demanding that he give into my request to fool around with someone else, because he wasn't "doing his husbandly duty and pleasing me." I can't imagine how shit-astic I made him feel and I never bothered asking, which fills me with shame. I'm not proud of cheating on my husband. It's definitely one of my five regrets in life, right there next to getting married to him in the first place.

However, I feel like I can safely say that by marrying Skeletor and subsequently cheating on him, I was inadvertently led down the path of finding my biggest passion: travel. We all make mistakes, some bigger than others. What matters is how we learn from them and recognize how mistakes can lead to glory.

Dear Catalyst,

Some women can name a singular man that lit up their world and changed the course of their life forever.

Apparently, I have an entire book filled with men like that.

Yet I can say, with confidence, that you were the game changer, the pivotal point that set so much in motion. You helped cultivate my travel bug, even inadvertently. You wrote me poems. I still listen to the songs you gave me with a smile. And honestly, so few men have matched our chemistry in bed. Even if you just came out to me as a gay man, you still screwed like vagina was your destiny.

The first time we saw one another was a sticky humid morning in Pensacola, on the bleachers by the football field of the naval base. I was on limited duty due to a knee injury and you were passing by, looking like sex on two legs. You had a playful smirk on your face, accentuating the gentle curves of your lips.

You were a "booter," fresh to the ranks, and I felt like I was definitely too good for you. I had been in the military for three years already and didn't *associate* with *booters*. You were a persistent little bugger though, saying hello to me any chance you got, ignoring the shining wedding ring I purposefully flashed in disdain every time you tried.

It wasn't that I was faithful to my husband—he'd already given me permission to canoodle with men while I was away at school—it was because it felt powerful to turn you down. You ignored my power play and tried to persuade me to have dinner with you, just once. I'd seen a diner I wanted to eat at on TV, so after two weeks of persistent attention, I thought why the hell not. I loved free food, anyway.

We clicked instantly, enjoying the restaurant as rolls were flung at us. I steadfastly refused to let you get romantically close, but our chemistry drew me in like a moth to flame. I already felt like I could tell you anything without judgment. You even laughed as I dramatically peed on the side of the road, terrified that I was going to get shot for peeing in someone's bushes.

I told Skeletor about all of this, assuring him that I wouldn't use my "hall pass" with you. I didn't even kiss you that particular night and didn't have any intentions to do so, but the more time we spent together the more I was completely smitten with you. I don't remember our first kiss, but when we finally broke the barrier, we kissed for hours, horses galloping in my chest every time you got close to me. I loved the way you smelled, the slow smile that curled on your soft lips any time you found me doing something you thought was adorable.

Without meaning to, caught up in all the pheromones and slow music, we had sex. I blame it on Adele's *19*—she just croons sexy vibes. It was a Thursday night. I remember the first time you just kissed my *knee* I felt fireworks explode behind my eyes and I lost myself. Sex with you was like getting lost in a hot spring—comforting and erotic all at once. The bliss was short lived, however, because reality came crashing down almost immediately.

The morning after, I was wracked with guilt. How could I have done this, become the cheater, the most detestable of marital enemies?

You left none the wiser, and after a day of dealing with my abhorrent guilt, I finally told my husband everything. Right after drying my tears, I texted you to let you know we couldn't do this anymore. You were *so* pissed. You told me I wouldn't have cheated if there weren't something seriously lacking in my marriage, which I also knew to be true.

I wanted to be selfish. I wanted to get lost in the softness of your affection and attentions. It was the first time since Mr. Chef that I felt cherished. I realized, after another couple days of soul searching, that my marriage was bound to fail, especially since you showed me a world of mind-blowing sex and emotional connection that I hadn't known existed. There wasn't a single chance of me being able to return to my old life with a selfish, clueless husband.

So began our affair in earnest, with you basically living with me at my hotel, careful to not be caught by anyone that might care about our adultery. You passed me poems during smoke breaks, dedicated songs to our struggle, and fucked me all the right ways two or three times a day.

The whole time I kept up the charade with Skeletor, not wanting to ask for a divorce over the phone. Should I have done things a little differently? Heck yeah. It's easy to blame how young I was, but in reality, I just wanted to all of the things I felt I deserved.

Our relationship moved incredibly rapidly, a fact neither of us seemed to quite grasp. We said "I love you" within three weeks and in total spent only six or so together. Instead of understanding that these emotions weren't genuine, I wanted to jump from one marriage to another, even took myself off birth control in hopes I would get pregnant with you. How stupid could we have been? You were a couple years older than me, but you seemed as lost as I was.

We hung out with your family before it was time for me to go back home and your mother said something I'll never forget: "Why are you with my son? You're too good for him . . ." I remember being offended, determined to either raise you to my level or fall down to yours. To be fair, she didn't know I was married. She probably would have sung another tune had she known.

Then it was time for me to graduate and head off to San Diego to see my soon-to-be-ex. I couldn't have been more wrecked. You dropped me off at the airport, tears streaming down my face, burning my skin. I'm pretty sure I got a few side-eye glances from alarmed passengers as I proceeded to cry for the entire flight, four straight hours.

There was a temporary respite when you visited me in Hawaii three weeks later. You stayed for a whole week and I paid for all of it, being so desperate for love and affection after demanding a divorce from Skeletor. I still laugh when I think about that time we were upstairs fooling around in the bed and realized he'd come home. Oh my god, I think I almost vomited from the possible drama, my brain visualizing possible scenarios that kept ending with murder-suicide. I shoved you into the closet while I tried to distract him. He never suspected, but I also never tried any kind of crazy shit like that ever again!

This time it was your turn to leave, albeit without all the dramatic tears of our last goodbye. I wasn't worried in the slightest about having a long-distance relationship with you. We promised to talk every day, and a couple weeks later I even bought a ticket to Virginia, to visit you over Christmas.

Then you butt-dialed me.

Your butt first dialed me at two PM on a Tuesday. I answered with a smile on my face, which slowly faded when I realized you weren't actually on the line. I listened a bit, because that's what a butt-dial entails. That's when I heard it—a woman's voice, a soft sigh, noises that sounded an awful like bed sheets rustling.

I hung up and dialed you again, furious, terrified that my suspicions were right. I imagined you with some buxom brunette, getting head from her luscious lips. Damn, I always knew my lips were too small! Did she have a nicer ass than me? Was her name something exotic like Natasha, or was it cheap like Star? My imagination pounded away at me, especially as you proceeded to ignore my subsequent fifty phone calls.

I went absolutely insane, like any woman would.

For years I've been convinced that most women are not as crazy as men claim them to be. Men make us crazy. They tell us we're crazy when our intuition tells us something is up. Men tell us that we're overreacting even as they hold a pillow over their dick and the skank in their bed crawls away in shame. They tell us we're too emotional when we empathize with all living creatures, including that damn Sarah McLachlan ASPCA video. If we're angry, it's because we're on our "monthly time," not because our emotions may be valid.

You disappeared for *two days*.

You resurfaced half a day after I'd finally given up and decided to end our relationship. I was on my way to work when you called, acting like nothing had happened. I was furious and laughed in disgust as I informed you that there was no longer a "we" in this equation.

"Oh yeah? I just lost my phone for two days! I see how it is! You're crazy."

I immediately doubted my decision and begged forgiveness. The prospect of being alone was daunting and I sobbed to you on the phone. It was your turn to be disgusted and mean. You hung up, probably feeling quite triumphant in your manipulations and deceit.

I was in a funk for a couple weeks, dealing not only with a divorce but now a rebound breakup. I had this ticket to see you during Christmas, which was only six weeks away. I'm grateful for that opportunity—though I couldn't muster gratitude at that time—as that ticket paid for my first trip out of the country. I was able to quench my thirst for travel because of your infidelity.

Let's be clear: I don't have a single angry bone directed toward you. We were so young! You awakened a drive inside me, a new understanding about how to connect with someone. You were also the inspiration for me to expand my passport. You were the true catalyst for some important things and I'm grateful for that.

A letter to a random hookup

Dear Guy with a Cast,

There I was, minding my own business, nursing my third vodka and cranberry and wishing I was anywhere but this grungy, cramped bar. I admit I'm so incredibly insecure when it comes to bars and clubs. That girl over there has a better ass. The chick over yonder has hips I wouldn't dare dream for. Me? I have white girl hair, limp and stringy on a good day. I have badass legs but swimmer's shoulders. My lips are too small, my nose resembles a witch's, my straight athlete's frame gets passed over again and again.

I wore my fear like armor, strengthening my resting bitch face, not letting anyone reject me. It worked 95 percent of the time. But then there was that one time, with the guy with the cast on his arm.

I sat at the grimy cocktail table feeling pretty low and lonely. I'd been to this bar, with its low ceiling and loud country music, more times than I could count. The light was low, the bar packed, and I was ready to go home. I turned to A, my best friend, about to ask if we could leave, when you walked up to her and whispered in her ear.

You weren't particularly tall but I remember you wore a white t-shirt, something out of place in that sea of plaid and flannel. You had soft, short blond hair and a white cast on your left arm. Energy seemed to crackle around you as you leaned into A's hair, talking with a smile. I felt a flare of jealousy. Another night's makeup wasted.

You walked away for a moment and I leaned toward A. "Looks like he was into you!" I said, trying to be the good friend. God, I just wanted to curl up into bed and read a book.

"Actually, he's super into you!" she said excitedly. I felt a sharp shock pass through me. The cute dude was into me?

You came back, drinks in hand, offering me one with a massive grin across your handsome face. "Hey, I'm Guy with a Cast." I laughed as you offered your hand, your firm confident grip catching my attention.

I wish I could remember your name, but I know it began with a J. We talked for a while and you explained that you were leaving in three days to move back to the mainland. I didn't care honestly; I just wanted to bask in your energy. You radiated happiness; kindness seemed to ooze out your pores. Jesus, I was so turned on and simply wanted to take you home.

So I did.

We spent the next three days together, shagging like animals, laughing and giggling all over the place. So few men are actually PRESENT during sex, most burying their faces into the pillow as they pump away. You were generous with your attentions, willing to laugh when things got silly, even sleeping beside me in complete comfort.

Of course, I wanted more but I cherished those three days. Most men aren't made like you. Sure, we fucked like rabbits and didn't really talk about anything meaningful, but it was clear that you were a good person, going out of your way to make me feel incredibly sexy. I felt wanted and beautiful—something not easily accomplished.

The amount of men that have appreciated me, entirely as I am, is so few and far between. If I knew where you were now, I'd buy you a drink. I hope you found a beautiful girl to do beautiful things with. Who knows, maybe you'll read this letter and go, "I slept with a stunning and awesome blonde after breaking my wrist/arm/elbow." If this is you, let's do a creepy Missed Connection email, craigslist style. Hit me up, even if you're with someone. You deserve a thank you.

Farewell, my wonderful blond man in a cast.

A letter to a southern gentleman

After the breakup with Catalyst, I spent that Christmas with my then-best friend Paris, whose family graciously hosted me in California. We explored Hollywood, even renting a limo to tour the different mansions owned by celebrities. The next day, Paris and I got incredibly drunk on free champagne and I got the bright idea to get my nipples pierced. I always say some of the best worst days of my life happen on champagne. When I returned to Hawaii, I started dating again and began a profile on Match.com. I went on some crazy dates, including one guy who told me I was the worst date he had ever been on. I still chuckle about that guy, because he was simply offended by the magnet I had purchased that said, "I may not have my virginity anymore, but I still have the box it came in." Scorpio was a welcome reprieve from the constant disappointment of dating.

Dear Scorpio,

The day we met, New Year's Eve 2008, signified the end of an insane year. My friends were having a New Year's party at their humble abode, giving me the bright idea to invite you for our first date. I've always been unconventional with my dating, much to the chagrin of my friends, but I didn't think it was unsafe to invite you to a party full of people.

You pulled up in your big silver truck, rolling down the window while I bounded toward you. "Park over there!" I said, my tipsiness slurring my words as I pointed to an empty spot on the road. You smiled and went to go park, while I, refusing to wait on a man, ran back to the party.

I didn't give two shits about impressing you. I had drinks that required attention!

The party wasn't too crazy, involving games of beer pong and, for a brief five minutes, my friends getting sassy and flashing our tits everywhere. I barely paid attention to you but you adjusted to my rude behavior, making friends with the guests and just making sure you gave me a kiss at midnight.

We went for a run the next day, both of us hung over. It was such a terrible idea—our muscles screaming in protest, sweat pouring down our faces, stinking of alcohol. We'd started something special though, somehow, and we began to date in earnest. Back then I dated like it was a sport, making it clear you weren't the only guy on the roster, sometimes forcing you to wait a week to see me. You weren't intimidated though, and instead started planning some great dates. I remember we went to a stand-up comedy show and I got drunk and heckled the comedian. We both know I was funnier than him.

The sex between was hotter than the sun's surface and sometimes rougher than a cowboy's life at a rodeo. Our chemistry was intoxicating, distracting, fulfilling. Your scorpio ways enthralled me, making me addicted to you. I've honestly spent years searching for something similar, everyone else coming up short. Within a few weeks, I claimed exclusivity and we became official. Maybe we moved too fast, and by maybe I mean we definitely did. More because I was young, freshly divorced, and really shouldn't have been in a relationship. I was constantly torn, because I could feel myself wanting to date other men, but with you, in your arms, I found safety. I found reassurance in your quiet steadiness.

The goodness could have never lasted, not at that point in my life. About two months into our relationship, I expressed my wish to date other men—in all honesty more fearful of finding happiness than needing new dick . I told you I had an itch that needed to be scratched and, with untold grace, you supported my insane request. I think at the time I just needed the façade of freedom, because we still spent all of our time together. I was falling in love with you—like really loving you. We probably wouldn't have run into any obstacles if not for the fact that you went home to visit your parents for a couple weeks. While I'm not blaming you in the slightest, the time away afforded me the opportunity to reconnect with a guy we'll call T-Bone.

You have to believe me—I didn't mean to hurt you. I was at the age where I should have been figuring myself out, rather than jumping from one relationship to another. I was self-sabotaging to the extreme and I think a part of me wanted you to find out. Why else would I have left the condom in the trashcan? I remember you paused at the doorway, peered into it, calmly asked me if I'd fucked someone else.

I nonchalantly answered yes. Because you *did* say it was all right. Oh, how naive I was. Now I know that when men say, "you can do whatever you want," it's really a test. Admittedly, women do the exact same thing. You didn't say much else on the topic and acted like everything was normal, but your demeanor toward me changed. You began to pull away emotionally, though so slowly that I didn't quite notice at first. I was so enamored with you; I saw only what I wanted to.

Instead, I struggled with the fear of knowing I was falling in love with you but not wanting to be the first to say it, fearing that you didn't feel the same way. After three months, I couldn't hold it in any longer. I can't remember the exact conversation, but I alluded to my feelings and you responded with a simple, "I could never love you." You said it with a matter-of-fact tone, as if observing that it might rain. You were dropping me off at home after having gone to the movies and suddenly, I was single. It, us, we . . . had ended. I didn't see you again for a very long time. My heart was like glass shattering into pieces. Third relationship ending in a year . . . that must be a record or something.

I spiraled out of control, dating like it was an Olympic sport. I drank every weekend, barely sleeping, focused on being absolutely devious. The summer of 2009 was filled with men whose names I don't recall. A lot of them make me feel really icky at this point in my life, like the guy who tried to give me to his friend or the weirdo who would insist on sex in complete darkness. These awful experiences in the dating world only made me realize how much I missed you. I would find myself crying at two AM outside of Señor Frogs in Waikiki, convinced that no one would love me. My friends would try to comfort me, but I only found comfort in wet T-shirt contests and shots of tequila.

As the saying goes, time heals all wounds, and eventually I moved on, choosing instead to focus on my future. It actually wasn't until after my second divorce that we reconnected. Taking advantage of your open door invitation, I took refuge in your home in an attempt to avoid my ex. I brought my dog, a border collie that you adored and smothered with affection.

You spoiled us with delicious grilled delights, let me drink your booze and choose the movies we would watch. Sometimes we fooled around, but it was more about simple friendship and conversation than anything else. I loved staying up watching movies, drinking whiskey, just leaning together and taking comfort in one another's presence. Our canoodling never led to anything, but at the time, the human comfort was a welcome distraction. Your decision to live the perpetual bachelor lifestyle hindered any forward progress, but that's perfectly fine. I prefer to have the memories we have of one another and not taint it with further drama. We would have never worked.

We've drifted in and out of touch over the years, with you always single and me hopping from dude to dude. You were always telling me to be single, making fun of my inability to be alone, but I never took your advice, despite knowing you were right. I've appreciated your friendship through the years, and while we'll most likely never hang out again in person— I recently deleted you from Facebook for supporting Trump— know that I appreciate how our relationship helped form me into the woman I am today.

A letter to ex-husband #2

Life is a funny thing, with an ironic sense of humor. I met Army Man literally the week in 2009 that I hung up my dating hat, sick and tired of the weirdoes that kept crossing my path. I had just tried to have an arranged booty call with a dude who ended up being an extreme racist, leaving me feeling dirty as fuck. The guy before that was a boyfriend for two weeks and legitimately had seizure-like orgasms in bed, which was terrifying. I was so tired from dating. I was over it. Men can be bizarre creatures. So when Army Man drunkenly swaggered into my life, I was in dating purgatory, hoping to never have to deal with shitty men ever again, but also hoping Prince Charming would come rescue me from the bad sex and loneliness.

Dear Army Man,

Out of all of my ex-husbands, you stand the highest chance of surviving a stroll in front of my car. How are things? How's your bitchy wife? Sometimes, when I think about our relationship, I search for ways I could have been better or different. It all boils down to failed compatibility, but it doesn't make me resent you any less.

You met me at a time where I was truly free, living alone and trying to be okay with the single life. It had been eight months since my last relationship and I had been putting way too much effort into dating. It was normal for my girlfriends and I to have a night out on the town and I was eager to just go out without a goal in mind.

So when Schwasty and I walked into Moose's Bar that fateful night, no one could have guessed where things were headed. I was wearing my infamous "boob shirt"—a single wrong move and out popped a nipple. I also had on my white pinstriped gangster hat from the previous Halloween, which I wore to gain approachability. Your drunken friend came up to us first, snatching the hat from my head and placing it on his own. I coquettishly giggled as I reached to retrieve it, but only half-heartedly. That's when I saw you, slightly cross-eyed from drink, positively dripping with confidence.

You bought me a drink, telling me about how you had just returned from Iraq three days before. I was trying to stay away from military men, but your smooth conversation intrigued me, especially when you showed vehement passion about going to Antarctica and playing with penguins. It was downright charming. I laughed at the absurdity of it all, informing you that freezing to death was the only possible end result. I couldn't help it though; I was smitten.

The bars shut down around four in the morning and, instead of going home, we decided to walk through Waikiki until the sun rose. We found ourselves sitting on a perfectly manicured lawn, kissing like it was our last sunrise, feeling drunk more from exhaustion than drink. We set our first date for only a few hours later, incapable of waiting to see one another again.

You were handsome, charismatic, and you showered me with compliments from the start, calling me your beautiful sweet lover. The continued compliments were a novelty, fueling my rapidly growing obsession with you. We fell fast for one another, reveling in long conversations, spontaneous fun, even easy political debates. You showed pain from your multiple deployments, losing friends in the sandbox. You drank far too much, losing yourself to blackouts almost every night.

Although at the time I lacked introspection and emotional maturity, I now recognize that I was attracted to the pain inside you, caused from multiple deployments, PTSD, and alcoholism. I saw you as a project, a fixer upper—someone to save.

The first time I realized how much work you actually needed would probably be that trip to Maui we took in October 2009. We had been dating for about six weeks and it was technically a girls' weekend, but my friend Hippie brought her boyfriend DickHead, so you weren't alone. DickHead had also deployed and at first, the enthusiastic military conversations were cute and entertaining. You both finished off a bottle of liquor and it stopped being cute, quickly becoming dangerous. Both of you began having flashbacks, struggling with your

PTSD. The night eventually ended with you collapsing into bed, sobbing. You began to cry, sharing horrific things about your deployment I doubt you've ever told anyone else. I swore I would keep your secrets and I meant it. My heart broke for you, wanting to heal and protect you. It didn't seem like a red flag at the time, because I understood the power of rage, of anguish. To me, it seemed like we were bonding, creating an indestructible connection.

Our first three months, like I said, were the best. Despite the drama in Maui, we made the best of it and enjoyed ourselves thoroughly. The following week, we took a staycation in Waikiki for Halloween. It was an incredible time. You continued to shower me with gifts and compliments, making me feel loved beyond belief. You were essentially living with me, waiting to process out of the military. Having done this myself, I knew the terror and uncertainty of it all, but at the time, the demanding perfectionist that I was, I didn't understand how your personality could change almost overnight.

It was a complete flip, the first Monday of outprocessing turning you into an angry, upset asshole, getting pissed at the smallest things. You hadn't started looking for a job yet, never once bringing up the impending empty bank account. By the time you mentioned being broke, it was too late. The government checks had stopped arriving and you hadn't applied to work anywhere. And because you had no real job experience outside of war, you were met with a wall of rejection from the civilian world. You eventually found a job cleaning grease vents, which barely covered the bills. But without any other options, you sucked it up and did what you had to. At the time, I was proud of you for pushing aside your pride, but now . . . I just wish you'd been an adult from the get-go and found a job before I was forced to support us both.

Despite trying to move forward in life, the stress of not having enough money began to gnaw at you. As a result, our passion dwindled and your alcoholism began in earnest; you resented that I paid for most of our bills while you could barely afford rent. Your heavy drinking reached a breaking point when you showed up in Waikiki one Saturday night with your friends so drunk you started screaming Arabic at taxi drivers. I had literally just been telling Schwasty that we were better, the irony almost unbearable when you showed up ten minutes later, embarrassing me so thoroughly I almost kicked you out of the house the next day. We had only recently found a place of our own, but when you came home from the bars, I told you it was over. I couldn't handle the intense drinking binges, the PTSD, the anger. You refused therapy but continued to humiliate me thoroughly. I looked like a fool for keeping you around. You got to your knees, begging me to stay, but I knew we needed a break. You moved into the second bedroom and we declared ourselves "just roommates."

While we pretended to be "just roommates," I started to date occasionally, even bringing some of them around, attempting to make you jealous. I know we both held out hope we could make it workout between the two of us, but I also knew you needed to learn your lesson. After a failed hook up with Lone Ranger, I came home and we talked. It was such a positive conversation, with you earnestly requesting a second chance. I've *always* been a sucker for second chances, having given mulligans to almost every relationship I've ever had. We talked constantly during the break and, as I go through our Facebook messages, my heart aches for how much we really wanted to love one another.

Me: *Well, I think it's a good sign when I'm completely obsessed with getting your replies. I remember when we first started dating, I was on cloud nine. I'd come to work with a smile stuck on my face. I'm sitting here with butterflies in my belly. I don't even know why. It's like, all of a sudden, I know we're going to start dating and I'm excited.*

Army Man: *I have the butterflies, too. It is funny but I like feeling this. We haven't talked on here this much since we met. I love it. I just want you to be happy. If you are happy, I am happy. I know we will figure this whole thing out as long as we stick together this time.*

Army Man: *This "you" that I speak of is also the one that gives me motivation to strive for better things for you and I. I lost that when I lost you.*

Me: *I know. I'd rather make you strive for better things for yourself, not just you and I. I want you to do well in your life. I like feeling like this, too. It's a good feeling, the anticipation.*

Army Man: *Yesterday was the first time I ever fought for you and it felt GREAT! I didn't know what would happen but I just knew I had to throw all my cards on the table and try. You are worth it though.*

Prior to meeting you, I had already been planning a three-week trip to England, Italy, and Greece. We were still on break, and while we'd been talking through our issues, I wanted to travel as a single woman with hopes that I would have a decent hookup or three along the way. But even as I made my way through parts of Europe, you were the only man on my mind. You had my loyalty, even when it wasn't warranted. The complete fuck up with Skeletor taught me that one should never just jump the bones of anyone nearby.

I went through Europe like a tornado, soaking up all of the sunshine, and sometimes even the rain! It was my second trip abroad and I decided to step out of my comfort zone by staying in hostels the entire time. You expressed apprehension, but supported my bravery. The beginning part of my journey got off to a rough start. As an inexperienced traveler, I didn't even look at the weather! I assumed that in May it would be spring-like weather, with warm breezes and sunshine. Imagine landing in London, with no sweater or jacket to speak of and only a single pair of jeans, already filthy from thirty hours of travel. I was jetlagged, freezing, and exhausted, but I forced myself to walk around the city. You remember the first time I Skyped you, chattering teeth and soaked to the bone, lamenting what an idiot I was for packing only skirts? I didn't want to explore London, fearful of hyperthermia, but it ended up being an incredible experience because by the time I made it to the London Eye, I had discovered something new in myself: self-worth. I looked at Big Ben and the Parliament and it hit me like a freight train: I was in London, a place I had only imagined in my dreams. I had saved for six months to pay for everything with cash, and despite the initial impulse purchase, I suddenly realized I could make anything happen. I went from being a drug-addicted teenager to a woman with a steady job traveling the world. It was a cataclysmic moment in my life, fortifying the foundation of the woman I would eventually become.

However, I definitely didn't like London, finding the weather and exchange rate disheartening. I left the next day to go to Rome, eager to explore Italian culture. What I found was definitely not what I expected: a metropolis spattered with ruins. I endured my very first culture shock, overwhelmed by pushy taxi drivers and forceful male shopkeepers. I thoroughly enjoyed the food, but found myself exhausted daily with the energy that Rome demanded. My hostel became a wonderful escape—it was relatively quiet and there were not a lot of travelers. I did meet one girl, an Australian, who invited me out one night, assuring me she had eager Italian men waiting for us. I put on my brand new gladiator-style Italian heels and we meandered through the cobblestone streets, excited at the whispered promises of the night. We found ourselves at Campo Di' Fiori, a bustling market during the day and restaurant haven at night.

Just as she had sworn, the boys were cute—both the typical smooth-talking Italian man. This guy, who we'll call Mario because I don't remember his actual name, asked me what I wanted to drink. Me being incredibly unfamiliar with ordering in strange bars, I asked what he would suggest. "A mojito?" he suggested, a sly smile on his face.

I agreed, clueless as to the potency of said drink. The rum and sugar rushed to my head and before I knew it, I'd had *nine*. Ironically, it ended up being one of the most fun nights of my life. After the fifth mojito, we piled into Mario's teeny tiny European car and drove to a hidden dance club. As he weaved in and out of traffic, I pressed my face against the window, staring in awe at the Coliseum lit up at night. Once again I was grateful for this opportunity, to travel the world alone.

We ended up in a badass nightclub, from what I vaguely remember. I could barely walk after all nine mojitos, let alone remember the random Italian man I'd kissed. I woke up the next day with a pounding headache, vowing to never drink again.

I grew tired of Rome after just a few days. While I enjoyed the novelty of having pizza for breakfast, the constant hustle was too much for my introvert personality. I eagerly boarded my train to Florence, ready to explore a new location. Florence, naturally, did not disappoint. It's the opposite of Rome, more quiet and quaint. I continued to eat all of the carbs and gelato in the city, doing wine tastings and going to museums. One of my favorite stories coming out of Florence was the day I accidentally took Ambien instead of Ibuprofen. I took the pill, hoping to stave off the knee pain I had been dealing with for months. I was on my way to see the statue of *David*, my tickets already bought, when I began to hallucinate. I realized suddenly that I'd mistaken my sleeping pill for pain medicine. Always one for a grand adventure, I decided to roll with it and walked up to the museum with a swagger. "*Act normal, it'll all be fine,*" I muttered to myself, plastering a too-wide smile onto my face. After my tickets were accepted without issue, I cautiously walked into the museum, bewildered by the different plaster artworks around me. I slowly made my way into the cavernous room that held *David* and slowly walked around it, gawking at its beauty.

Then it winked at me.

Shocked, I found my way to the adjoining room filled with other smaller statues. I imagined each of them were humans that had accidentally been covered in plaster, punished for offenses I couldn't imagine. Tears filled my eyes as I began to cry for these plaster-covered people. I left the museum, incapable of realizing how ridiculously high I was, and tried to find my way back to my hostel. I weaved in and out of the maze that is Florence, finding myself in a leather shop. I stared, mouth agape, at the soft leather jackets hanging on the walls.

"Is there anything you like, signora?" An Italian man approached, eyeing me with a well-trained gaze. I tried to look confident as my eyes crossed and speech slurred.

"These are pretty jackets," I mumbled, staring at a light brown one. It felt soft as buttery heaven.

"Yes, yes, these are lamb leather jackets, the finest in Florence!"

A little voice in my brain reminded me that I was against the slaughter of baby animals, but the Ambien piped up. "YES! I'll take one!" I shouted while I was high on Ambien, confusing the hell out of him. Now that I think about it, I probably yelled, "THIS TURKEY IS DONE!" which would explain his confused expression.

I called you afterwards on Skype, elated at my purchase, bragging about how *cultured* I was now, with a new soft Italian leather jacket. I'm pretty sure you laughed at me. I woke the next day with a headache and a new two hundred-dollar jacket that didn't fit my broad swimmer's shoulders.

A week had passed and it was time to head to Greece. I greeted the warm climate with overwhelming joy, fleeing the intensity that Italy is known for. I fell in love with Athens almost immediately, the Athens Backpackers hostel being one of the best I'd ever visited. They had a gorgeous rooftop bar, with hookahs and shots of Ouzo for happy hour. I found a new passion for meeting other travelers, exploring the ancient ruins, swimming in the Mediterranean. I was proposed to by random Greek men, who were just as forward as Italian men, but strangely enough not as creepy. My time in Greece was lovely, up to the point when I realized I had forgotten to book a hostel for my return from Santorini. I begged my hostel in Athens to let me stay, but unfortunately they were full for the night. The girl at the desk was kind and jumped online to help find me a new place. She found one in the Pláka, down the road, but when she called to find out if there was space, the man told her I first had to inspect the room. He refused to book me otherwise.

So I show up to the hostel and ask to see the room. The hostel was simple—a small reception area, with some stairs to the left and to the right. I introduced myself and asked if he still had space available.

"Yes, but you must see the room first. We are full, so we only have overflow beds available."

"All right," I agreed. "It doesn't matter though, it's this or I'm sleeping in the streets with the dogs." I laughed but he still looked apprehensive.

"Go up the stairs, cross the room, go down the stairs. Keep going down until you find a green door. Then continue down those stairs. Come back when you're done and tell me what you think."

Shrugging, I followed his directions. The first set of stairs led me upstairs to an area of rooms and a common area. The walls were lined with doors, each one a hostel room. I peered into one, seeing a small room that fit a set of bunk beds. I passed through the common area, which was just an open space in the center of the other doors. I reached the next set of stairs and began walking down. The steps grew narrower as I traipsed down flight after flight, searching for the green steps.

Finally, after four flights, I found the set of green stairs and started to get nervous. Something felt off, but I couldn't put my finger on what. As I slowly went down, the air grew more stifling, more intense. I found myself in a large, windowless, airless room with six sets of bunk beds. I wanted nothing more than to NOT stay there, but I didn't have a choice. So I made my way back up to reception and agreed to take the room.

After setting up my belongings, I hurried to my old hostel, eager to drown my sorrows in Ouzo at the rooftop bar. By the time I was sufficiently sloshed, it was almost midnight and I had to be up at seven in the morning. Miracles of miracles, I got back to the new hostel, passing out in the deathly quiet and creepy room. My alarm went off too quickly, it seemed, and I brought all of my things upstairs. After a shower, I went to check out, eager to get going to a new location. Somehow, the person at reception was the same guy as before.

"Enjoy the room?" He asked as he checked me out.

I laughed loudly. "Well, I survived somehow! It was creepy though, to be sure."

He gave me a tight smile and handed back my credit card. "Yes, some people find the electroshock therapy room to be disarming."

I stood there, dumbfounded. "Wh-wh-what?" I barely stammered out, my heart racing. "Please tell me you're kidding. You just made my story *that* much better!"

This time he gave a warm smile and chuckled. "Unfortunately, I'm not kidding. This used to be a mental institution. You slept in what was the electroshock therapy room. People find it incredibly creepy, actually, which is why you needed to approve it first."

The rest of the trip passed uneventfully. We spoke almost every day, thanks to Skype. We also emailed every day, our words only reflecting how much we missed one another. My wanderlust had only just begun, but I came home, ready to begin anew with you.

We were so happy at first, picking up where we left off, but better. That is, until I found out you had applied through the National Guard to deploy to the Philippines during our break . . . and you were given orders to deploy at the beginning of 2011. It was only June 2010, but the short time we had together seemed to narrow down into nothing. I cried on the phone, befuddled with the thought of living without you for 180 days.

I don't know who brought it up first, but suddenly we began discussing the idea of marriage. This is such a normal reaction in the military lifestyle: rushing marriage like you might die on any given day. Since we were so sure this second chance we had allotted ourselves would finally be the ticket, we began to plot the engagement, after you promised to find help for your alcoholism. You attended one Alcoholics Anonymous meeting but insisted that you weren't like "them." You continued to drink every single night, gaining weight and making false promises.

You proposed in October 2010, after we'd done extensive ring shopping a few weeks prior. You tied the ring to our dog's collar and ushered her into the kitchen while trying to maintain your cool in the living room. I needed a shower, and when I saw the ring on her collar, I refused to acknowledge it. What girl wants to be proposed to while stinking to high heaven?!

I went upstairs, pretending not to know what was happening but grinning like a maniac as I washed my hair. My "ignorance" exasperated you, with you demanding I remove Kayrah's collar and me hollering back you should do it yourself. I got dressed and brushed out my wet hair in the bedroom, waiting for you to lose patience. "Kayrah! GO SEE MOMMY!" you insisted, pushing her down the hallway. I laughed and feigned surprise at the bling hanging from the metal. It still remains a good memory for me, making you sweat for that "yes."

Rumor has it your wedding to your second wife was a bit more upscale and reportedly happier than ours. Ours was held in the backyard of a friend's house in Kapolei, most of the money spent on food and booze. I was such a coiled bundle of nerves, terrified and stressed. Behind my back, people whispered *"bridezilla,"* but I was so nervous and praying everything would be perfect. It is still one of the top 150 best moments of my life, walking down the aisle to Penguin Café Orchestra. You looked so handsome in your cornflower blue tie and vest, a smile breaking out across your face when you saw me.

I looked damn good, too.

You left only two weeks after we were married, deployed for six months. The goodbye was incredibly bittersweet, hugs lingering and tears wiped quickly away. You left at nine in the evening, resulting in a lonely drive home. I sobbed into my pillow for two straight days.

Around this time, the frustrations I had with the military had come to an unbearable precipice, robbing me of sleep, the stress leeching my energy every single day. A week before you left, on a Tuesday night in January 2011, I called while you were at training, begging for permission to not reenlist. I couldn't do it; I couldn't agree to the emotional and mental abuse of the military for another four years, moving to Washington and being stationed on a ship. I was so miserable, so incredibly unhappy. Some of my coworkers treated each day like an episode of *Survivor* and I found myself hiding in the bathroom to avoid confrontations. The mental warfare of the military was never for me. I want to either beat down walls with brute force or find a peaceable solution; manipulations aren't my style.

I called that fateful Tuesday evening, sobbing. "I can't do this, I can't reenlist. I don't want to go to Washington. Can I just get out of the military?"

"Okay . . . but what will you do?" you asked.

"I DON'T KNOW!" I wailed into the phone, adjusting the comforter around me. "I'll start my own business! I'll create a photography business!" It was like a puzzle piece clicking into place and suddenly I realized that I knew how to move forward in my life. Admittedly, I didn't have a lot of photography experience, at least in the professional sense, but in my absurd logic, I thought that because I'd managed a few good photos out of the thousands taken while traveling that I had an eye worth money.

"That's fine . . . you can get out, as long as you can get the bills paid."

Receiving the green light, I gleefully put on the label of entrepreneur. I cancelled my reenlistment and began the arduous process of getting out of the military. I spent nights feverishly researching photography, purchasing expensive equipment, and gave away photography sessions to build my portfolio. I had zero business experience, but I felt drawn to the hustle, reveling in the steady thirteen-hour days. I felt pulled to the marketing side of things; I signed up for networking meetings, built a website, had a logo created, poured money I didn't really have into my craft. Everyone at my day job in the Navy scoffed, having only witnessed the lazy and irritated version of my personality. This only fueled me further, determined to take their rejection as an energy booster.

I easily worked over a hundred hours every week those first few months. I became versed in licenses, insurance, permits, and the vast world of branding. I actually knew nothing about the wedding industry, so I spent days, weeks, researching everything related to the industry. With you gone and often out of touch for a day or two at a stretch, almost all of my energy went into this endeavor. I knew I could make it work, but it consumed me to the point of driving you crazy. You joked that you "couldn't wait to come home to talk more about photography," but I didn't care: I could feel it in my gut. It was worth the struggle.

While you were gone, we had to decide whether or not to stay in Hawaii. It was left up to me, since the Navy would pay for my belongings to be returned to Texas. Neither one of us was ready to leave the white sand and turquoise water. The decision was clear and unanimous: we would stay. However, as your deployment progressed, things between us started going downhill. Three months after you left, you informed me via Facebook that you actually didn't want kids anymore. Because Facebook is the appropriate medium for such conversations, I suppose.

> **Army Man:** *I haven't read your blog yet but why are you getting baby fever? I really don't have that right now.*
>
> **Army Man:** *I love you babe!*
>
> **Me:** *I dunno I just kinda want a baby LOL I love you too <smile emoticon> I'm gettin toned for ya today!*
>
> **Army Man:** *No kids for this guy. I am happy without them.*
>
> **Me:** *Excuse you?? You don't ever want kids now???? WTF?*

Army Man: *We talked about this. Anyway, how was the partying tonight?*

Me: *Yeah we talked about how you would probably want kids . . .*

Army Man: *Probably but not for sure and sure as hell not now.*

Me: *Wow . . . I feel tricked.*

Army Man: *How do you feel tricked when I have been saying that about kids the entire time you have known me?*

Me: *'Cause the ONLY reason we got married is that you said most likely you'll want them . . .*

Army Man: *But we never fully agreed on the kid thing. And I didn't know that we got married to have children. That is news to me. I should say I didn't realize that that is the only reason we got married.*

Me: *It wasn't but I thought I married someone who wanted to start a family in the future. I feel sick now.*

Army Man: *And I thought we were at the understanding that that was something we still needed to look into and discuss more. Apparently we didn't communicate this to each other as well as we had thought.*

Me: *I guess not . . .*

Your admittance at actually never wanting kids haunted me. At first, I reasoned that I would rather not have kids than admit we were already divorce worthy, three months into matrimony. I began to train myself to dislike children, pretending their grimy faces weren't charming. Subconsciously though, I began to resent you. If you weren't willing to give me children, then I expected to be treated like a goddess. If I couldn't physically create someone who would love me unconditionally, then I would demand that you meet my insatiable need for love. My insecurities followed me everywhere, forcing me to make demands that you couldn't meet. I would grow irate when a couple days passed without an email, especially if you hadn't previously informed me of a communication blackout. We would have nasty, vicious fights, after which you would attempt to assuage my rage with compliments.

But that moment of refusing me kids, Army Man, started us on our journey to the end.

When you returned from deployment after being gone for six months, things were awkward and tense. This is normal and expected for military couples but it was exacerbated by having to put down Kayrah, our American pit bull terrier, for her increased aggression toward infants and small toddlers. I'd adopted her with Skeletor, but kept her after the divorce. I had tried to manage her aggression for years, but when she started showing aggression toward infants . . . I knew we had to put her down. You weren't sure, though. She'd become your emotional support dog, helping you deal with your deployment PTSD. But it had just become too risky to take her outside of the house. What kind of life could she have led never being allowed on walks?

Putting her down is one of my few regrets in this life. We gave her McDonald's as a last meal, as well as pita bread, which she loved, and took her to a secluded beach where she ate the waves like she was chasing cats. When we were ready, we brought her to the veterinarian together, neither of us wanting to look the other in the eye.

Holding her as her legs buckled out from underneath her, feeling my heart wrenched into slices that would never quite fit together again . . .

You didn't want to be around me after that. You preferred to contend with your demons alone.

I'm so fucking sorry we had to do that. Maybe we could have kept her alive, but she could never again be safely walked. The option for children would absolutely have been removed, with her visually locking onto infants like they were cats ready to be eaten. Yet . . . knowing it was the right decision doesn't make the ache any better. I want you to know, I still honor her. I have her picture on the fridge, the one where she's sitting by a beer, ready for some booze. She was my first canine soul mate and I'll always miss her.

I think Kayrah being put down broke the camel's proverbial back. We stopped having sex, going months without it, fighting about everything under the sun and the stars. You stopped looking for a job, preferring to be on unemployment and stay home all day. I strived daily to make my business flourish while working on my degree full time, meanwhile you preferred to stay home and drink. Admittedly, you cleaned the house every day, but without any viable income outside of government assistance, the strain between the two of us became intolerable.

The day we decided to get divorced, I was sitting at the top of the stairs, looking down at you as you stood just a few steps below. We'd tried therapy; tried writing; we even tried all kinds of relationship exercises. Sex had become an unappealing burden. You'd gained about sixty pounds and wouldn't even let me see you without a shirt on. It felt like we were in limbo. Decisions had to be made.

While we sat there on the stairs, I looked at you with a weary soul and said, "I think we should just get divorced."

I could see the acknowledgement in your eyes. You knew I was right. We weren't happy, and just thinking about divorce eased the pressure in my gut. I felt relieved, being able to move on, and I could see that same feeling apparent in your own body language. You didn't even argue, giving me a hug instead as we both cried in complete defeat.

We were always better friends than lovers, something we should have recognized at the beginning. Despite making the intelligent decision of getting a divorce, we botched it by continuing to live together for almost a year. The end result was hateful words and resentment, undoubtedly fueled by trying to date other people in front of one another. It was a relief for both of us when you were deployed again—back to the same place in the Philippines. You were eager to leave America and put our hurts behind you.

Sometimes, I wish we'd stopped speaking when you left for deployment, but instead we took the time to heal, gaining good ground on our friendship. We made plans to eat at our favorite pizzeria when you returned and I gave you some relationship advice about the girl you had been "dating" (i.e., met in person and kept in touch). You told me how it was almost moving too quickly, since you hadn't ever dated her in person and being long distance made you wary. You asked me if it was too fast and I said that it sounded a bit quick. You thanked me for my friendship, assuring me that because I'd been your first wife, you would always trust and appreciate my opinion.

A month later, you blocked me on Facebook, claiming she was uncomfortable with you being friends with me. I felt so betrayed and resentful, as I do whenever I'm friend-dumped. I had hoped she at least was a decent person, but soon after, she started talking smack against my business and writing threatening emails, entirely unprovoked. You never quite apologized for her childish behavior; one could only assume you supported her insecure insanity. She did something for you, something I can't put a name to. Since our divorce, you quit drinking, got your degree, got a job, and even lost that weight. She may be a bitch, but she got you to shape up! I feel like the starter wife now more than ever.

I hope you find yourself in Antarctica one day. One should never give up on their dreams, no matter how silly they seem to others.

Authors note: *I reached out to Army Man right before the release of this book, to give him the courtesy of letting him know this book was coming out. He was grateful that details were changed and after chatting a few minutes, I realized how much of the good I didn't include in this letter. I focused on the bad, because there was a lot of it. I can honestly say we have respect for one another and even though I strongly dislike his wife, I am very grateful to her for making him happy. He deserves it. As he told me, when I tried to apologize again for Kayrah, "we were all selfish back then." My heart still hurts over this divorce and I think in some ways, I still grieve it. The only thing we can both do now is move on and refuse to make the same mistakes, I suppose.*

A letter to a nerdy virgin

The divorce from Army Man was incredibly hurtful. It's easy to recognize now that we both gave up, the work too daunting for us in the long run. Now that I've experienced a healthy relationship where both of us put in the effort to make things work, I realize I was usually too quick to the punch to give up if the other person wasn't putting in the effort I felt they should have been. This continues to be a struggle, if we're being honest.

Nerd Boy was a semi-typical rebound, although I had been single for about four months before I met him. I was still hurting over my divorce though, trying to figure out how I'd become twice divorced before hitting thirty. I was also dealing with horrific flashbacks from my father, waking up in cold sweats with dreams that would haunt me in the daylight. This is now a recognizable sign that my brain is trying to deal with some shit, but that didn't make it suck any less. I was still searching for my savior, my Prince Charming, that one man that would be the perfect bandage to my invisible wounds. Clearly, I hadn't learned my lesson.

Dear Nerd Boy,

By the time we met, I was already an asshole when it came to dating. In the aftermath of my second divorce, I'd been dating periodically, remembering why it was I desperately didn't want to remain single. Some dudes are assholes. You almost didn't pass the first initial test I have when it comes to dating: contacting me within twelve hours of getting my phone number. It's twelve hours down to the minute. Any more and I pretend I don't know you. You called me at hour thirteen and I legitimately gave you attitude on the phone.

"Oh I thought you weren't going to call. I assumed you had a legion of women in your life distracting you."

You stuttered on the phone, flabbergasted that I was already being sassy. I didn't care about impressing you; I just wanted to not be hurt again.

Our first date was actually magical, meeting for the first time at my favorite Japanese BBQ joint. You greeted me at the door, your eyes widening when you saw me walk through the threshold. For three hours, our conversation covered a wide range of subjects including bathroom jokes and *Star Wars*. "Smitten as fuck," would probably be the best way to describe how we felt. I saw your large nose and ears as charming, your affinity for plaid refreshing from the hideous Hawaiian print shirts that surrounded us.

After a few drinks and hours spent laughing, you walked me to my car. I skipped with excitement, thrilled at the idea of a first kiss. I was completely enamored by your slightly asymmetrical face, your slow and thoughtful smile, the flannel shirt that almost wore you instead of the other way around.

You walked away without kissing me.

I got into my car, buckling my seatbelt, disappointed but hopeful that all wasn't lost. You texted me almost immediately—an excellent sign that I hadn't fucked things up with you. This was actually rule number two in my dating handbook: if the guy didn't text within twelve hours of the date, he wasn't that into you. If he texted within two hours, you were guaranteed a second date.

You still wouldn't kiss me, even after two more dates had passed. By our third date, while the roar of your motorcycle did make my heart flutter, all I wanted were your lips on mine. One our fourth date, we rode up to the North Shore of the island, parking on the side of the road so we could walk through a forest in the dark before settling on the beach atop our jackets. The moon was full and the wind was brisk enough to move the clouds into shapes. We snuggled to stay warm and used our imagination to envision different creatures in the clouds. I felt safe and would have walked through fire for you.

Our first kiss was so tender and soft, with a hint of giddiness. It was so incredibly amazing to be excited once more like a teenager, our hearts galloping a billion miles a second. Without coming right out and saying it, we agreed to take things slow and relish in the newness of everything. Dates were fun excursions around the island, like snorkeling at the beach or listening to live music. We immediately started what could have been wonderful traditions, like waking up on Sundays and making cinnamon pancakes, drinking coffee, relaxing in bed while we talked for hours. I found you fascinating; envied your time spent living abroad, jealous that you could speak multiple languages. You engaged me intellectually, while making me feel so incredibly important and sexy.

We had sex for the first time a couple weeks later. It was bumbling, tender, and at some points amusing. I knew you were inexperienced, your nerves at times getting the best of you. You fumbled along in the bedroom in a way that was slightly baffling. Feeling generous, I spent the next few weeks giving you guidance. Eventually, I succeeded in morphing you into the perfect lover.

On our second date, I nervously told you that I still lived with Army Man and that our divorce wasn't official yet. This was likely the first red flag for you, but you were so into me, I imagine you shoved your apprehensions aside, willing to even meet him at home. As time passed, you both learned to casually engage in conversation. I realized later on that you had a lot of reservations—you just didn't verbalize them. The only time I can recall you being candidly honest with me was when you told me that what my father had done to me was a red flag for you.

I remember being so hurt by your judgment, despite knowing full well I was only a child and had no control over being raped. *"He's just never experienced anything hard,"* I thought bitterly, which was true. What had you experienced in life that granted you the ability to judge me by my own trials? Nothing.

Sometimes you talked about your mother, always exasperated by her neediness. You expressed frustration when she poured on the guilt, convincing you to purchase a trip to Hawaii for her and your sister. I struggled—and still struggle— to understand how people can put up with various forms of abuse and just explain it away as "well, they're family." Why the hell would you do that if you didn't want to?

Certain family dynamics will always elude me.

The first "I love you" came approximately five months into our relationship. I remember the moment perfectly: it was a Sunday morning, mid-November 2012, and I was slated to fly out later that day for a work-related trip to Ireland. Up to that point, things had been wonderful. We'd never fought and instead spent time at the beaches, watched movies, and took rides around the island. This particular morning was slow and filled with our favorites: coffee and pancakes. We stayed in bed listening to music, the AC blasting despite it being November. You nestled closer, soaking in the peaceful moment before I had to leave.

"I just want to tell you I love you."

I was about as light as a feather in that moment, bubbling over with glee and joy. I instantly said it back to you, nuzzling you and grinning from ear to ear. Basking in your love, I felt so incredibly lucky to have you in my life.

"I have to tell you something though," you said hesitantly, your face lined with worry. "It might change how you feel about me now."

I laughed, the mere thought of not loving you ridiculous. "Tell me!" I insisted.

"So, you know how I dated that girl a few years ago?" You took a deep breath. I nodded, waiting for you to continue. "There was that girl, then a couple years later I had that long-distance relationship. We never went further than third base. I dated that other girl, but we also never went very far. Then . . . I met you."

The phrase "pregnant pause" was incredibly fitting for this particular moment. I lay in silence, still naked from our early morning canoodling. Suddenly I sat up, the implications hitting me like a brick.

"Do you mean I took your innocence?!"

You nodded in affirmation, cringing. "I don't like that term, but yes, I was a virgin."

My heart and mind raced. "WHY DIDN'T YOU TELL ME?" I wailed, frantic at the thought, thinking of the first time we had had sex. The nervousness, the bumbling, the uncomfortable moments . . . it suddenly slid into place like a finished puzzle.

My god. You were my third virgin. I was the Virginator. I demolished virginities like it was hunting season. They were probably going to give me a badge for Christmas.

My reaction didn't exactly please you, but I was furious that you had lied by omission, that we couldn't have made the experience something more special. Yes, we had waited to have sex, but the moment of copulation wasn't anything special or meaningful to the scale of losing ones virginity. Perhaps this is just me being stuck in the societal mindset that virginity means something, but I felt that by not letting me in on the secret, while all your friends knew . . . it felt like a huge lie.

I began dissecting all of the times we'd had sex. I realized the third time you ever had sex was on a bench in the park, where we got caught by someone pulling up in a car. I was instantly grateful for my previous patience, but still I felt betrayed. The lying bothered me, especially as all your friends knew I was your cherry popper yet I'd been completely in the dark.

I calmed down after a few hysterical minutes, not truly voicing my worries. I meant the three words when they passed my lips, and despite you not telling me that something was amiss, I believed you would be honest from here on out.

Later that day, I boarded the plane with no apprehensions, still on cloud nine, shoving aside the "lie of omission"—the red flag I refused to acknowledge. I had a styled wedding shoot planned with an event planner in Dublin, one of the biggest projects in my career up to that point. I had met her online after emailing twenty different wedding planners. C was the only wedding planner that responded, but that promised to be extremely fortuitous. You were so nervous about this risky endeavor. What if she never showed up? Yet, in true Irish hospitality, she picked me up at the airport, immediately feeding me home cooking and bottles of wine. I was exhausted after forty hours of travel but elated to be in a new country, meeting new people. I slept nestled in a warm, soft bed, waking up seven hours later to shoot at castles and horses with different models. I ended my first day in Ireland exhausted, but elated, celebrating with delicious Indian food. The following day, we drove down to Dingle for a venue tour and ultimately got wasted in two different pubs. I don't remember a lot about that night, but I do know that C, who was the same age as my mother, drank me under the table. I had made the drastic mistake of forgetting I wasn't in America anymore and that they served pints of beer. I guzzled down the Carlsberg like it was going out of style, occasionally getting shots of whiskey to mix it up. I recall dancing by myself on an empty dance floor, jeered on by a drunken stag party, followed by holding a gay Irish man who cried because he couldn't be open about his sexuality in his own country. I cried with him and bought him some whiskey, hoping that would make it all better. Yes, somehow I found the lone gay man in a bar and cried with him.

We woke the next day clutching our foreheads and moaning for relief. The traditional Irish breakfast of greasy protein did little to abate our hangovers from hell.

When C and I weren't discussing the wedding industry, I filled the quiet with conversation about the sexy Nerd Boy waiting for me at home. She warned me to be cautious, but I dismissed her concerns, confident in our perfect relationship. We had been talking the whole time I was gone and you were visibly crazy about me, available to chat almost all the time.

Nerd Boy: *Hey. Still miss you. Just wanted you to know.*

Nerd Boy: *Hi. I wanted to to tell you that I love you. Just FYI. I do. You're cool.*

Me: *Hi* ☺

Nerd Boy: *HEY!!! I MISS YOU!!!*

Me: *Just woke up. Tell me sweet things because I had a bad dream :(*

Nerd Boy: *You are beautiful and awesome and I love you and I can't stop thinking about you and I can't sleep because I miss you so much.*

Me: *Thanks babe . . . I don't know why I have these dreams about you but I always wake so depressed.*

Nerd Boy: *What dream? What are you dreaming about?*

Me: *That you leave me :(last night you left me and had another girl. It was so bad I couldn't sleep anymore*

Nerd Boy: *lol. That's dumb. Remember what I said to you right before I left your house after I spent the whole weekend with you? I am freaking crazy about you. Stop worrying about me and try* *to enjoy me. That's why you're having this dream. When I think about you I don't worry, I feel excited and happy and that's what I dream about.*

I dream about how I feel about you. It's happy, and nervous, and excited.

You don't need to worry. believe me?

Me: *I know . . . I know. I'm so in love with you and you're everything to me. You've changed my life and made me a better person. You treat me so phenomenally and I want to be with you forever. But I'm just so scared :(I think on a level I know that without you, I would break :(*

Nerd Boy: *No you wouldn't. You're too strong. But I'm crazy for you, so you don't have to worry about that.*

I was only in Ireland for four days, a stay so brief I left with serious FOMO, but I was also eager to return to the man that proclaimed his love for me almost every waking second. I left C in Dublin with promises to return, feeling even more inspired to travel the world.

Because you only had a motorcycle, you couldn't pick me up at the airport, but when you roared up to my apartment, we were more than enthusiastic in making up for lost time. It had been 144 hours too long. My love for travel inspired you and we began planning a trip to the Big Island after your trip home for Christmas, which was in less than a month. With a load of apprehension, we also braced ourselves for your mother's arrival. You'd have thought we were prepping for an impending storm.

Within just twelve hours of her being in Hawaii, I could feel myself beginning to lose you. The adoration you loudly professed before her arrival began to peter out. My first impression of your mother was a nasty one, as I watched her manipulate you, while letting your sixteen-year-old sister drink herself silly. I loathed how she laid on the guilt, heavy and thick like icing, whispering lamentations into your ear with me across the room. I was a threat to her, the girlfriend of her baby boy, and I hated the conflict.

Our first and only fight was the day she threw a fit about us spending only a couple of hours alone, complaining that she flew all the way there and didn't appreciate being ignored. *Yeah, okay.* Even though you were flying home for Christmas only three weeks later, you still couldn't help but jump right up and submit to her manipulations. When I challenged your decision—the only time I ever actually challenged you on anything—you were infuriated and left without even giving me a hug.

Mommy issues, party of one?

That particular argument, with me challenging your inability to set healthy boundaries, started to put a serious strain on us. We didn't discuss it like a healthy couple and instead just apologized without really being sorry. Three weeks later, you flew home and basically avoided speaking to me the entire time you were gone. I began to feel threatened, as if my very existence was at stake, especially since the whole time I was in Ireland you constantly messaged me, telling me how much you missed me, how you couldn't exist without me, etc. Suddenly, I was a bother because you were hanging out with people that you really care about and don't ever see. I felt befuddled, how three weeks could change your behavior toward me. I knew that the longer we were apart, the higher the chances of your mother brainwashing you away from me. This was December 2012, and despite being so broke I couldn't afford much besides ramen, I was attempting to chug along like a goldfish stuck on land, breathing in a puddle of shit. The misery of living with my ex and constantly being hungry was weighing heavily on me. My business wasn't doing as well as it needed to be and I was over thirty grand in debt. I had picked up a second job, on top of my business and attending school full time, to try and make ends meet. On top of it all, I was struggling with constant flashbacks from my father and dealing with the anger that came along with all that. I never took my anger out on you, fearful of losing you, but I also didn't talk to you about it. You had no clue how defeated I felt every day.

In hindsight, as a result, I think I got too clingy and I'm super sorry about that. We met at a time when my life was real shit and my loneliness was all consuming. I wanted you to *make* me happy, which wasn't fair. It isn't healthy. On Christmas Eve, when I was feeling incredibly down and low, pet-sitting someone else's dog in someone else's guest room, I tried to reach out to you on Facebook. My approach must have not worked for you, because instead of consoling me, you told me to "go make more friends."

Nerd Boy: *Hey, babe, my phone died.*

Me: *Hey ☺ Could you make me feel better please?*

Nerd Boy: *I'm showing my friends some of my videos. Me and J are video guys. That zit on my bottom lip got really big and now my lip hurts really bad ☺*

Me: *Sorry*

Nerd Boy: *What are you doing the 29th? ;)*

Me: *Hanging out with you, I think...*

Nerd Boy: *Oh for real?*

Me: *But that doesn't make me feel less lonely tonight ☹*

Nerd Boy: *Aww...*

Me: *I'm having a really big pity party here.*

Nerd Boy: *Gross. Stop being mopey.*

Me: *Says the guy surrounded by friends and family.*

Nerd Boy: *Hey, make some friends.*

Me: *Hey, I've been trying. Cut me some slack.*

Nerd Boy: *FINE...*

Me: *☹*

Nerd Boy: *I just want you to be happy without relying on me. You need to be able to find joy from within. I want to add to your life, not be the reason for you being happy.*

Me: *Nerd Boy, I was without you for twenty-six years. I CAN be happy without you. You just make me happier.*

Nerd Boy: *Ok. I just want to be sure. I'm glad you miss me tho.*

Me: *Do I come off that needy and dependent?!*

Nerd Boy: *Sometimes.*

Me: **sigh* Fine. Then I'll back off.*

Nerd Boy: *lol. You're fine, babe. You just worry me sometimes. I don't want you to need me. I want you to just want me.*

Me: *I personally don't think it's healthy to be with someone and not need them. How will a love last if there isn't a little need there? But okay. I'll start making plans on the weekends and such.*

Nerd Boy: *Good. I want you to do stuff!!!*

The next day was Christmas and honestly, I was a hot mess. I hated that we had fought, knowing how important this holiday was to you. You were a Christmas nut, the kind to watch *Elf* every day during December. We had even hosted a holiday party before you left for our friends and I knew that spending Christmas with your family was the highlight of your year. I tried to respect this, but my insecurities snowballed out of control.

Nerd Boy: *Merry Christmas! I'm keeping my phone off this am.*

Me: *Merry Christmas.*

Nerd Boy: *I have a volcano growing on my lip. This zit is out of control. I'm keeping hot compress on it, but it hurts . . .*

Me: *It may not be a zit then . . .*

Nerd Boy: *It's a zit!*

Me: *Okay. Lol.*

Nerd Boy: *When are you going to your friend's house?*

Me: *Later today. I'm still at the client's house.*

Nerd Boy: *How are you?*

Me: *I don't want to talk about it. I don't want to upset you today.*

Nerd Boy: *Yeah you do, but I won't drag it out of you.*

Me: *No, I really don't. I don't want to upset you on Christmas. I love you and your happiness means more to me than that.*

Nerd Boy: *I'd rather you tell me.*

Me: *I know. But it's not a text conversation.*

Nerd Boy: *My phone is dead. It won't have a charge for a while and Christmas is about to start. Can you try please?*

Me: *Fine, I'll try. But it'll probably piss you off.*

Nerd Boy: *Let's hear it.*

Nerd Boy: *?*

Me: *Nerd Boy, dating you is hard. Not because you are mean to me, but because the things an average person learns about a relationship, you're learning through me. I have to be enormously patient but I also live in constant fear that you'll leave me or begin to resent me, because of who I am. I'm a girl and I'm emotional. I'm irrational. I need constant love and adoration and if it doesn't happen, I get insecure. But you always tell me to stop being weird, when I'm just being who I naturally am. Which makes me question if you really like me for me, or who you think I can be.*

Last night, you told me you think I'm needy at times. That hurt so bad, because it's taken me months to get to the point where I'm comfortable sharing excitement that you say you feel sometimes. I have been hurt, physically and emotionally, by almost all the men in my life and it's been a journey to trust you. Then you tell me you don't want me to need you. Then I thought, "he has said he's needed me before!" And then I realized it was only when he needed sex. Then I got even more upset.

Then you tell me I need to find happiness from within and I realize you take the current Jenna for granted. Despite people telling you how much I've changed this year, you want more. Sometimes I feel like you're waiting for the Jenna I can be and not enjoying the Jenna that I am at times. Not all the time or else you wouldn't be with me, but it stresses me out trying to better myself to the standards you seem to have.

I was upset, because you haven't put yourself in my shoes. I'm spending the holidays alone and while it may be easy to drunkenly tell me to "make friends," I live in Hawaii, where most of my friends go home to the mainland. I DON'T rely on you for happiness and for you to even assume so, let alone voice it, stung phenomenally. I run my own business, which gives me joy. I ride horses, which gives me joy. I travel, which gives me joy.

I do more than most people in a month. I don't RELY on you but I have been in relationships where forced sex was a thing, ignoring me was normal, hitting me was okay and making fun of me was affection. So when I found you, I slowly allowed myself to be happy. Maybe I took it too far and now you think I'm needy. Maybe we should spend less time together. I don't know. I don't know because all you do is tell me to find more things to do, which stresses me out because I already struggle to do everything else and now you want more. I fear that when school starts you'll just assume all I do is stress out and leave me.

You put a tremendous amount of pressure on me and all I got on Christmas Eve was to be told to stop being needy. When we had spoken a collective fifteen minutes that day. Someone actually needy wouldn't have tolerated so little contact during the holidays. That stings and makes me feel like you don't care.

I know you care but like I said, the things your average person learns earlier, you're learning now. You may think you show how you care, but if it isn't in my love language, I'm not going to see it or get it.

Nerd Boy: *Well, that's a lot more than I expected. I have to go open presents and do breakfast with my family. I'll get back to you as soon as I can.*

You avoided talking to me for six hours. You turned off your phone, dismissing my concerns and worries, instead choosing to eat French toast and open presents. You eventually called me on the phone and when I voiced the same concerns all over again, you just sighed on the phone and said you had to open presents with your family.

"I thought you just opened presents with your family? That's why we haven't spoken in hours?"

"Jenna, we were waiting on . . . I just have to go, okay?"

I felt like the size of a pill bug, wanting to roll up into a protective shell to prevent this hurt, this abandonment. Up to this point, all of my life experiences were accumulating into a nasty brew of despair. The hurt and betrayals of my failed relationships sat upon my shoulders like heavy weights, affecting everything in my life. I couldn't stand being alone, demanding your attention every waking second. Christmas seemed to be the last straw for you, especially when you refused to talk to me most of the day, choosing to spend it with your family sans cell phone. It was a phenomenally lonely Christmas for me and my only reasonable response was to write five paragraphs of insecure crap that most likely made your stomach roil in revulsion.

You got back from your trip, chipper and seemingly 100 percent into our relationship, the Christmas debacle forgiven and forgotten. We left for our trip to the Big Island, excited to adventure together, squealing when we saw the big hot tub in our cabin. We got drunk, had sex by a roaring fire (a luxury in Hawaii!), and spent two days exploring what the island had to offer. We went to a winery, the black sand beach, and some lava tubes. I was on a balloon, floating through time and space, feeling like nothing could go wrong.

The trip ended and for the next few days, we celebrated the new year by watching fireworks and enjoying the remaining days you had off from the military. Both of us were so sure that 2013 was going to be an amazing year. I greeted the new year with vigor, tired of being broke and unable to afford lunch meats. On January 8, we went to California Pizza Kitchen for a date that was, *apparently*, our last.

I picked you up since it was raining, and despite being excited to see you, I noticed that you were slightly off. You were avoiding eye contact and sat quietly in the passenger seat of my car. I became concerned and asked multiple times if you were all right, but you insisted that you were just fine. I could sense something was off but didn't want to keep pushing. I chattered about inane things, such as work, future plans for the upcoming year, even how I wished we'd gotten the fried macaroni as an appetizer. You would only respond with single-syllable words or grunts, paying for dinner with a sense of finality, making our trip back to the barracks awkward and worrisome. I parked my car and turned to you, hoping for a kiss. You looked at me with sad eyes.

"Jenna, I think we should break up."

A fugue set over real life. Your words weren't real. Nope, not real.

"I just don't see myself getting married any time soon. It seems like that's where you're headed and I don't want to waste your time."

My lower lip quivered. The leaky faucets behind my eyelids threatened to overflow. Instead, I bit the inside of my cheek and said with a steely voice, "Are you done?"

You nodded. You looked so crestfallen, but who was I to beg you to stay?

"You can get the fuck out now."

Hurt flashed across your face, but I was determined to have my breakdown elsewhere, away from you, on my forty-minute drive back home.

"I really did love you, Jenna."

The door closed and I waited until you were out of sight before letting the sobs wrack my ribcage like pounding gorillas, my chest feeling like it might explode with the pain of loss. I attempted to drive through my bleary vision, dialing Schwasty, who was my go-to when it came to breakups.

"NERDBOYBROKEUPWITHMEEEEEEEEE," I wailed, already hyperventilating. She sighed sadly, muttering profanities under her breath, understanding how devastating this was for me.

"Are you driving right now?" I hiccupped in the affirmative and she demanded I pull over. She offered soothing words ("he fucked up," and "you'll find someone better!"), and after a while I'd had enough time to collect myself so I was no longer a moving road hazard. It was three in the morning on the east coast, so Schwasty said she needed to go back to sleep. I bid her goodnight and hung up.

I've had some long drives in my life, but that was definitely top five. Why would you do that? Make me drop you off and dump me on your way out? That's a big dick move, bro.

The subsequent breakdown and depression was awful. The beginning of 2013 has gone down in history as "The Time Jenna Almost Ruined Everything." I found myself sleeping most of the day, even accidentally fucking up my second job as a dog walker. I walked around in a hazy reality, crying every time I imagined life without you. Sure, now I realize that we most likely don't have one true soul mate, but I genuinely thought you could have been the sole provider of my future security.

We didn't speak for a long time, except for that one time you insisted on coming by to pick up things you'd left at my house. Naturally, I made sure I was dressed to go out on a date, because heels and lipstick are always wonderful forms of revenge. You looked so hurt when you saw me dolled up, which bolstered my determination to sleep with your roommate. I figured if lipstick could make your heart hurt, what about doing the nasty with your roommate? The logic was probably not the *most* sound.

I'm not normally the chick to revenge fuck her way through a guy's buddies, but in the span of forty-five days, you had professed love and then crushed me. I wanted to hurt you as bad as you had hurt me. And to be fair, I *did* back out before anything happened because I knew deep down it wasn't truly me. Revenge isn't my MO. Regardless, I'm sorry for how that made you feel when you found out.

The first few months following our breakup I did some terrible and awesome things, like a week of "yes" at a photography conference, where I actually made a fool of myself and solidified my reputation as a lush in the photography industry. I canoodled around with a famous photographer in an attempt to feel important. My stomach roils when I think about 2013 Jenna. It really is quite miraculous how much a person can change in even three years.

In hindsight, I recognize that I just wasn't ready for a healthy relationship. Maybe if we'd met at a different time, but at this point it's moot to speculate. I just hope you're happy now. I hope you found ways to better communicate with the wife that you married only six months after our breakup. So much for *"not ready to get married,"* eh? No, you just didn't want to marry *me*.

Sincerely,

The Starter Girlfriend

A letter to a man-child

When I met Walrus, I was two years away from finishing my Bachelor's Degree in Advertising and Public Relations. After the first six months of 2013, which were filled with struggles, my business was finally taking off, and in glorious ways. I moved out of the house that I shared with Army Man and began living with one of my good childhood friends close to Chinatown in Oahu. I had been single for six months at this point and actually hadn't slept with anyone, choosing to wait until my next relationship. I was so proud *of myself for this, being able to discern some real change in how I behaved when it came to relationships and random hookups. I was becoming* mature, *y'all. The only thing I knew was that my next boyfriend had to be better looking than Nerd Boy, as payback for him marrying a woman who had the face of a horse. This letter is about the time I thought I could have my cake and eat it too.*

Dear Walrus,

Ours was easily one of the most fucked up relationships I've ever had the misfortune of enduring. Writing these letters has helped me accept that I tend to pick narcissists, but it wasn't until the most recent crash and burn that I realized this fully. I might have felt enlightened when I first met you, with my newfound *maturity*, but our relationship definitely proved I knew *nothing* about life.

Where do I begin with this impending train wreck? I suppose our first date is as good as any. After chatting online for a little bit, we finally met at a local southern BBQ joint "only for drinks." You walked in, wearing a blue plaid shirt and jeans, a sprinkling of stubble lining your handsome jaw. *You were the best looking guy I had ever been on a date with* and I almost couldn't stand all of your perfection—your bright blue eyes, your biceps, your infectious laugh. We laughed hysterically over baby goats, your eyes twinkling as I snorted in delight watching them do back-flips on YouTube. We found ourselves sitting there for four hours, unwilling to say goodbye even when the clock struck midnight.

At this point, June 2013, I had been single for six months. My heart was still trying to recover from Nerd Boy's breakup and subsequent marriage, but I greeted our budding relationship with as little baggage as possible. I hadn't even had sex since the breakup, choosing to wait for the next real thing in my life. You came into my life, the embodiment of the handsome replacement I told myself I deserved.

On our second date, we went to see one of my favorite bluegrass bands perform, but your job, which was in the oil industry, made it so you worked crazy hours, and you had to leave before the set was even over. I walked with you back to your car, accepting your invitation to be driven back around to the front of the bar. When we got there, you slid the car into park and said, "Come here," beckoning me closer. I wanted to play hard to get but my curiosity won out. Your kiss made me feel woozy, lights exploding in every nerve all over my body. I hadn't felt that way in years, and I wanted more of it.

Your office was close to my house and you often stopped by on your way back from work, sometimes in between jobs. We had sex for the first time a couple weeks later. It was perfect, if not a little vanilla. "We could do this every day," you promised, your voice light and sultry. At the time, the mere idea of awesome vanilla sex every day with a man who made me laugh sounded like an incredible gift. We had so much fun together, those first few weeks. I still laugh when I think about how you fit I believe it was . . . nineteen grapes in your mouth? Your cheeks were stuffed to bursting, making chewing impossible. You went from a handsome Abercrombie model to resembling a desperate starving hamster. I almost peed myself. Your antics often amused me and kept me on my toes.

We even reached a point of goofing off together—when we said something outrageous but true, we would laughingly add "WALRUSES!" to show we were telling the truth. Sometimes we even used this code word to punctuate the seriousness of conversations. "You're the best thing that ever happened to me. Walruses." Even when we were fighting, we would occasionally use this special code, to show how much we cared or how angry we were. Your nickname became "the Walrus" to my friends, the fun jokester who always had a laugh to bestow.

The honeymoon phase didn't seem to last long, though. A month into our relationship, I began noticing red flags all over. You could never discuss anything outside of the topic of gasoline and how much money you made. You imposed random yet constant stops at my house, where you expected me to put my work and school on hold. If you did a favor for me, you expected one in return, your Libra nature overpowering any natural kindness a relationship should contain. I was torn, attracted to your pretty face but also wishing I could have more time alone. I remember talking with my friend, who was a stylist, telling him I thought I might just have to break it off. We had only been dating for about a month, but something felt off.

"You're crazy," he told me. "He's gorgeous. If you don't date him, I will."

For some odd reason, I thought my worth was measured by how handsome my boyfriends were. I foolishly thought that your handsome could defeat your red flags.

Only a day after talking to my friend, we got into a fight. You had once again stopped by spontaneously, my resentment stewing as we watched television. At the time, I was struggling to balance a budding business and full-time school at Hawaii Pacific University, so taking five to seven hours off spur of the moment was at times debilitating. For a long time, I thought trying to prioritize my success and education was selfish, but in hindsight, I realize *I* wasn't the selfish one.

On this particular day, I asked for a foot rub. Instead of obliging, you slammed your feet toward me and whined, "What about me? Do I get a foot rub? I brought you ice cream and I've been working all day."

There I was, mid-work day, trying to appease you while thinking about the 346 items on my to-do list. You had brought ice cream as a consolation prize, but I was expected to cook dinner as well. I didn't think that asking for a foot rub was out-of-this-world kind of crazy.

I rubbed your fucking feet.

Then I made you dinner, one of my famous cheesy pasta concoctions. It was an easy meal but still took about thirty minutes to make. You didn't even seem grateful, accepting the hot meal as if it was your due. I knew right then and there we wouldn't be a good fit. I lamented to friends about your behavior and I remember one of them saying, "He sounds insane." Taking a deep breath, I called you the day after you demanded the foot rub, ready to break it off.

"Walrus, I just don't think this is working?"

"What—what do you mean?"

"We just aren't the right fit. I like you, but I don't think I'm going to be able to give you what you need. You're exhausting me."

"I promise I'll get better. I'm not myself. I'm working these new hours. I promise I'm not normally like this."

"I don't know . . ."

"Please, Jenna, trust me!" His voice was pleading, the deep baritone soothing and convincing.

"Fine, but I need more space. I need you to stop telling me things like how I'm selfish when I need to focus on school and my business. And I need you to stop demanding things."

"Okay, I will, promise."

But promises are merely words, I've learned. Within two weeks, you were back to the same gimmicks and I was lost as to what to do. You didn't seem to care as much about how I felt and gave no thought to certain things, especially when it came to your mother and how she viewed me. Our introduction was forced and abrupt, the grin on your face wide while we awkwardly introduced ourselves in her living room. Since neither of us had anticipated meeting, my hair was askew and I wasn't wearing a bra. She wasn't either, a fact that thoroughly embarrassed her. Maybe if we'd had a better first impression she wouldn't have made a snap judgment about me. Whether it was that particular moment or another, one thing was clear: she didn't think I was good enough for her baby boy.

I'm not sure why. You were a recovering weed addict, with barely an associate's degree, and had spent your twenties just cooking in restaurants. I don't say this as a reflection of chefs or people with only an associate's degree, but fuck, I had my own business. I had pulled myself out of the muck of addiction, served my country, and was finishing my bachelor's degree. I even made her food and occasionally helped clean her house.

How the hell was I not good enough?

The meeting with your mother was only the beginning of our troubles. During the long sixteen months we were together, I think we broke up around a dozen times. I wish I were kidding, but the count is undoubtedly in the double digits. I tried to leave you so many times, but you continuously sucked me in with promises and lies, changing for a week or two before slipping back into your manipulations. Fighting became our way of life, strife morphing into reality, the calm moments more alarming than the drama. You never stopped touching me and always made sure foreplay was more the main show rather than simply the preview, which made me pretend you were more generous than you really were. We were so unhappy together; I don't know how we kept it going.

The cheating began early in the relationship, starting with a woman you claimed was *just* a friend. You introduced her as K, a girl you'd met before me but declared you had no interest in. Yet the one time I saw you interact with her, the chemistry and looks that passed between you simmered in the air. A niggle in my brain told me something was off. I did what any paranoid woman would do: I waited until you went to sleep, took your phone, and began searching. I didn't feel comfortable asking, in case I was just having a case of "the jealousies."

However, my fears were confirmed almost immediately:

Walrus: *My girlfriend is driving me crazy again.*

K: *Why don't you leave her?*

Walrus: *I can't. What are you doing?*

K: *Chillin'.*

K: *I have a friend you might want to meet.*

Walrus: *Yeah? Who?*

K: *A doctor. Blonde.*

Walrus: *Pics?*

Walrus: *Just curious.*

There were also texts where you asked to sleep and shower at her place, despite her repeated reminders that you had a girlfriend. After reading those messages, I slipped out of bed and left. I drove home, lost in my own thoughts, wondering where to go from here. I was still at that point in my life where I couldn't stand to be alone. Somehow I reasoned that since it didn't seem like anything had happened, that your transgressions could be forgiven. I confronted you the next day, marking our fifth or eighth breakup (*who the fuck knows at this point?*). But in the end, I stayed. I stayed in a relationship that was beyond the realms of healthy, all because of fear.

I slowly began to lose myself, each breakup chipping away at my self-esteem and sense of right and wrong. I came to think our relationship was perfectly fine, despite all the signs saying that it wasn't. Do you remember our first Christmas? We were supposed to spend it with your parents', but your mom was so stressed and overworked, I suggested we go clean up her house to make her feel better. So on Christmas Eve, we spent three hours cleaning the house. I also asked to go to the store so I could bake scones for the morning, loving the idea of maybe, *just maybe*, having a good Christmas. My father had spent my entire childhood tormenting me on Christmas and it had become the shittiest holiday of my life. I just wanted to make fucking scone, damn it.

We got into a fight over the idea of scones, with you telling me that I didn't have time to do it and shouldn't even bother. I threw a fit because I just wanted to do this small thing for myself and everyone else. I cook to show my love and you weren't understanding of this facet of my personality. We had been together for six months, but you never paused to really understand me.

Instead, the fight was so nasty I almost bailed on the holiday. I cried that night, in bed, while you rolled over and ignored me. For the millionth time, I was reminded how shitty holidays were for me. I was alone in this world.

We still went to your parents' house the next morning and had a good time. I skipped baking the scones but no one noticed. For a present, you got me a beautiful Tiffany's ring and I got you a gorgeous watch that you had been eyeing at the mall two months before. I always felt like our happiness was forced, but on this particular day, as long as we avoided anything below the surface, we were happy. It was one of the fakest holidays of my adult life and somehow, sadly, the happiest.

The next day, we got into another argument, my inability to drop the issue of the scones casting a dark cloud. It wasn't *really* about the scones and I'm sure you eventually realized that. We legitimately almost broke up again, with you sitting on your couch, terror etched into your face when you realized I was about to leave.

"Please, Jenna. Don't. I love you."

It was the first time you had said those three words. The world stopped for a second. *This isn't how it should be done*, I heard a voice whisper in my head. Why did you say it after another fight? Couldn't you have lent the moment better timing?

Shyly, you handed over the Christmas card you had intended to give me only the day before. I opened it and glitter sprinkled out of the envelope, covering the fabric of the couch. My mouth dry, I read the card, seeing the large "I Love You" printed over a red ornament on the front, covered in red glitter.

Was I going to ever receive better treatment from a man? Had I peaked in life, stuck with a card professing love? Was this my future? *Did I deserve this for my past mistakes?*

Despite my serious apprehensions, I accepted your proclamation, my need for love overpowering my need for sanity. Nothing was ever easy with us, but I hoped once again things could change. Sixth breakup and reunification is the charm, yes?

In December 2013, we began to dance around the topic of living together, but you were held back by fear, having never lived with a woman. I wasn't entirely interested in being another starter girlfriend, but I definitely began to consider being the starter female roommate.

Your demands on me continued, our unhealthy interactions piling up like dead bodies. It began straining my mental wellbeing, and I struggled to balance school and business. You were working sixty hours a week, but I easily worked twenty more. I was going to school five days a week on top of serving clients. Your anger seemed to grow as if in response to the lack of time I could afford to give you.

My friends were tired of hearing about our bullshit drama. Even Facebook refused to acknowledge our relationship status changes, since they occurred almost monthly. In April 2014, I had hit my limit with the most recent breakup, returning all of your belongings, determined to make this breakup stick. I put you on radio silence and turned my focus on my impending trip to Thailand, which I was so sure would change my life. I activated my online dating accounts and even began having conversations with other men. Despite enjoying the room to breathe, I had to admit that I missed you.

After a couple weeks' hiatus, you began to try and woo me back, realizing that I was one of the best things you'd ever had. Your promises had more flourish this go-around, declaring that you'd like to marry me some day, and that you admired me for my work ethic and talents. You swore to change, promising to respect my time and needs, even going so far as offering to move in together. Against my better judgment, I took you back before I left for Thailand. What the fuck was I thinking? Even though I was on the true path to healing from what my father did, I still saw my worth as being wrapped up in the men that loved me. I use the term "love" loosely here, of course. I left for Thailand, hoping to find some perspective and space. You were so supportive from the get-go, which made me feel better about taking you back for the one-thousandth time.

In May 2014, I boarded a plane for my dream trip to Thailand. This particular journey began years before, while I was still in the military. I'd found a website showing volunteer opportunities working with elephants. It was one of those few times I felt the Universe providing me with a calling, a lifetime goal suddenly clicking into place. At the time, due to military security measures and limitations, I wasn't permitted to go to Thailand. But now that my business was growing like a snowball rolling downhill, I could afford to take the time off to achieve some dreams.

I arrived in Bangkok around midnight, so I paid for a personal driver to collect me in an effort to avoid possible taxi scams. The first thing that hit was the heat; it was like stepping into an oven. My driver took me through streets where I saw dogs dodging tuk-tuks in the streets, trash littering the gutters.

Brave shopkeepers sold their wares to late-night drunks and food carts stirred up smells that made my mouth water. Something about the energy in the country stirred my spirit and I felt a smile began to curl across my face. It turned into a full-blown grin when we arrived at my five-star hotel, the Chatrium. I was greeted with soft words like "Madam," and quietly led to my suite overlooking a stunning river. Around one in the morning, I curled into my fluffy, cool sheets, free from the burdens of you, of my job, of any type of stress. I was *home*.

Alas, that infatuation was short-lived. The next day, I decided to brave the bustling city of Bangkok in the brightness of day and was immediately scammed by a taxi driver. It started simple enough: I was leaving MBK—a huge mall in the heart of the city with seven floors of bargain shopping, wall-to-wall electronics shops, and a food court with over twenty cultures to choose from—when I walked past some tuk-tuks. A small Thai man eyed me shrewdly and stood up from his slouching position.

"Hello! Tuk-tuk?"

I looked at him, assessing the situation. I didn't get a particularly bad vibe about him, so I asked the one question everyone should always ask: "How much?"

"Oh, not much. Two hundred fifty baht."

I laughed at him and began to walk away. "I just paid sixty baht to get here. You're insane."

He began to follow, which didn't alarm me. I watched him out of the corner of my eye as he pulled out a pen. "Wait! Okay, let's make a deal!" Interested, I turned around, curious to see what kind of travel story I could get myself into that afternoon. He began to scribble lines on his palm.

"Okay, see, we here. Your hotel here. Over here, is custom dress shop. I take you there. If you buy something, your taxi ride free."

I saw the scam but welcomed it. I had originally wanted to see if I could get a custom dress during my short stay in Bangkok, so I saw this as a possible opportunity. This, of course, was my first mistake. My second mistake was climbing into the front passenger seat when we got into his visibly ramshackle car. I was used to driving passenger with taxi drivers, never being afraid. I hadn't considered the culture I was in; I was wrapped up by the prospect of losing money for a good story.

We weaved in and out of the traffic while he pestered me with questions about America. I watched our surroundings and answered with vague responses. All of the streets looked the same, with crumbling walls, faded posters, and a plethora of wires that seemed to bleed from rooftops. After about fifteen minutes in traffic, we finally pulled up in front of the dress shop. Despite my concerns, I found it to be clean and the staff helpful. I ended up picking out a pattern, with the seamstress promising next day delivery. It cost me around sixty dollars, far more than it should have, but I shrugged it off. Sometimes it's about the experience, not the cost.

I piled back into the taxi, satisfied and feeling confident. Sure, I'd been swindled, but the skirt was bound to be pretty and now my taxi ride was free. We started making our way back to my hotel when he again pelted me with questions.

"So who else are you traveling with?"

A little bell went off in my head. This question seemed innocuous enough, but then he put his hand on my thigh. My survival instincts kicked in and I became instantly wary.

"A bunch of friends!" I lied. My body language became standoffish, but he didn't seem to notice.

"Men or women?"

The bell rang more loudly. "Both. Six men and two women. We're traveling around Thailand."

Luckily, backpacking groups of friends being commonplace made this a plausible lie. He nodded. I tried to change the subject, mentioning the flower markets noted on a tourist brochure placed on the dashboard.

"Oh yes, the flower markets! I can take you and your friends!" he said, eagerness dripping from his words. Again, I was uneasy.

"How much?" my words were laced with wariness, which he noticed.

"Oh don't worry, it'll be fine. I give you good price."

"No, how much?"

"You can decide how much!" he promised.

There was now a fire alarm going off inside my head. I envisioned the taxi stopping on the way to the markets and getting robbed or worse. It made no sense that he wouldn't give me a price. I tried to placate him, promising him I would talk to my "friends." He became incredibly insistent.

"So tomorrow, eight AM? You'll be there? You not a liar?"

I smiled my bravest smile and agreed. Then I bolted from the taxi, feeling bad and scared at the same time. If he just simply lacked knowledge of American women and our fear of kidnappings, then he was going to be so upset the next morning. But I'd rather trust my instincts than regret my choices.

Navigating the insanity that is Thailand was an endeavor in itself. It was my first "Third World" country, albeit I've now been to actual Third World countries and would argue Thailand is a Second World country. Sure, it's cheap as hell, but you don't have to hunt for toilet paper like you do in Morocco. Yet the culture shock was still incredibly intense. After two days in Bangkok, I was ready to explore Chiang Mai, a place of calmer waters. I called you in between stops and hotels, searching for WiFi in every spot I found myself, keeping in touch the best I could. I wanted you to know I hadn't forgotten about you, even during my journey.

The true purpose of going to Thailand was the elephants up in the northern forests of Thailand. I could feel the culture of Thailand breaking me down and building me back up, making me confident that two days with elephants was just what I needed. The bumpy traffic-riddled ride to the sanctuary made me jittery, but I kept my calm by imagining the large, gray pachyderms in the jungle waiting for me. Upon arrival, we were shuffled to the main building with a concrete lookout balcony, the perfect height at which to meet elephants face to face. I could hear trumpets in the distance and looked around, overwrought with emotion at the prospect of touching my first elephant.

We were brought as a group to buckets of melon and told the rules of interaction: no placing food directly into their mouths, no touching their faces, and stay behind the red line. I hopped excitedly from foot to foot. When would they show up? The suspense was killing me. After a few minutes, I saw some excited tourists pointing somewhere behind me. I whipped my head around and saw them: a family of four, with a baby elephant!

I burst into tears—thank goodness I was wearing sunglasses. They walked up to the building, their movements slow and deliberate. Being sensitive to energies, I felt myself reaching out for theirs and being wrapped up into the warmth. I grabbed a piece of melon and offered it to a female who wasn't interested in my transcendent experience; she just wanted the fruit. Everything in my life fell away, my focus being only on this curious trunk in front of me, probing my hands for more treats. Words are completely inefficient for this moment. The mere presence of elephants has transfixed humans for thousands of years. They've been used in battles; carried cargo; abused in circuses; worshipped; and most importantly, they've been killed. It's said that they have a better memory than humans and mourn their dead even decades later. They're simply remarkable.

This particular sanctuary does not permit elephant riding, because of the inherent cruelty of the practice, but we got to feed and bathe them, as well as just hang out in the fields as they ate and interacted. I cared for an elephant whose hips had been broken in a forced breeding. I gave fruit to elephants that were blinded as punishment. My heart was breaking and healing every single minute. Somehow, simply by existing in their presence, I was starting to find the peace I'd sought my entire life.

What I found so inconceivable was that every single one of the elephants had endured unimaginable abuse. Most females had had babies taken from them too young. There were ten blind elephants, none of which had gone blind from natural causes. A particular elephant named Jokia had been forced to carry logs while pregnant. She was even carrying a log uphill while in the process of giving birth. The baby eventually died, and mother was so heartbroken she refused to work. Her *mahout* punished her insubordination by jamming his bullhook into her eye until she was completely blind.

Yet this old matriarch was gentle, her energy like a deep, warm pool of liquid that I never wanted to leave. I was struck by the endless forgiveness elephants have, despite how horrifically they'd been treated. The revelation came to me in a fury: it does not make me weak to forgive the abuses of the men in my life; it makes me strong, like an elephant. I saw myself in these gentle giants, capable of tearing down entire buildings but choosing peace instead. Could I choose peace too? Could I choose forgiveness and finally heal from the pain my father inflicted upon me all those years ago?

I fell asleep that night with a herd of elephants rumbling and squeaking right outside my window. It was hot, sticky, and mosquitoes buzzed outside my netting. I slept like a baby, a soft smile plastered across my face. It was one of the best nights of my life.

I woke early, eager to not miss a moment of time with the elephants. I grabbed a cup of coffee and sat down on a bench, attempting to ignore the army of flies that ruled the roost. The sun peeked it's orange head above the mountains, a soft mist covering the fields as the elephants were let out of their pens, allowed to roam for the day. It was probably one of the most relaxing moments of my entire life. I also found some strong WiFi and FaceTimed you, showing you some of the elephants and stray dogs that ran around. It felt so good to show you a little bit about what was changing me into a better person. You seemed thrilled to be included!

My group had to leave later that day, after walking around with elephants most of the morning. I climbed into the transport van feeling morose, wishing I could stay longer. It took about an hour to get back to my hotel, most of which was spent trying to keep my shit together. I somehow made it back to my room with my luggage before having a complete breakdown and sobbing for an undetermined amount of time, emotions rolling over me in unrelenting waves. I think, after all the work I'd been putting toward healing, being stuck in a stressed life with you, it all accumulated and came down on me at once. I wept for who I was, for my lost childhood, my poor, hateful heart that ached to be soft again. I took a look at myself, at the choices I'd made, and wanted nothing more than to be happy. Everything up to this point had been a battle, not just with you, but every man I had ever tried to be with. I was so incredibly tired.

I called my mother, sharing my devastation, tears smearing my cheeks. I didn't know how to process anything; everything inside felt broken. She laughed softly, sadly, at my heartbreak, not understanding why I was so hysterical. I don't think anyone could have understood. Even I have difficulty grasping how my personality had shifted in such an outstanding way, in two short days.

I had tried so hard to include you in this trip, FaceTiming you when WiFi permitted. I even tried to video chat while at the elephant sanctuary, to bring you into my slice of heaven, but I came to realize the journey was all my own. The change inside me, or soul fracture as I call it, was so expansive that for a period I thought you and I could overcome anything. I temporarily forgot that you hadn't just experienced a similar life-changing moment and were still stuck toiling in America. I tried to not be resentful, but I couldn't help it. Even our normal interactions frustrated me, especially while I was still abroad.

> **Me:** *Hey babe :) It's been tough with the internet, so I borrowed a friend's :) I knew you'd be worried, so I wanted to check in :) I miss the shit out of you. We HAVE to come here together. It would blow your mind. I've never been so at peace :)*
>
> **Walrus:** *Don't worry babe! I miss more shit out of you! Do your thang and just contact me when you can.*
>
> **Me:** *I can't wait to hug you again.*
>
> **Walrus:** *Just reach your arms out and pretend I'm there.*
>
> **Me:** *Then I would just be hugging either a tourist or elephant ;) I got chased by a baby elephant. They're little buggers hahaha.*
>
> **Walrus:** *Ok I'm more like the elephant so hug that one!*
>
> **Me:** *Haha yeah you do have a big nose ;)*
>
> **Walrus:** *Wish me luck for tomorrow!*
>
> **Me:** *What's tomorrow???*
>
> **Walrus:** *My championship game . . .*
>
> **Me:** *Oh! Sorry it's Sunday here and I can't keep track. Well good luck ☺ you'll be amazing!!!*
>
> **Walrus:** *You are my girlfriend, right?*

> *Me: I don't think I'm just your girlfriend. I don't feel like just a girlfriend.*
>
> **Walrus**: *Really?*
>
> *Me: Yes really. Spending time thinking here made me realize how much I really want to be with you. And how much I love you.*
>
> **Walrus**: *Why do you love me?*
>
> *Me: Haha why do you ask? Have I not listed enough reasons previously???*
>
> **Walrus:** *I just want to hear.*
>
> *Me: Okay, well unfortunately, I don't have time. I just hope you can take me at my word??I have to go eat lunch now . . .*
>
> **Walrus**: *What?!?!?!?Wow . . . That much huh?*
>
> *Me: You're weirding me out.*
>
> **Walrus:** *Ok . . .*
>
> *Me: Uhm . . . I'm going to go now. I'll talk to you later.*
>
> **Walrus**: *Bye, babe.*
>
> *Me: Walrus, I understand you feel insecure while I'm gone, since I don't think you're used to being separated from someone like this, but it hurts me that if I don't have time to explain why I love you, you seem to get upset. That isn't fair. I love you and I hope that at this point, through everything, I don't need to justify or explain it. It gives me anxiety to even think you're upset because I didn't have the time to explain it. I love you and I know y'all will rock the championships.*

Nothing infuriated me more than having to always reassure you of my love and consistently being asked to explain it. I said it every day and even took the time, usually, to explain why I loved you. Were you just insecure with how much fun I was having without you? Despite my concerns, I returned from Thailand with hope of moving forward. Hope had blossomed in my soul and I imagined that somehow it would transfer to you by osmosis. After Thailand, I had wanted to live more simply and put more of an effort into traveling. I dropped my name-brand obsession, striving to give up my selfishness and undesirable personality traits. Disappointment came like a stab in the gut when reality came crashing down. You, unfortunately, had not come to the same conclusion and instead wanted to go right back into the drama. I didn't want the same things as before—the Jenna from two weeks prior had disappeared forever.

You remained the same money-obsessed boy you'd always been, focused on anything gasoline related, avoiding any kind of self-reflection.

Despite our glaring incompatibilities, we began discussing moving in together in earnest. This time you suggested we live with your parents for a couple of months while you saved more money, and then get an apartment of our own. *I didn't want to fucking do it* and you knew that. I didn't want to have to put my things in storage, even if I'd be able to save a little money in the meantime. Your mother hated me, refusing to even go to lunch with me when I invited her.

In June 2014, we got into a massive argument because even though we'd been discussing moving in together for a bit, you refused to tell your parents about the plan. Their house wasn't prepared to host another human and two dogs, the spare bedroom full to the brim with knick-knacks from thirty years prior. In that moment, I realized that you would never be a reliable part of my life, covered in the façade of broken promises and ideas that would never happen. Like a bird taking a shit in my hair, I knew this wasn't going to work out. I suddenly saw myself living with you every day, dirty laundry and dishes a constant, fights happening at every single opportunity. That was *not* what I imagined for my future. I tried desperately to crawl out of the situation. I called friends, begging for a place to stay; I looked all over the internet, trying to locate an affordable place for me and my two dogs, but found nothing. Hawaii was a horrendous and impossible place to live alone, especially with two dogs. Some places wanted a deposit for the same amount of rent just to have the dogs, not including the security deposit. We're talking over six grand, just to move in. I didn't want to live without them; the idea of giving them up filled me with agonizing sadness.

Acknowledging defeat, I agreed to move in with you. In July 2014, around the time of our first anniversary, I packed up my belongings and put the larger pieces into storage. We drove to your parents' house, where I had another breakdown. The house was not prepared, because you had delayed until the last second in telling your parents about the plan and me moving in. We had to spend hours just moving things around the house, shoving ten-year-old magazines out of the way and carefully moving around receipts from fifteen years ago. My friend Sarcasmo came to help me bring items in and had to step out while I screamed every nasty word I knew, disgusted at the state of things. She was so sad for me and left after giving me a tight hug and whispering "good luck."

    I later discovered that you had told your parents that I'd made poor choices and was in a financial pickle, so they only let me move in with the perception I was down on my luck, when in reality I had just made the massive mistake of not being strong enough to leave a year before.

Coo-Coo-Ca-Chu Part Two

Dear Walrus,

Throughout the majority of our endless arguments, you usually declared at least once, "I don't mean to be an asshole!" Do you recall my rote response?

"For not trying, you're sure as fuck succeeding."

Except I wasn't allowed to use the word "fuck," because you "refused to be spoken to like that." Foul language dirtied the perception of who you thought we were. You seemed as trapped as I was, in a perpetual merry-go-round of misery. I feel like when I was with you, I spent my time trying to diminish myself, to make myself average. I slowly lost important parts of myself, like the strength to walk away. I began to think our constant fighting was the new normal, the way things just had to be.

That summer spent living with your parents passed quickly, with me frequently traveling for work. I threw myself into my photography company, accepting almost every gig that came my way. I closed in on my degree, anticipating graduation in less than a year. I hope that if I worked hard enough, I could just walk out on you. I genuinely didn't want to live with you and my resentment only fueled our arguments. You tried being cheery with me, but I had become sour. I felt like my life was a train doomed to run off the tracks and I didn't know how to get off before it wrecked. My vicious anger, complete and consuming, confused you every day. You couldn't fathom that the root of my rage came from the constant game of, "will Walrus let me keep this space clean for longer than six hours?" Your mother was equally ungrateful when I cleaned expired, five-year-old food from her cupboard. She never confronted me but instead went to you, wondering why I thought it would be okay to clean the kitchen in the first place. I would spend three hours cleaning their house, as a thank you for temporarily hosting me, and they would trash it again without even acknowledging the time I'd put into organizing everything. I was losing a battle with my sanity, with no end in sight. I secretly searched Craigslist for places to stay, hoping to avoid signing a lease with you. The costs of Hawaii filled me with hopelessness.

In August 2014, I flew to Colorado to photograph a wedding, leaving you to find an apartment for us. Your parents were growing impatient and frustrated with my existence, no matter how hard I tried to shrink myself. The trip to Colorado came at a fortuitous time and I arrived in my hotel with my then-friend Rude, looking forward to hanging out after traveling for about fifteen hours. You'd promised the week before that I could trust you to find a place for us to live in and I took a leap of faith, deciding this would be the deciding factor on whether I could rely on you.

First, you picked a small cottage with a landlord who was fucked out of his gourd. He began to make demands, like access to the yard any time he wanted or insisting we use his shitty internet service. You couldn't handle the adult necessity of bargaining and called me, lost in the stress. You began verbally abusing me, telling me how selfish I was for not being there to help you with this. You ended the conversation by telling me we were over and that I had a week to find a new place to live.

I sat in the hotel, dumbfounded. Rude tried to comfort me, telling me how much she didn't like him and I couldn't help but agree. "What will I do?" I asked, knowing that I didn't have the thousands it would require to move in just a few weeks. A temporary solution presented itself: you called me fifteen minutes later, apologizing for everything . . . not even caring how your emotional abuse affected my job.

In September 2014, we moved into the small cottage you'd been negotiating and losing your shit over. You promised it was perfect, raving about how quiet the neighborhood was, how much I would like the quaint feel of it all.

"It has beautiful French doors and a yard!"

It was actually a glorified shoebox, with two half closets, a kitchen without counter space, a sexist landlord, and barking neighbor dogs. I walked in the front door and was immediately repulsed. Once again, I was stuck in a situation with no perceivable way out. I remember taking a deep breath and saying to myself, "Jenna, we can do this. We'll find a way out. Let's start over and try to make the best of it." So I brought my remaining things out of storage and began to decorate, trying my best to make it a home, hoping things would get better.

I was fucking delusional. *Delusional*. It became apparent from the get-go that you had zero intention of being a grown adult. I had become your new mother. The evidence of your disgusting way of living was everywhere, from the dirty dishes in the sink to the mound of laundry that threatened to suffocate us all the way from the closet. That first week I honestly didn't know how I was going to survive. I didn't want to nag you but I was working fourteen-hour days and couldn't also take care of the man-child sitting on my couch. I grew desperate, hoping to find a way out.

The Universe heard my pleas and presented a solution: a ringing iPod.

It was nine in the evening on a Wednesday and there I was, minding my own business, when I heard a ringing from your closet. You were at work, due home in about an hour, so I knew it wasn't your phone. I walked to the bedroom and searched for the source of the ringing, which hadn't stopped. I opened your soccer bag and found an iPod stuffed inside, lit up from texts. I saw that it was from one of your soccer teammates and I knew this particular guy owed you money, so I entered the passcode, figuring I could text you what he was saying. Instead, it opened straight to messages, with strange unlabeled numbers. You were the type to label every number and so my suspicions were spurred. I opened them. My horror mounted with every interaction, every word: "beautiful," "send a pic," and even, "let's meet up." There were multiple messages between you and two different girls: one from five months prior and one from only two weeks earlier. You'd sent them photos; they'd sent photos back, dirty words shared by both. I was devastated, mentally thrashing myself for being such an idiot. I called you, feeling violent and vengeful.

You answered promptly, a smile in your voice.

"Hey, babe, what's up?"

"What. The. Fuck. Have. You. Done?"

"What do you mean?"

Your concern brought a sneer to my face. My voice deepened as my anger grew. "I found the fucking text messages. WHAT THE FUCK HAVE YOU DONE?!"

This time, I heard panic seeping into your voice, gears whirring in your tiny brain. "What are you talking about?"

"I found your fucking iPod, you piece of shit."

Quick to switch blame, you turned accusatory. "You went through my iPod?"

I laughed, not letting you put the blame on me. I wasn't being nosey intentionally, so I knew I wasn't in the wrong. "Yes, and thank goodness I did, you lying cheating piece of shit. WHAT THE FUCK HAVE YOU DONE?"

"It's not what you think. What are you talking about?"

I opened up one of the messages—a pretty girl who lived on Maui—and started reading. "Does this sound familiar? 'Hey, baby, send me a pic . . . oh, you're beautiful. Do you have something sexier you can share? Let's meet up!'"

You paused, panicking. "I'm coming home."

"Don't fucking bother. I'm packing up. I'm fucking leaving you."

I hung up, ignoring your protests, shoving clothes into bags, not even registering what I was grabbing. Unfortunately, you arrived just in time to stop me from heading to the car. You begged for the chance to explain, practically dropping to your knees. After over a year of this drama, I didn't know how to just shut this shit down. Old habits die hard—the weak part of me relented. I gave you ten minutes to explain your shit, keeping one eye on my belongings sitting by the door.

"I have a problem, Jenna."

"No shit, Sherlock." I snorted in derision, already deciding I wasn't going to like whatever bullshit you told me.

"No, really, hear me out. I have a problem. I'm insecure. I discovered dating websites a few years ago and became addicted to the rating system. Most of the time, I would just use it as a way to talk to girls, people I would have never met otherwise. It built up my self-esteem when girls were attracted to me and said they wanted me. It's why I kept in touch with K, and I did it at the beginning as well. I stopped for a long time, but lately you've been distant and we've been fighting so much. We barely have sex anymore. If you gave me more sex I wouldn't have to do this. I just wanted to feel good, to feel wanted. I knew it was wrong; I just couldn't stop myself. Moving in with you was like a do-over for me—I promise I deleted all of the apps. I just want to start fresh with you!"

Yes. You literally laid the blame at my feet, unwilling to admit that this was entirely your fault. Lucky for me, you also successfully shifted something inside me. I couldn't do this anymore—I couldn't live with a man who blamed our lack of intimacy entirely on me. If I avoided anything resembling intimacy, it was because I was too busy disliking your daily manipulations. After you confessed to emotionally cheating, you turned the conversation toward chastising me for "snooping." You gently admonished me for starting shit when I didn't need to. The subject was deemed *done* and I was virtually forbidden from bringing it up, because you felt *so* bad and wanted to just start over. Once again, I pulled the wool over my own eyes and just stopped caring.

We tried to be amicable, and for the next few months we almost succeeded. This is mostly due to you getting the game *Destiny* and playing it every available moment. I would leave for school at seven AM and come back at five to find you in the same exact position and the dishes still not done. "Stop harassing me, I'll get it done!" you'd yell, making me wait another day. You were the most irresponsible and disgusting man I've ever lived with. I exhausted myself, being an adult full time and cleaning up after you as well.

As my good friend Sarcasmo once told me, after enduring the dozens of phone calls from me, crying about how poorly you treated me, "At one time, you might have been strong enough to leave him. But he wore you down until you just couldn't anymore." The emotional and mental abuse had been a slow burn, searing away my self-worth. I didn't know how to escape. What would I do with my dogs? How would I survive? I didn't have the answers yet, but I was finally ready to fight back.

My natural and immediate response was to *plan a motherfucking trip*. I started planning a three-month trip to Southeast Asia, with a move to Seattle where I would then buy a house. I presented it to you like it was *maybe* going to happen, terrified you would try and talk me out of it. I pretended that you could join me, without really involving you in any of the research. I began to secretly save money for both the trip and the move, knowing it would be a struggle to figure everything out, especially when it came to pulling the trigger on moving forward. It's one thing to plan; it's another to take action. The kick in the ass happened on November 29, 2014, in a Starbucks with my client and friend M.

I had just ordered a gorgeous leather album for her and wanted to deliver it in person. She and I sat there for a while, discussing her Kauai wedding and other miscellaneous topics, until she brought up her close friend that spontaneously embarked on a trip around the world. I lamented about how short the trip was that I was planning, wishing I had the guts to do what her roommate did.

"Why don't you just travel, Jenna?" she said.

The question was simple.

The answer was obvious.

Why the hell not?

I came home and excitedly told you about my plans to travel the world for six months. I knew in my heart of hearts I needed to do this and tried desperately to convey this. Your first response was, "What about me?" Followed by: "Who will I have sex with?"

You, of course, tried to convince me to stay, but I steadfastly refused. I just couldn't continue it any further. I needed to be free and do my own thing, my own way. I had caught you talking dirty to other women too many times, which I consider cheating. Too often you'd made me out to be the bad guy, but I knew deep down I had nothing but the best intentions. Through time and effort, you had worn me into a nub, a woman just trying to survive and rediscover herself.

After careful consideration, I planned the breakup for December 2014, to give a thirty-day move-out notice. I didn't even have an apartment set up, but I knew that in order to escape you without declaring bankruptcy, as well as to afford the move off island, I would have to re-home my dogs. But somehow, you presented the solution. When you informed you parents that we were splitting up, their first words (according to you) were, "We'll take the dogs." While it wasn't ideal, as they disliked me, they also adored my dogs. Roarke loved the pool in the back and would toss the ball for himself for hours. Aslin loved the constant affection your mother showered them with. While I knew it meant I wouldn't be able to see them ever again, I knew they would be in good hands.

After the breakup, you put yourself back together rather quickly, heading back to the gym and giving up video games. Within a couple of weeks, you even went on some dates, meeting the girl to whom you're now engaged. We still lived together and I was devastated, watching as you quickly became the functional adult I'd dreamed you could one day be. I doubted my choice, whether this was the right move. What if, this time, you really were going to change? I couldn't help myself; we began having sex again, hot and rough. We were surprised by how good it was, making us both pause and wonder if we should give it another go. I became so confused with what I wanted, and my impending move loomed.

Admittedly, I hate change. I've always hated change because it so rarely leads to good things. Rehoming my dogs was shattering, but I knew it was the only way I could escape this abusive relationship and find a place to live that I could actually afford. The idea of losing them crippled me emotionally at times. I lashed out at you, angry that I'd put myself in this situation—angry with you for not being enough, for being lazy with us in the first place. I even reversed my stance in an attempt to avoid losing my dogs; I begged you to take me back, humiliating myself and not even caring. I just wanted my dogs.

The breakup was mostly amicable, though it came to a head the week before I was slated to move out. We began screaming at one another, with you telling me once more how selfish I was, how all of your friends and family hated me. You told me how self-involved I was and I believed it. Every man I had ever been with had said the same thing, so I just sobbed in agreement. "You push everything away. You destroy everything. You don't deserve good things!" you shouted as I lay on the laminate floor in a fetal position, hyperventilating, agreeing to everything hurled at me.

For years, I let myself be as selfish as possible, thinking I deserved everything good because of what my father had done to me. I felt the universe owed me shit, good shit, and I stopped at nothing to achieve it. It was an insanely entitled way of functioning, but I wasn't enlightened enough to do anything about it, despite feeling like an asshole every single day of my life.

In hindsight, I realize that the men I've chosen, the ones that made me behave selfishly and feel like shit, were my recompense. I see now that I was unwittingly punishing myself for not saying no to my father as a child, for not being strong enough to tell people about him. As a result, time and again I chose men who couldn't possibly love me. I searched for a way to tell my father that he couldn't break me while inadvertently breaking myself into nothing. Your words rang true, but I was too exhausted to fight back. I hadn't wanted to hurt you. I never wanted us to get to this point of no return. I tried to walk away so many times but *your* selfishness wouldn't let me. We were both of us selfish assholes.

You eventually took pity as I lay there, prone, offering me soothing words. "Don't worry, you're not that bad. You're a good person. I love you. I want to be with you. I know you're struggling to move on from your father. You need to just move on. I love you, always will. Walruses." You said the last word softly, emphasizing how serious you were with your proclamations, your subtle manipulations. You stroked my hair, calming me down while my heart cracked and then hardened. I felt cold and empty inside, incapable of moving. Resting my head in your lap, I felt everything just melt away until nothing was left. It was probably one of the lowest moments of my entire life. A part of me recognized your manipulations for what they were, but another part of me wanted to believe that I was the biggest asshole alive. I deserved it, didn't I? I hadn't told my father no and was therefore doomed to a lifetime of purgatory.

This was one of my lowest points. I've picked myself up again in the time since—it's been almost two years since our breakup and I feel nothing but disdain for you. I should have been stronger that first month, but I still had a lot of growing to do. You? I'm betting you're still the same selfish dickhole you've always been. Does your new wife know that on your first date together, I was sitting only a few feet away on a date of my own? Does she know you fucked me while the two of you were just starting to get to know one another?

I don't miss you. When I see photos of you, I feel a sense of removed familiarity, as if looking at the photo of a stranger I've seen one too many times. I'm completely apathetic to your successes and failures. While I am 100 percent culpable in letting us fall too far down the rabbit hole, my biggest regret is losing my dogs. I don't think I can ever forgive you for manipulating me so deeply that I felt I had no choice but to escape and leave them behind.

Sincerely,

Fierce Tiger

> *"I weep for you," the Walrus said:*
> *"I deeply sympathize."*
> *With sobs and tears he sorted out*
> *Those of the largest size,*
> *Holding his pocket-handkerchief*
> *Before his streaming eyes.*
>
> *"O Oysters," said the Carpenter,*
> *"You've had a pleasant run!*
> *Shall we be trotting home again?"*
> *But answer came there none—*
> *And this was scarcely odd, because*
> *They'd eaten every one.*

"The Walrus and the Carpenter," by Lewis Carroll

A brief respite from the crazy men

This book only briefly touches on the major key male players of my life. It tells only maybe 1/3 of my life, so please don't see this as a tell all. I was surprised, however, how some dudes expected to be in this book, merely because I let them penetrate me whenever it was ago. As if they were somehow profound enough to be written about, when in actuality, I remember only about half of the names of the men I've slept with and remember about 20% of the men I've just kissed. But I figured the self-centered men should be included in this novel, so they can know I think they have small dicks or mediocre bedroom skills. Because let's be honest: if they were amazing, they would have been in this book.

Dear Men who treated me like crap, but not crappy enough to get a letter, yet felt like they should have been included because they think their dick is magic:

Lol

A letter to my past addiction

Dear T-Bone,

I had this whole letter to you typed up and I've debated for months whether or not to include it with the other chapters. How can I explain our unhealthy connection? How you excited and destroyed me all at the same time—multiple times? Pen to paper, the letter seemed disjointed and didn't quite explain everything.

In the end, I decided to nix the contents of that letter. A big reason why is because you just got engaged to an incredible woman, who I had the pleasure of meeting last year. And really, after she and I spoke for hours about you, I realized trudging this shit up would do nothing but hurt you. I want to give you a fighting chance at happiness without throwing all of our drama out into the world. You at least deserve that much.

However, because you've been mentioned, and on top of that you've been a formative man in my life, I want to say thank you. Thanks for treating me like shit, a *lot*, all those years ago. But also, thank you for being a real friend, despite everything. Your fiancée recently told me that sometimes, you seem to feel the pressure of friendships that only want you around for entertainment value. You're vivacious, hilarious, thoughtful, and sincere. You're the center of the show when you arrive and how could you not be? We're both Leos—born on the same day! I want you to know that our friendship, to me, was never a dog and pony show. I have thoroughly enjoyed your friendship, to the point of not smattering your story all over these pages.

Thanks to you and your fiancée, I was able to get this damn show on the road following my divorce from Psychopath. You helped me get my car in California, you let me chill with y'all for a few days, feeding me, talking to me, making me laugh. Honestly? I think those three (four?) days with you both was transformative. I appreciate you.

I also appreciate you taking the time out of your day in November, to tell me to just be single for a year. I think you referred to my habitual dating life as "herpes." A type of "herpes that takes a year to fix," and "would you want to give this herpes to someone you really like?" You made me realize that I had been giving my baggage off to each guy, the pile of issues just getting larger after each relationship.

I don't want to give my next husband herpes. Literally or figuratively.

I can't say I'll last a year (because I'm *such* a catch ::eyeroll::) and I certainly won't spend a year celibate, but I appreciate your advice and thoughtfully blunt words. I wish nothing but the best for you, my friend. Keep being yourself, keep finding your truth, keep living life with a smile.

And don't fuck this up with her. Or I'll skin you alive myself.

A Letter to Ex-Husband #3

The story you're about to read has been written as truthfully as possible, although I am human and therefore fallible. I paraphrase only about 30 percent of the conversations, able to pull directly from messages and emails for much of it. I cannot be accused of making this shit up; I'm not that imaginative. My search for love, my quest for a devoted mate, has been filled with ridiculous folly, mishaps, and mistakes. My third husband is no exception, and is actually the most glorious crash-and-burn experience of my life.

Our connection definitely wasn't in my head, though I definitely ignored every red flag. This chapter, these letters, tell the tale of my rebirth. I'm not the same woman I was when I met this man. No man will ever treat me like this again—this I promise. I highly encourage you to make the same declaration should you see ANY degree of mirroring with your own relationship within these paragraphs.

Judge kindly, for my demons are plenty.

Dear Psychopath Adonis,

I hate you. Since we divorced, multiple people have come to me to find solace in the ways you've hurt them as well. It's as if I've become the leader of the Psychopath Adonis Recovery Support Group. From our first meeting, I secretly wondered why you didn't have a lot of friends, but a random high school friend of yours found me on Instagram and told me that you were a class-A dick back then as well . . . which explains why you have, like, maybe two friends. And even then, you talk shit about them. I find solace in knowing that you only get away with your bullshit because of your good looks. This consoles me because we both know that time will wear down your face and eventually you'll be nothing more than a crotchety old man, dying alone at a nursing home. Maybe I'm sacrificing some karmic brownie points by saying this, but I sincerely hope you die alone.

Apologies, I'm getting ahead of myself. Your story is my favorite to tell and I would prefer to not rush it.

I remember the first time I saw your photo online, your big wide smile that seemed to invite conversation. My heart skipped like a stone across a pond, pitter-pattering like a teenager. I don't know what it was, but I felt drawn to you. You were magnetic, charismatic and humorous. Beautiful hazel eyes that held a hint of mischief, and biceps that threatened to engulf me. I will admit: your sexy muscles appealed to me.

What's cooking good lookin? I messaged, hoping against hope that you would reply back.

You responded: *I saw you like to eat steaks, which is good, because I like to make them!*

It was fate, truly. A good steak is what binds people for forever, right?

We planned to meet for tacos at a place I loved. Running a bit late, you stepped out of your gray jeep, flashing your pearly whites. God damn it, I was smitten as fuck: your biceps bulged in ways that made my mouth water; your laugh startled my heart.

Our first date was *fifteen* hours long. Tacos led into drinks at the nearby beach bar, which led to walking along the beach under the gaze of a full moon. We laughed nervously when you botched our first kiss, but you made up for it by making the second one entrancing. I didn't want a relationship; I wasn't looking for one. I just figured I would get laid and move on. The moment before we actually began having sex, you cradled me in your arms, showering me with kisses, and asked, "Do you want to wait until the morning? I don't want you to regret this."

"No, I figure that even if you never call me again, I'll get good sex out of it."

You laughed, shocked at my crass response, but it was true: if you'd never called me again, I would have been okay with it. I would have continued on with the rest of my life, calling you The Adonis Who Fucked My Brains Out.

I wish now you had left me alone.

My love for you came quickly, roaring like a brush fire, burning through my defenses like dried kindling. I fought it, already realizing you were a skittish fella, letting you set the pace. We had a few more dates, each one better than the last, the fun increasing each time. Two weeks after our first date, we decided to make it official, with you slipping your hands between my thighs as I drove to dinner, whispering promises in my ear. While lust blurred my vision, my heart was pitter pattering, whispering, "maybe . . . just maybe."

Almost three weeks into our budding relationship, on a Thursday night, you disappeared for a few hours, virtually incommunicado, your texts short and abrupt. I thought it was odd but I didn't push it, hoping you were just watching sports on TV. Instead, you called me later that night completely breathless and harried.

"Hey, sorry I've been busy."

"It's okay. Where are you?"

"Chinatown. At a bar."

I felt my stomach drop to the floor. "Oh. Everything okay?"

"It doesn't matter. Don't worry, I'm not cheating on you. Maybe I'll tell you one day . . . maybe."

I said nothing, knowing immediately you were with a girl. Why else would you spit out "I'm not cheating on you"? I didn't push too hard for details, but the following day made it very clear I expect to know when my significant other hangs out with another woman. You steadfastly refused to share why it was you were at a bar in Chinatown on a Wednesday night, but agreed to do be transparent in the future.

Despite that singular blip, those first couple months were utterly fantastic. We spent hours in bed talking, drinking on the weekends, sunbathing at the beach during the days. While you worked on papers—homework for your MBA—I worked on my bachelor's in advertising. I was set to graduate in three months and hunkered down every day to study. As I learned the Spanish meaning of "pantalones," I watched you with hungry eyes, soaking in your carefully sculpted body, playfully distracting you during our study breaks. I loved bantering with you, learning from you, trusting you to tell me about worldly things. You were a refreshing change after Walrus, who couldn't discuss anything outside gasoline.

We were playful in everything we did, skimming over serious topics, preferring crazy sex and booze over legitimate conversation. Do you remember that time I tried to do the dishes and you took me from behind? I giggled as soap and water splashed everywhere, trying halfheartedly to scrub the plates. I remember thinking, "this would be wonderful to do all the time . . ." I never pushed you for anything those first few months, preferring you to set the tone of our relationship.

Even after showing you I could be a great companion, I felt the wall you had up, which was infuriating. We were so good together—how could you not see that? I took care of you every day, bringing you meals, giving you backrubs, listening to you complain about your friends and family. I began looking for red flags, searching for reasons as to why we weren't connecting.

In March 2015, we went to Maui together for two days and instead of enjoying the adventure, we found ourselves arguing where to drive to, because you were afraid of getting "lost" on an unknown road. I fantasized about adventure, while you rejected it outright. It was a fucking island—where did you think that road was going to lead? I quietly turned the car around, wondering if I could be with someone so afraid to be lost.

At the airport heading back home to Oahu, your phone buzzed but you picked it up and tilted the screen away from me. That minute movement triggered my wariness; it's crazy how something so seemingly innocuous felt as threatening as an impending tidal wave. As I write this, I realize maybe that was when I should have walked away. You gave me a side-eyed glance, to see if I was paying attention. I pretended to be oblivious, instead turning into myself, wondering what you could be doing behind my back.

We returned to the real world, with you barely speaking to me, claiming your new night shift schedule was exhausting you. I seemed more of an after thought, which is a position in life I could never tolerate. Between your self-imposed distance and the creepy phone behavior, I decided to call you on your shit.

Me: *Psychopath Adonis, I'm crazy about you. You make me happy. But I'm just not sure how you feel. The only emotion I'm ever sure of is when you're pissed. I bite my tongue, desperate to get a kind word from you. Because when you're frustrated or worked up, you won't even touch me. And I'm desperate for you to touch me more.*

I don't want to be with someone who doesn't want to be with me. I want to be with someone who knows I'm a catch. Because I know I am. If you actually want to be with me, I need to know. But if you're unsure, then let's seriously not drag this out. If you can't handle us not agreeing on things, then let's not drag this out. Because if we move further, I'm going to become emotionally involved and it won't be fair to me if you aren't even remotely close to being emotionally involved. We've spent two months together—vast amounts of time. More than most. If you're unsure of whether or not you care, even just slightly, then let's not drag this out.

I sent the message, holding my breath, but already knowing the answer.

Psychopath Adonis: *Ok then, let's end it. (Which I hate to do via text.) You have a ton of good qualities and will make someone happy. But I'm unsure, and you're probably right—if I'm unsure we shouldn't be together.*

Me: *You didn't have to do it via text. You could have FaceTimed, but whatever. My only advice is to learn to let go of your fear, because it consumes you. Learn to let go more, like actually let go, and good things will follow. It was nice while it lasted. Bye.*

I cried that night—for about eight minutes. I lay in bed, staring at the ceiling, wondering why I didn't miss you more. Maybe I'd romanticized everything to the point of insanity, which is my worst relationship habit. Instead of looking into it too deeply, I hopped right onto Tinder and started dating again. I unfriended you on Facebook in an attempt to move on, and you in turn blocked me, which stung but I brushed it off. I began dating a sexy Latino man, who was an enthusiastic lover and a kick-ass dancer. I liked him a ton and honestly, I didn't think of you once.

Never the type to dwell, I decided to finally begin planning my move to a new city, which I would do after the six-month world trip I had planned. I was torn between Seattle and Austin, both being wonderful cities (although I had never actually been to Austin). I made a YouTube video—best two out of three coin toss to decide my next location. Austin won, and while I found myself ambivalent at the time, that coin toss would end up saving my life a year later. I began to plan my move to Austin, announcing it on my business page, prepping for the move to take place in just six months.

My life continued until you texted me one particular Wednesday, three weeks after we'd broken up.

Hey, how have you been?

I squealed, feeling a mix of shock, happiness, and anger. I screamed to my roommate, "YOU WON'T BELIEVE WHO JUST TEXTED ME!" When I told her, we both laughed, and maybe even high-fived, because this was a sign: *I won the breakup.* I played it cool though, replying, *I'm awesome! How are you?*

You played a cat and mouse game with me, remorse plain as day, though you couldn't admit it. Finally, after a little cajoling, you offered me some absolution.

Psychopath Adonis: *Do you want to know why I had to break up with you?*

Me: *Duh.*

Psychopath Adonis: *A month before I met you, I was dating this girl. Remember that Thursday I couldn't talk about? She and I had met up at the bar and she told me she was pregnant. I didn't know how to tell you, since we were so new. I really liked you but I thought no one would want to date me if I had a kid. I was afraid you would walk away. I'm sorry, I should have told you.*

I ran to my roommate, yelling to her about how I KNEW there had been another chick. My instincts were on point! You and I texted back and forth for a while, admitting that we missed each other and wanted to revisit our relationship. I was so nervous as I shaved my legs before our date, but I refused to shave anything else. You didn't deserve the cookie.

I showed up at your house with some baked goods, worried and euphoric at the thought of what might happen that evening. Your smile was just as tantalizing as it had been three weeks earlier; you flashed it as you hugged me and took the brownies out of my hands. Our energies were literally vibrating at close contact, my heart rattling against my rib cage as I eyed your biceps, imagining them in my mouth.

You grilled us up a dinner while I practiced for an upcoming Spanish exam, quietly reviewing the verbs on my handwritten flash cards. Suddenly, I was overcome with a genius idea. "Do you think you could get dressed in some of these words for clothing I need to know? I think it will help me learn," I asked, innocent in my request. What can I say; I'm a hands-on kind of learner. You laughed, agreeing to the idea. After we ate, we went up to your room where I picked out a suit and matching tie, muttering the words in Spanish. "I have to shower real quick!" you said, sweat coating your skin. I would probably have licked you clean if you'd asked.

I barely noticed when the shower ended and you walked out completely naked, trying to stir a reaction from my perfected resting bitch face. Finally observing your naked Adonis ass standing right beside me, I squealed and scooted away from you. "Put your clothes back on!" I laughed, showing you the suit I had chosen, trying to ignore your third leg. You gave me a knowing smirk, the sparkle in your eye telling me that the best was yet to come.

You didn't shave anything, I reminded myself, huffing at Past Jenna's stubborn refusal to fully utilize a razor.

We were in your closet, putting a tie on you, when you whirled me around and gave me a fierce and possessive kiss. My stomach dropped and my knees weakened. I was utterly helpless, lost in lust as you took me right there, in the closet doorway. Half the suit hung from your muscles while you whispered promises and apologies, and I gripped your tie for leverage. I surrendered to you in that moment—not against the painful doorjamb, but to you as a man. I was yours. I forgave everything, wanting this passionate new man in front of me. You lifted me by my ass, taking me to the bed, still apologizing and promising to be a better man. I ate up your words, clinging to them like a life raft. You didn't even care that I hadn't shaved. Life was perfect again.

You put in such an effort once we were back together. I reveled in the shower of compliments and encouragement, finally feeling like I had struck relationship gold. You were more open to communicating about your life; I took advantage of your new openness, asking endless questions. We spoke about your new Baby Momma, speculating in length whether she had tricked you into impregnating her. You'd only been together for a couple of months, but your aversion to condoms, compounded with the prenatal pills in her bathroom, made us realize that maybe you had been duped. I felt so bad for you! Naturally, I also struggled to come to terms with the fact that I would possibly have to share my boyfriend with another woman. I knew women did it all the time and I pulled strength from knowing I wasn't alone. Notwithstanding, we were so happy together we made everyone around us sick. Sometimes I would cry from the overwhelming joy in my heart; never around you though, as you got uncomfortable when I cried.

Despite our apparent happiness, I wondered where we were going. My trip was swiftly approaching and while we were communicating more, I never pushed you for something more than what we had. While I was easily the happiest I had ever been, with a smoking hot boyfriend and finally graduating from college with my bachelor's in Advertising and Public Relations, we still needed to deal with reality. What if my love for you became so consuming that we broke up before my trip and I was completely crushed? It wouldn't be about me anymore, but about our breakup, about something disastrous. I was working too hard to scrimp and save for this adventure; I needed this trip for myself and no one else. Realizing we couldn't avoid the topic forever, I decided to be as clear as possible with you.

"Psychopath?"

"Yeah." You sat by me, reading one of your many school-related books.

"Can I say something?"

You stopped reading and gave me a look of concern. "Of course. What's up?"

"My trip is in three months and I just want to say that it's okay if you don't think you can stay with me. Long distance is hard and we haven't really known one another a long time. Just don't make it a breakup trip."

You nodded solemnly, acknowledging the gravity and sincerity of my request. I trusted you to be a mature adult, confident of my assumption, having not been given cause to believe otherwise. You understood how important this trip was to me, for which I counted my blessings.

How lucky am I? I thought. Finally, a man who understood my roaming spirit! I even shortened my trip by two months because I didn't want to be apart from you any longer than necessary.

Every day I woke up feeling more fortunate than the day before. With your unending support, I even finally felt empowered to move on from my father. I knew I wanted to move on from him and heal before entering my thirties, and you supported every effort I made.

There was just *one* little hiccup.

Your parents and Baby Momma still didn't know about me. Flag, meet the color red.

We had been dating for four months and despite me voicing my apprehension at being hidden from a big portion of your life, you brushed off my concerns like an annoying gnat. How could we possibly move forward with a heavy anchor holding us back? Why didn't you feel proud of having me as well?

By June, it felt like we were on an uncontrollable train bringing us toward the end of our relationship. We avoided the topic of my impending trip, preferring to delude ourselves with the idea of endless days together. I prepared myself for the breakup, bolstering myself against the possible heartbreak. You gave me no reason to think otherwise.

Two weeks after Memorial Day weekend, we were at our favorite beach, swimming in the warm azure water. You watched me intently, your head bobbing up and down with the lazy waves.

"A ton of my friends just got married, you know? And they got to move out of the barracks into a real house. It just isn't fucking fair."

You were on another one of your tirades. I had grown used to them, listening patiently as you ranted about politics, your friends, the military—whatever was pissing you off at that particular moment. I used to pride myself for quietly letting you vent, thinking what a loving girlfriend I was. Today's particular tirade was focused on how oppressed you felt in the military, being treated like a kid.

"I mean, I'm twenty-nine and living in a room the size of a shoebox. They inspect the room every day and they're always after me. They pick on me!"

"You think they pick on you?"

"I know they do! I just want to get out, you know? I may go insane if I can't get out of the barracks." You wiped the sweat off your face in frustration.

"I'm sorry, baby. I wish I could help." We continued to swim in the ocean, quietly contemplating your words. You were always complaining about how *hard* life was for you and I knew better than to try and give advice.

"You won't be able to come back to Hawaii after your trip, right?"

I nodded, knowing I wouldn't be able to afford Hawaii rent on my own, without support from the military. Even though we were together, I still continued to plan the move to Texas, where people were friendlier and the rent was more affordable.

You treaded water thoughtfully, moisture beading across your smooth forehead. Every time your gaze fell on me, I felt like I wasn't pretty enough for you. My lips were too small, my chin too droopy. I swam a little closer and wrapped my thighs around you, hoping to assuage my insecurities.

"Well, if we're going to get married, we should probably do it soon," you said with a matter-of-fact tone.

I stared at you with a carefully schooled face, removing any possible emotion from it. Thank god I'm used to having to hide emotions in my field of work, because otherwise my jaw would have dropped. We'd never even *mentioned* marriage before and here you were, basically proposing. Yet . . . not actually proposing. I waited for you to continue, not trusting myself to speak.

"I don't want the only reason you don't return to be because you couldn't afford rent. I'm just not ready to let you go. If we got married now, we could get everything done before you left for the trip. You would have insurance and we could rent a place. You could store all your things instead of having to pay for them to be shipped. Then you'd be able to afford to come back to Hawaii."

I continued on in silence, wading in the warm, blue water, wondering if you were joking. None of my other husbands got down on one knee. I kept hoping my third proposal would have been different.

"Yes . . ." I began, carefully choosing my words. "That makes sense." I couldn't elaborate further; I was afraid I might scare you off. I looked at you like a doe lit by headlights, shocked at this proposition. I had the opportunity to marry and create spawn with this Adonis? My first thought: our babies would be fucking gorgeous. My second thought?

You hadn't even told me you loved me.

I pushed that thought aside, reasoned with myself that couples didn't always confess their love. Granted, that was a time when women were sold to men like chattel, but that didn't matter. Sometimes love was just *known*, you know? It happened in movies and books all the time! I knew you loved me. I had to believe you loved me. Why else would you want to marry me?

So we began planning this foolish endeavor, getting the marriage license just two days later. We bent our heads together in conspiracy, both of us with independent ideas as to what we thought would happen. I can't speculate as to yours, but I imagined a lifetime of hot sex, giggling, being the yin to the other's yang. With apparent understanding of the gravity the situation held, we'd discussed our impending lives together, agreeing on finances, children, where to move—all of the good stuff. I was under the impression we had it drawn in blood, completing in agreement when it came to everything.

Then I called my mother. My stomach filled with dread, weighing me down.

"Mom . . . Psychopath Adonis and I are getting married," I said. I waited for her response, already knowing what she was going to say.

She paused, thinking about my declaration. "Are you sure?"

At the time, I was more sure of us than anything in the whole world. I told her how we never fought, and when we did, it was always quickly squashed. You were more mature than the others, encouraging me to spread my wings. You were excited to travel more and try new foods. You taught me about topics I didn't understand. What the hell else more could I ask for in a life mate?

Despite my reasonings, my mother remained unconvinced. I sobbed on the phone, angrily rejecting her apprehensions. I hung up, determined to marry you despite that tiny voice in my head that whispered, *"but he hasn't said he loves you."*

You also told me that for now you weren't going to tell your parents or Baby Momma about us, because your parents were still recovering from the surprise of having a grandchild born out of wedlock. A new wife would have just muddied things, you reasoned. I forced you to agree to tell them by the time I returned from my trip. You accepted my condition and I moved on, hoping that you would one day proudly declare my importance to your family. I wanted you to be the fantastic end to my search for real love.

We got hitched at noon on a Tuesday in June 2015. Deciding to skip the fanfare, we were third in line at the local courthouse. I wore bright pink lipstick, curled my hair, and pranced around in my brand new heels like a delighted pony. I was looking fresh to death, excited to seal the deal on this madness. You looked like walking sex, in your blue shirt and tie, khakis hugging your carefully sculpted butt in ways that made me lose my thoughts. Damn, you were some kind of pretty.

As the Justice of the Peace spoke the vows, we held hands tightly and I laughed nervously at her monotonous voice. I stuck out my tongue to make you smile and you crossed your eyes in turn. I have no idea what was said—she won the award for most boring officiant ever! When she finally announced that you could kiss me, you grabbed my hips and dipped me as I giggled like a school girl, relishing the big smooch you planted on my lips. We practically skipped out of the cramped, fluorescently lit room, my excitement bubbling over.

I loved the fuck out of you.

I would have done anything for you.

I genuinely thought you were my soul mate.

A sexy Adonis soul mate.

You still hadn't told me you loved me, but I pushed that thought aside and focused on what our future couch would look like. We were on the hunt for an apartment and since I had already committed to celebrating Pride in New York City with my gay best friend, I flew across the world while you found us an excellent place on the seventh floor in the 'burbs of Oahu. When I returned, elated from champagne and parade dancing, we went on the hunt for the perfect couch. You tried to be generous and let me pick out the couch while grumbling that it was two hundred dollars more than the one you preferred. It only compounded the fact that you seemed distracted and distant, avoiding any talk of Baby Momma. It left me unsettled, but I figured you wanted to keep our budding marriage separate from a girl who tricked you into fathering her child.

I imagined the experience of moving in together to be like our first meal in the apartment: easy and simple. We ordered a pizza and ate on the floor, toasting our future with water in Styrofoam cups. It seemed so surreal, living with the man with whom I would spend the rest of my life. You seemed uncomfortable and I asked you what was wrong. After a moment of consideration, you told me.

"Baby Momma asked if we could try to make it work last week."

I know you thought about being with her when she initially told you—we'd talked about it many times. But I had no reason to question you. I was adamant that we just needed to be transparent with one another. I felt bad for this mysterious woman, who thought you were free for the taking, not knowing I had staked my claim. Psychopath Adonis was all mine!

Moving in together was a blur. You later admitted you *hated* me that first week, because I was too "lazy," which explained your constant resentment and the little confrontations here and there. How was I lazy? Maybe I *was* lazy. During that week, I only had the time to meet with the landlord, got the bills started, got the deliveries made, filled the house with food, organized everything so it looked homey, and got my office set up, all while working a full-time job. Sorry it wasn't enough. You're right; I was absolutely the definition of "lazy."

The second week of marriage, we went down to the beach at dawn in an attempt to have a romantic moment and exchange some vows. We were supposed to do our own vows on our wedding day, but you had "forgotten," and then repeatedly asked for more time to write yours, claiming that you wanted to make them right. So we waited two weeks; I was eager to finally, hopefully, hear that you loved me. I'd had my vows for three weeks already and was proud of the sweet words I had written:

On February 9th, I wrote the following in my journal: "So I met a man. And if I could keep him forever I would . . . he has a smile that makes my heart beat faster and he made me laugh so hard I'm sore. I'm terrified that I'll never see him again because I like him THAT much. His name is Psychopath Adonis, and if we keep seeing one another, I think I'll be in trouble"

Last month, I married you and I feel like I've won the lottery. From the moment I saw you come out of the car, I've been yours. I hope you understand how much I love you because it's terrifying to me and the power you have over me makes me weak and strong all at the same time. I've said it before and I really mean it: I've never felt this way ever. Laugh all you want, but I manifested you, down to your smile and kindness.

I married you without knowing if you loved me. But I realized my love has never been dependent on whether or not you love me. It has simply existed in dedication. We may have moved quickly but I just know we are going to be unstoppable. You're my center. And the moment you dipped me in a kiss, you were silently gifted my loyalty, my fierceness, my passion. From now on, I am yours.

I remember how awkward it was, since we had the intimacy of relative strangers. After I said my vows, you smiled at me and pulled out a piece of paper. Oh my goodness, you wrote them on paper? How sweet!

Your vows were mostly robotic, reminiscent of rote vows given by a minister. You made promises to travel more and try new foods . . . but the first time you told me you loved me came from the phrase "I promise to honor and love you . . ." A knot formed in my stomach, leaving me feeling so let down and upset that you couldn't even come up with something that you hadn't heard in every rom-com ever. Was I being persnickety? Hell yes. But I felt as if I had every right to be picky! You married me so spontaneously, before ever admitting you loved me. This was your grand moment, the pinnacle where you could have just lowered your barriers and told me how you felt. Instead, you came up with some lame bullshit that just left me feeling sad. It sounded as if you had just pulled them from the internet. Afterward, I became so frustrated that you still couldn't just say the words, even after we'd married. This inability to be intimate and trusting set the tone for the remainder of our relationship.

It became quickly apparent that my worst nightmare was manifesting: marrying someone and he changes into a completely different person. You were my very own personal Lifetime movie. It started with little things here and there—nothing alarming at first. You made demands that I keep the house clean like you wanted, or you would become upset, even if I left only a couple of dishes in the sink when it was *just so fucking easy to put them in the dishwasher*. Or if I watched what you deemed as too much TV when *there was so much to be done*, like vacuuming.

Our first big fight was over my "inability" to clean as quickly or as well as you thought I should. The sun was going down as our fight turned up in volume. I had already apologized multiple times, but you continued on your rant, claiming that you worked harder than I did and that because I worked from home, *I* should be the one keeping things clean. You stood seven feet from me, waving your hands and screaming maniacally as I sat in a corner in our master bedroom. Fear came down on me like an anvil. What would you do next? Would you hit me? I was *terrified* of you. You stomped out of the room then, leaving me to quietly cry. I recall whispering to myself, "What the fuck have I done?"

You weren't who I thought you were. We had done the same thing hundreds of people do every day, marrying after too short a period of time. We'd talked about our hopes and dreams before getting married, and we had never had a fight. However, you had hidden your controlling personality from me until after I was locked down. I should have walked away then but I didn't—the thought of three divorces was absolutely terrifying. Who the hell would love me? How would I explain that to a future man? "Hi! I have tons of good qualities but alas, I've been rejected by every husband. Oh, how many? Here, let me show you my Marriage Membership Punch Card!"

I was ashamed at the very idea, to the point that I picked myself up off the mattress and apologized profusely. I promised to vacuum more, find a place for my purse that was suitable for you, to shower two times a day like you did. I began mentally reciting the things I needed to do every day to avoid an argument: *do the dishes, keep the washer door open so it doesn't smell like mildew, don't watch TV if there are things to be done, make dinner, wake up early so my work is done before you get home, work out, don't get too fat.*

My promises seemed to satiate your need for control, at least for a little while. I settled into my role as the dutiful wife and tried to not ask for too much. The following weekend, you'd planned to go golfing with some work buddies after work on a Friday. "Have fun! I'll make dinner," I declared, excited to act like a good little wife.

"I'll be home by four," you promised, kissing my cheek. I went shopping and bought steaks, couscous, and some vegetables. We would have ourselves such a good night!

Psychopath Adonis (3:23): *Maybe like 5.*

Me (3:27): *Uhhhh okay,*

Me (3:33): *so I guess I should stop making dinner now?*

Me (3:40): *I'm not trying to be an ass. I just kinda have a sexy nightgown on. I'm making dinner and just want to hang out with you.*

> **Me** (4:00): *All right. I'll just put it all aside then.*
>
> **Me** (4:16): *Just remember how pissed you've been before when I've done this.*
>
> *I'm taking off the nightie and just making dinner. I'll see you whenever you come home.*
>
> **Psychopath Adonis** (4:17): *Ok . . . Yeah, sorry. Not my fault. We met a general who wanted to talk to us.*
>
> **Me** (4:17): *Umm. All right.*
>
> **Psychopath Adonis** (4:21): **some weird shocked emoji**
>
> **Me** (4:35): *I don't know what the fuck that means.*
>
> **Me** (4:37): *Look, I don't want you to come home and we fight. I'm putting a pin in this and we can talk about it tomorrow okay?*
>
> **Psychopath Adonis** (4:57) *Ok what day is the house warming?*
>
> **Me** (4:59): *August 15.*
>
> **Me** (5:37): *So . . . I'm guessing not 5:30 either???*
>
> **Psychopath Adonis** (5:38): *We just finished.*
>
> **Psychopath Adonis** (6:18): *On my way!*

During this whole exchange, I raged and ranted, muttering profanities and imaginary insults to an invisible you as I paced the apartment. We had only been married a couple of weeks. Why was I not a priority? Why couldn't you at least text me in a timely fashion? And why did it take you thirty minutes to come home when the golf course was only five minutes away?

You opened the door and stumbled in, drunk, at 6:30. Unapologetic, you poured yourself into the couch and turned on the TV. You seemed to be under the impression that my suggestion to squash it two hours prior would still be honored, not realizing this offer expired after the second time you didn't show when you said you would.

"Hi, Baby!" you chirped, a goofy, ridiculous smile on your face. I gave you my best glare, steam practically whistling out of my ears. I stomped past you, muttering under my breath. You ignored me, pretending that my anger wasn't worth addressing.

My feelings never quite mattered much, did they? I was DEFINITELY not open to squashing this anymore—you were two and a half hours later than promised. I not only had to eat alone, but you drove home drunk as if nothing was wrong. We couldn't have been more of a cliché if your name was Bob and we lived in a double-wide.

I marched into the bedroom, loudly stating that I didn't appreciate your behavior, and then collapsed into the bed, still ready to tear you apart. My feelings of inadequacy were raging, which further fueled my anger. I heard the door jingle and you swung it open, eyeing me with a mean-spirited look. You shut the door and fell into the bed, announcing it was time for you to go to sleep. I ignored you and continued reading a book.

While the next words we exchanged are a bit fuzzy, it became clear to you that the window for passively squashing your rude behavior had closed. You were itching for a fight; you said things like, "calm down," and "you're overreacting." Really, those are the best words for an enraged woman. We *love* that.

I must have said something that triggered your anger, because you finally got off the bed and stormed out, screaming at me, telling me you would sleep in the next room. I felt vindicated in finally making you feel the way I felt. You slammed the bedroom door. I heard some noises from the living room and then the spare bedroom door slammed shut. I waited a moment and then quietly went to inspect the source of the noises. Some of my things were spread over the living room floor, seemingly tossed in anger. I checked the door to the spare bedroom but you'd locked it. *If he can lock his door, I'll lock mine!* I thought.

I texted you while hiding in the bedroom with the door locked, hoping I might get a reaction.

Me: *I'm going to find somewhere else to stay for the weekend, with friends who actually care about my feelings. Then you can go on pretending you aren't married. That'll be fun.*

Psychopath Adonis: *Ok bye.*

I went to call my sister, but before I could hit the call button, I heard the doorknob jiggle. It held against your push. You loudly swore and slammed into the door, the wood creaking under your weight. The door smashed open on your second powerful thrust, the lock flying across the room. You looked around, your eyes landing on me as I lay on the bed, completely petrified. You turned to the closet and grabbed a bag.

"What the fuck are you waiting for?!" you screamed, grabbing my clothes and throwing them into the bag. "Fucking leave if you want! Be with someone who cares!"

Feeling as if I were in some kind of nightmare and that my new husband couldn't possibly be screaming at me like this, I pulled the blanket up to my chin to shield myself. You tossed the bag at me and motioned to the door. "Well? What the fuck are you waiting for? Get the fuck out. Leave. Get the fuck out. Out. Out now!"

Scrambling out of bed, cowering as I walked by you, I grabbed the bag in your hand and slinked out to the kitchen. Satisfied that I fully understood your manly power, you stormed back into the other bedroom. When I heard that door close, I rushed back and grabbed clothes I could actually use. I also snatched up my phone charger, some shoes, threw on a jacket, and grabbed my keys.

I gently closed the front door, trying to not disturb you, hoping that I wouldn't have to face you again. As I waited for the elevator, I finally called my sister.

"I don't think I can do this," I wailed, feeling like the situation was hopeless. She tried to pacify me, asking what had happened. I filled her in on everything, even the daily arguments we had over things like dishes, clothes, and whatever you felt was important.

"Has he always been like this?"

"NO! I would never have married him!" I insisted, knowing it was true. You had never screamed at me, broken things, or thrown me out. For most of our pre-marriage relationship, you always did the dishes and were flattered when I took the time to cook for you. I couldn't understand what had changed.

"Look, my husband and I fought a lot at the beginning. Maybe this is just growing pains."

The whole time you texted me, blaming the entire argument on me, telling me that I had promised to squash it but that because I got angry, you had no choice but to get angry, too.

Psychopath Adonis: *I see why you got divorced twice.*

Me: *And now a third.*

Psychopath Adonis: *Fine.*

Psychopath Adonis: *We can do the paper work whenever you want.*

Psychopath Adonis: *Good to know you can be understanding.*

Psychopath Adonis: *And reasonable. Love you too.*

Me: *You don't love me. This isn't love.*

Psychopath Adonis: *You're right you have shown none.*

Psychopath Adonis: *It's not like I was out with some random ppl. I was playing golf and an hour late.*

Psychopath Adonis: *Totally a legit reason to divorce.*

Me: *Go look at the shattered door and my thrown around belongings and then ask yourself why your wife just fled in fear.*

Psychopath Adonis: *Oh you love me and appreciate me cleaning and doing everything for you . . . Bullshit you want a slave not a husband.*

Psychopath Adonis: *You're not scared. I never even raised my voice.*

Psychopath Adonis: *I pick up and clean for you and when I don't do exactly what you want you get mad . . .*

Psychopath Adonis: *Point in case . . .*

Psychopath Adonis: *You drank too much and probably smoked and have lost your common sense. I can believe this is what you want.*

Me: *I don't want to divorce you. But I also don't want a violently drunk husband. One who says vicious things to me.*

Me: *Don't you lie to me or yourself.*

Psychopath Adonis: *There is a mat in the door.*

Psychopath Adonis: *Not violent. The door was giving I thought it was jammed you didn't say anything.*

Me: *You don't want to talk. If you did, you would have called. Or asked me to stay.*

Psychopath Adonis: *You said you left I came to see.*

Psychopath Adonis: *Again . . . Didn't know you were in there.*

Psychopath Adonis: *And I got in saw you were there . . . Not here to play games Jenna.*

Psychopath Adonis: *You're either my wife or you not.*

Me: *You're either going to respect me or you're not.*

Me: *You've treated me like shit this week.*

Psychopath Adonis: *I do. I was talking to a general . . .*

Me: *You can't even be an adult and call me.*

Psychopath Adonis: *What do you want me to say? Hey thanks for giving me your time and card. Bye.*

Psychopath Adonis: *You left and said you left not me.*

Psychopath Adonis: *I tried to come to bed.*

Me: *You don't respect me. Your behavior all week doesn't show love and respect.*

Me: *No, you came to fight.*

Psychopath Adonis: *Like yours does.*

Psychopath Adonis: *No I came to sleep.*

Psychopath Adonis: *I work at midnight.*

Psychopath Adonis: *You don't.*

Psychopath Adonis: *You always forget about that.*

Me: *Yeah. Your life sucks. I'm a forgetful bitch, a cunty ungrateful wife. You've made your point.*

Psychopath Adonis: *You have no clue what it's like.*

Me: *Because I do know what it's like to be emotionally beaten up by you.*

Psychopath Adonis: *Oh cause I want you to help out.*

Psychopath Adonis: *Yeah real mean.*

Psychopath Adonis: *Again not your slave.*

Psychopath Adonis: *You husband.*

Psychopath Adonis: *But clearly that's not what you want.*

Me: *You aren't a husband. You don't treat me like I'm going to be the one with you for the rest of your life. You treat me like I'm temporary.*

Psychopath Adonis: *I tell you to not be lazy. Oh fuck me. I don't be sweet and cuddly cause I'm tired and worn out from picking up and working . . . Just like last night.*

Psychopath Adonis: *Then you need to act like I am.*

Me: *Yeah. We already established I'm a lazy woman. I do nothing for you.*

Psychopath Adonis: *No. You do a few things . . . But I have to do twice as much. Clean up after the one meal. Plus the others you leave around. And then put all the dishes away. Not even talking about laundry.*

Psychopath Adonis: *Get it out of your head!!! You watch too much greys anatomy and other crap for me to even think you don't have time for simple things.*

Me: *Yep. Okay. I'm super lazy. Got it. You can never answer why you married me. Because I don't think you know.*

Psychopath Adonis: *I said I love you and don't want to be away from you! I wanted you to come home to me.*

Psychopath Adonis: *This is the 4th time.*

Psychopath Adonis: *I don't make you justify yourself.*

Psychopath Adonis: *That's bullshit.*

Me: *That's because you've never had to question my feelings and devotion.*

Psychopath Adonis: *I rushed this cause I wanted to make sure you would get taken care of ok your trip!!*

Psychopath Adonis: *I show you daily! I work my ass off then come home and make sure you are living in the best place I can give you.*

Me: *Okay. So now I don't love you. I'm lazy. Nice. I should win an award for best wife.*

Psychopath Adonis: *No some trashed apartment.*

You want attention then want time (when I'm gone is not enough) to work.

Psychopath Adonis: *Pick!!! I can't be up 24 hours a day!!!*

Psychopath Adonis: *I haven't seen my friends but once outside work!! You can stay up and see yours... Then come home and bitch about them.*

Psychopath Adonis: *That's reasonable . . . Thanks.*

Me: *Yep. I'm unreasonable too. I'm known for it.*

Psychopath Adonis: *So it's not just me.*

Good to know.

Me: *Nope. I'm a total cunt. You've made your point. Thanks.*

Psychopath Adonis: *I came in to sleep next to you.*

Psychopath Adonis: *To be sweet but you wanted to fight.*

Psychopath Adonis: *After you said you wanted to pin it.*

Me: *The question now is, who will you beat up and yell at when work stresses you out? Or you've had too much to drink? Or Baby Momma stresses you out? Or your parents judge you? Who will you have now?*

Psychopath Adonis: *I came home ready to make love to my wife.*

Psychopath Adonis: *I got a shit door.*

Psychopath Adonis: *Shut.*

Me: *You can't make love if you don't understand love.*

Psychopath Adonis: *Well I wish you thought that before we got married.*

Well I guess I'll just do like I did before and work out.

Me: *Guess you have it all figured out.*

Psychopath Adonis: *Nope. But I can accept I don't know what tomorrow holds.*

Probably more crappy cards but hey I've had them my whole life.

Me: *I wish I got to use the crappy life card as much as you do.*

I don't want to fight anymore. Leave me alone then. Stop hurting me.

Psychopath Adonis: *Come home and just love me for all my craziness like I love you.*

Me: *I'm sorry, Psychopath, but everything you just said . . . that wasn't love. That was downright cruel.*

Psychopath Adonis: *In my heart I thought you would be the one. And I've never put a hand up to hurt you. Nor would I. But I'm done fighting. We can reshuffle things and make this work til you get back from your trip.*

You have been abused in the past but that's not a reason to blame me.

Me: *You don't get to be a martyr. You don't get to pretend I'm the reason this happened.*

Psychopath Adonis: *I'm adjusting to my marriage and living with a woman for the first time.*

You can't expect me to know all the things you do. Not fair.

Me: *If you had cared, you would have called me. You still won't. Because you're so prideful that you're willing to ask for a divorce over text.*

Something inside me broke then. I wanted so badly for this to work. Maybe it was just growing pains, you know? We didn't really know one another, even though we had fooled ourselves into believing otherwise. I knew you were too prideful to come find me in my car; I hadn't actually gone anywhere, too emotional to drive. You later admitted you knew I was down there still, but just didn't want to come down.

I slowly went upstairs and opened the kitchen door, where you were waiting for me, a soft smile on your face. You took me into your big arms and we went to the bedroom. We lay quietly on the bed, cuddled up tight. You told me that you knew you needed to grow as a husband, that you needed to learn how to love me as your wife. You apologized for your anger issues and laughed when I said you needed to fix the door. "We'll get better," you said, and I believed you. I needed to fucking believe you. What was the alternative? Divorce?

A continuation of the insanity saga

I told Psychopath on our second date that I would be leaving in the fall for a trip around the world. Time and again I made it clear: I had zero expectations from him, asking only that he not turn my trip of a lifetime into a heartbreak recovery trip. He promised, repeatedly, that this wasn't the case, and even asked me to marry him.

My theory, in the end, is that he married me to get out of the barracks. Do I think he truly loved me? I think maybe yes, in his own way. His ideas of what a marriage should be were skewed, his idea of compromise usually swayed in his favor. I don't think I've cast a fair shadow at times, because it takes two to argue. However, I gave this relationship 110 percent. I lost myself at times, wrapped up in the idea of him being my soul mate.

Dear Psychopath Adonis,

One of your favorite pastimes was ranting about the world—how life had done you wrong, how it didn't matter how hard you worked. You had very little faith in humanity. "Everyone is evil. Even little children. I worked with children . . . they're awful!" This declaration left me dumbfounded, knowing in my heart of hearts that you were wrong, that this world is filled with a *lot* of decent folk. I contended that people aren't evil but you maintained your stance, always so sure of your own opinions. I dropped the subject, determined to show you that life was about love, not hate. I thought if I could love you hard enough, bathe you in my light, I might soften your hard edges. I thought you could learn to love me enough to accept my light with open arms.

Instead, you tried to fucking squash my light, like a demon hell bent on destruction.

In the beginning, I saw our marital strife as growing pains, necessary stepping stones. "The first year is the hardest" seems to be common advice given, especially as I never shared with anyone the full extent of your angry barrages. Those couple months before I left for my trip were filled with even more arguments over ridiculous bullshit, like dishes and laundry. Our housewarming party provided more fodder for resentment, with you ranting about how I could have been a better hostess, outraged that you had to make the margaritas—despite me making *all* of the food. In your eyes, you were constantly doing all of the work, no matter how hard I tried to keep things equal.

Marriage isn't easy and I was rising to the challenge, cutting down parts of myself while simultaneously hoping to help craft you into the loving husband I needed. I planned activities for us, encouraging a Friday night tradition I called "Margaritas and Weird Sex Night." Often, you couldn't be emotional with me unless you were intoxicated, so the solution was to get you hammered *all the time*. Plus, you liked weird sex. Remember that time you admitted to having a threesome and letting a guy go down on you?

On weekends, in between arguments, we embarked on adventures like hiking up mountains at sunrise, diving with ten-foot sharks, going to nice dinners occasionally. We went to Morton's for my birthday in 2015, but you were furious when I became so ill I couldn't finish my meal. I was lactose intolerant but didn't know it yet . . . so the food was wrecking my body and we didn't even realize. You simply focused on the amount of money you spent on a meal I was too sick to consume.

Our biggest bonding activity was working out at the gym. Because you worked nights, we woke up at three in the morning most weekends to head to the gym. Thankfully, my job permitted some flexibility when possible. We never really spoke while we were there and you refused to actually work out *with* me, but it was nice to have a shared activity. It was probably the only time we weren't arguing. As the day of my trip grew closer, our fights became more accusatory and nonsensical. You withdrew emotionally, our only real time to connect being every Friday while incredibly hammered on margaritas. The trip was greeted with both relief and fear, from both of us.

That fateful day, August 31, 2015, came too quickly. Before taking me to the airport, I secretly spent fifteen minutes covering the house in sticky notes. I put some in your food, your shoes, cleaning supplies, even the washing machine. I wanted you to find uplifting and lovey words for the next few weeks, to know I loved you even when I wasn't there. At the airport, you hugged me tightly at the TSA line, wiping away some of the tears on my cheeks. Foreboding hung over me like a heavy rain cloud. I felt like I was saying goodbye to my best friend—and I was, in more ways than I realized. I remember trying to be brave, but fuck, the thought of five months apart from you practically ripped me in half spiritually. I almost canceled my trip so I could stay with you. If you had asked, I would have done it in a heartbeat. But you frequently and fervently promised that you supported my trip.

I'll wait.

I love you.

You're worth waiting for.

Go have fun. Be adventurous.

I miss you.

Your words gave me the fortitude I needed to embrace the adventure. Your love, as difficult as it was in certain moments, gave me strength. There was one time, over Iceland, I thought my plane was crashing—because not all pilots are good at their jobs. Anyway, I thought I was dying and continuously muttered to myself, "Everything will be all right. My husband loves me. My husband loves me and I won't die." Your love literally helped me through fearful moments: I would lie in bed at random hostels, recalling your smile, your laugh, your hugs, and my heart would squeeze painfully. I cried myself to sleep at nights, in between tours, because it was slowly becoming apparent that I was losing you.

Only three weeks into my trip, I was in Dublin at C's house, the Irish friend that I met while dating Nerd Boy. We were sitting in her kitchen, having a cup of coffee, and I was excitedly chatting about you . . . but there was doubt in her eyes. She'd doubted Nerd Boy, and there she was, doubting you as well. At the time, I resented her for it, but she had a fair point: you had disappeared for twelve hours and refused to explain where you'd been. This had slowly become a common thing, ever since I left.

Writing these letters, I pored over our texts, looking for patterns, answers. I can only speculate as to what you were doing, since you've still never been quite honest with me. I saw though, after having been gone only two weeks, that something had shifted. Usually, we talked every day, sometimes twice a day, but you would disappear occasionally, sometimes for twelve to fourteen hours. I'd ask where you'd been and you would respond with indignation: "Do you have a question you want to ask me, Jenna?" I felt helpless, trying to enjoy my trip but wondering where it was you disappeared to. I couldn't hug you, touch you, or fuck you. The only power I had was to smother you with words, hoping it would help.

I love you.

You're my soul mate.

You're my center.

You're so sexy.

I miss your butt.

I want a hug.

I would share reasons why I loved you, making time *every single day* so we could FaceTime. I brought along Julio, our shared stuffed parrot, taking photos of him in various places. You always ignored them though, as if my efforts to include you didn't matter. I turned down drinking events, afraid to put myself in a compromising situation. I went to fucking Eastern Europe and never experienced the nightlife because I never wanted to give you a reason to wonder or worry.

In mid-October, while I was in Hungary, Baby Momma gave birth to a baby boy. You both chose a cheesy redneck name and, unbeknownst to me, you bestowed your middle name to your first-born. As your wife, who desperately wanted a real life with you, I felt so lost. You never told me he would get your middle name. You also never sent me a photo of my stepchild. Sure, Baby Momma had no clue of my existence, but I already felt tied to this new life, willing to do whatever it took to make this weird situation work. I just wanted to be involved!

The birth of Baby Psychopath . . . wait, that's not fair. The birth of Baby Totally Screwed . . . wait . . . Baby Bamboozled.

Yeah, Baby Bamboozled. Because the poor thing will most likely not realize until it's too late what a fucktard you are.

I digress. Becoming a new father seemed to trigger severe depression in you, I think. I'm only speculating, although your texts show a serious degradation in anything resembling positivity.

Psychopath Adonis: *Baby, I need you more than you know. I miss you.*

Me: *You okay?*

Psychopath Adonis: *Yeah. Just overwhelmed with things.*

Me: *Oh baby. Maybe I can help from here?*

Psychopath Adonis: *Do you want to see Baby Bamboozled?*

Me: *Sure, babe.*

Psychopath Adonis: *No you don't have to. IDK. I fee unwanted.*

Me: *lol let me see him.*

Psychopath Adonis: *I'm sorry. I just got sad then drunk. Not a good call.*

Me: *Don't be sorry. Why do you feel unwanted? You know I would do anything for you.*

Psychopath Adonis: *I just want a hug.*

Me: *I wish desperately I could hug you.*

Psychopath Adonis: *Me too.*

Me: *But you know, I'm pretty convinced you're a soul mate. Maybe you don't believe in that but we are too good to not be. I want you. And I need you.*

Psychopath Adonis: *I miss you.*

Me: *I miss you too, baby. My heart aches to know I can't help you right now.*

Me: *Where is Baby Bamboozled?*

Psychopath Adonis: *I'm sorry. Not trying to make it hard on you. Just sad.*

Psychopath Adonis: *I can do that you know.*

Me: *Hey baby, it's okay. It's okay to be sad. I just wish I could hold your head in my arms and kiss your forehead a billion times.*

Me: *It's okay for me to see Baby Bamboozled.*

Me: *You wouldn't have asked if you didn't want to show me.*

Psychopath Adonis: *Oh yeah.*

Psychopath Adonis: *Ok going to bed.*

Psychopath Adonis: *Kiss.*

Me: *Okay . . .*

I never did get to see my stepson. During our divorce, I cried for that lost opportunity. I know it sounds ridiculous, but I was excited to enter that part of my life, the one filled with love and family. Just another something you took from me. Our conversations became more forced, tiptoeing around anything serious. After Baby Bamboozled was born, you seemed to become even more closed off, unwilling to connect with me on the simplest of levels.

In an attempt to connect to you, I tried showing that I was present by sending you nasty, dirty naked photos of me, and trying phone sex. I just wanted to keep you engaged, and as a result sent photos I should never have sent anyone—especially after the Hockey Freak debacle. You would get so excited and happy when I did it though, so I pushed away any worries, hoping you would guard them carefully.

Everything permanently changed after Halloween. I'd been gone for two months and had just arrived in Prague, sharing a hostel room with six other girls who were being absolutely ridiculous. The internet was stressing me out, like it normally did, and I texted you to feel normal, to stave off the homesickness that seemed ever present.

Me: *How are you?*

Psychopath Adonis: *Well . . . You would love to see me in my outfit.*

Me: *Why . . . WHY?*

Psychopath Adonis: *Cause I love you and your super tight pissy.*

Pussy*

Me: *What is your outfit?*

Psychopath Adonis: *Bruce Jenner.*

Me: *You didn't.*

Psychopath Adonis: *Love you.*

Psychopath Adonis: *I love your tits!!*

Me: *I am now furious with you.*

Psychopath Adonis: *You give great head.*

Me: *I don't care how drunk you are. If you dressed as Caitlyn Jenner, I'm not talking to you for the next few days.*

Psychopath Adonis: *I'm kidding.*

Psychopath Adonis: *Wow.*

Me: *What are you then?*

Psychopath Adonis: *Nothing we aren't dressing up.*

Me: *Really? Why not?*

Psychopath Adonis: *But glad I know where you stand.*

Psychopath Adonis: *Cause we don't care.*

Me: *Hey. You said Bruce Jenner because you knew it would piss me off. So don't get mad when you get the exact reaction you expected.*

Psychopath Adonis: Oooooo

Psychopath Adonis: *Well we are heading out. Good night. Have a good day.*

Me: *Send me a photo!*

Me: *You're mad at ME now?*

Me: *What happened to my great skills at blow jobs?*

Psychopath Adonis: *No. Have a good day.*

Me: *Fine. Whatever. Don't die.*

You disappeared off into the evening (in America) while I had to go to start my day, wondering what the hell you were doing. I decided to give you space, while simultaneously testing you. Would you swallow your pride and break the silence? I constantly felt exhausted, as if I was always the one to placate you, to apologize and end our arguments. I'm not innocent in our conflict; I admit I was always trying to trigger something emotional in you, even if it was just anger. On this particular day, I just needed you to apologize for purposefully pissing me off. You knew your joke would upset me. Of course, waiting for you to lose your pride is like asking Donald Trump to not wear hairspray for a day—it just wasn't going to happen. After fourteen hours, I relented and broke the radio silence, on my own childish terms.

Me: *Hope you aren't dead. Night.*

Psychopath Adonis: *Wow.*

Psychopath Adonis: *Glad you're alive. Glad you think I was trying to piss you off.*

Psychopath Adonis: *Thanks for taking a joke and making it weird and starting a fight.*

Me: *Thanks for having such a big ego you couldn't apologize for a shitty joke you knew would upset me.*

Psychopath Adonis: *Didn't think you would respond like that.*

Psychopath Adonis: *I'm sorry.*

Me: *Right. Except you know how I am about equal rights and kindness to others.*

Psychopath Adonis: *That had nothing to do with equal rights.*

Me: *Ok.*

Then the following day:

Me: *I'm not being weird. I'm super hurt that you went out of your way to make me mad, won't apologize for it for two days now. I'm already struggling right now and I feel like you just so easily pretended I didn't exist. That really hurts.*

Psychopath Adonis: *Wow. Really? I have a wife that's gone for five months. That chose to take a trip. I can't help that you're gone.*

Me: *You just went out after making me mad and I didn't hear from you for fourteen hours. In fact, if I had gone to bed last night without texting, you'd probably still have not texted.*

Psychopath Adonis: *Wow, Jenna, you say you're so independent yet you want me to check in like you're here. I don't tell you what you can and can't do there.*

Me: *Fine then. Do whatever you want. Attempt at saying hi once a week, okay?*

Psychopath Adonis: *You did this crap in Ireland. This is you acting the same way. I didn't do anything wrong.*

Me: *Okay fine. Whatever. "I didn't do anything wrong." Okay. Whatever helps you sleep at night.*

Psychopath Adonis: *I, just like you, had something going on, and you don't like me having fun without you.*

After this, our conflicts began in earnest. You complained that I was needy, that I drained you, that you had *so much* going on. Granted, you were working nights and trying to get your master's degree. I thought asking for only thirty minutes a day wasn't too much of a burden, but you felt differently. Sometimes I asked you to stay on the phone just a little longer and you'd yell at me, declaring that I asked for too much.

Finally, in Poland, things came to a head. I discussed wanting to cut my hair, dye it, perhaps even shave the sides. You said you didn't want to "fuck a boy," and that you wouldn't be attracted to me if I cut my hair. I began feeling suffocated, not even able to express myself the way I wanted to. I wanted piercings, tattoos, bright pink hair. You told me that I needed to be cautious in case there were days we needed to be "conservative." I kept pushing, hoping to change your mind, knowing I couldn't do any of it without your permission. After the third time I brought up wanting to make some drastic changes, you got so mad you texted me the following:

> *Write, wear, cut your hair, get tattoos, pierce, smoke, eat, drink, do whatever you want. Show how strong and independent you are. Just know you can't control my reactions to those actions and we'll go from there. Be safe. Have fun.*

Who the fuck do you think you married?

My reasonable response was to get drunk and get a forward helix piercing in my left ear. It didn't matter; we had agreed to go silent for three days. I'd hoped that you would break and be the first to text me . . . but I was the first to break after only a day and a half. I came up with a bullshit emergency and texted you; I think I pretended to be sick, just so I could reach out to you. You didn't seem to miss me in the slightest, which really hurt. Maybe this was my fault. I can be headstrong and *incredibly* capricious. In fact, if you look up the word capricious in the dictionary, there is a photo of me in there giving you the finger while smiling. Anyway, I pretended to be sick and while you complained that it hadn't been a "full three days," you gave me the requisite thirty minutes of FaceTiming and texted me a little bit afterwards. The issue of my weight popped up. I was unhappy with my weight, especially when compared to your Adonis-like pecs and biceps. I felt fat when I stood next to you—something that you never corrected when expressed. I suggested going to the gym more and maybe finally going on a diet.

Psychopath Adonis: *I'm fine with where we are, but you're not. If that's going to change, I feel you would need to change your habits as well. Like I said, why I married you is not 'cause you're a trophy wife.*

Me: *Oh.*

Psychopath Adonis: *You're very pretty and yes, you turn me on. But you lust after my body more than I do yours. Your mind and personality are what makes me want to be with you.*

Me: *Well, I suppose that's a good thing.*

Psychopath Adonis: *I know it's hard and not what any girl wants to hear. I really hate even saying it.*

Me: *Well, I always suspected it.*

Psychopath Adonis: *I love that I can talk with you all day, and for the long game, that is always more important to me. We can go for hours and engage each other. Most couples I know can't.*

Your words tore through me like Michael Myers in *Halloween*. I wanted to be a trophy wife! I started counting calories the following morning, which eventually led to losing ten pounds in forty-five days. I was determined to look like those women in porn you admired so much. You remember how when we talked about porn and you admitted it probably gives you unrealistic expectations for me? Then kept watching it anyway? Yeah, you suck.

One day, you mentioned in passing a woman you met at the gym. Let's call her . . . Cunty McTwatterson. She was an "older woman who does art and would like some marketing help." You talked about her a bit, a few times actually, always referring to her as, "this older woman named Cunty." I actually thought it bizarre how you emphasized her age, but I imagined her quite a bit older, with drumstick arms and purple frizzy hair. So I said, "Sure, tell Cunty she can email me and I'll see if I can help!"

Cunty ended up sending me a lengthy email. You remember that email? It was ten paragraphs, with like a dozen questions—information she would have to purchase mentoring to receive. However, that wasn't what bothered me; it was the way she said, "Well, as Psychopath Adonis knows . . ." or, "We've spoken multiple times . . ."

Psychopath Adonis, when we went to the gym together, we barely spoke. Yet somehow, between a spectacular numbers of bicep reps, you found time to talk to a frail, old woman who was struggling with her dumbbells?

You're such a saint!

I called you, wondering why she seemed so familiar with you. "What are you accusing me of?" you retorted, as if ready for round thirty-seven of our fights. I felt bad, like I was being possessive and jealous, so I just apologized and didn't bring it up again. It was like the time I playfully accused you at cheating while playing *Words With Friends*. You sent me a vicious text saying, "*You always think I'm cheating on everything,*" and when I replied that I was just kidding, you responded with, "*we already have issues and trusting I'm playing fair shouldn't be questioned all the time.*" I apologized a second time, keeping in mind to never question you again. You gave me no reason to ever worry.

I sent Cunty a quote for mentoring and waited days for her response. During that time, you admitted you went to Cunty and asked her what she said that upset me so much. I was humiliated, feeling like some marriage honor code had been breached—*Thou shalt not share with other women your wife's fits of jealous rage.*

I felt betrayed but tried to not let it bother me. However, when she responded and refused to pay for mentoring (probably because you made me look insane), I noticed her Google+ account photo.

Wait—what's that? Cunty was pretty? And resembled Baby Momma? Is that blonde hair I see? And profoundly sexy shoulders in a bikini?

What the actual fuck?

I texted you, baffled, knowing something felt erroneous.

Me: *You made her sound ugly. She isn't ugly.*

Psychopath Adonis: *This is you avoiding fights and walking on eggshells? Accusing me about a woman you haven't mentioned—nor have I—in weeks? Lord, what is it you really want to know? Really?*

I felt crazy, wondering why I was acting like an insane person. I apologized, feeling idiotic and stupid. Why did I keep doing this? Was I going to be that wife that didn't allow her husband to converse with other women? I vowed to not be like that.

On November 25, while I was in Paris, you texted me, trying to express how drained you felt. We fought every day and it was so challenging, affecting every part of my trip. Instead of being eager about seeing the Eiffel Tower, I worried about the most recent scuffle. My trip-of-a-lifetime had become *all about you.*

Psychopath Adonis: *I'm sorry. I'm just really struggling after this last fight.*

Me: *I know. I get it. Take all the time you need, baby.*

Psychopath Adonis: *idk. Time's not the point.*

Psychopath Adonis: *I feel drained a little more each fight we have. My hope dies out a little more . . . it's like you don't even appreciate the fact I'm paying out bills for our house, and doing my best to save money for our move. I'm not buying things for me. I'm not going to trips to Maui or big island. I'm not buying video games or movies. I'm not buying a new computer that I actually need since mine is literally broke. But you keep talking about all the stuff you need! And instead I'm told I'm not loving you enough or making you feel appreciated. Yet you get mad because you don't get a purse* (side note: I had bought one for myself and he refused to pick it up at the post office for two weeks, so it was sent back.) *Like there will never be another sale. Kay spades stock has been in real trouble . . . They have too much merchandise not selling. You can get another purse. I'm hurt. You said I feel like you're being a burden . . . well when you keep taking you kinda are. You're getting all the time in the world to do what you want. I have 6hrs after work to get things done. I gladly give you an hour and yet you tell me I've not tried. I'm a slow reader and a slower writer. I actually should have been diagnosed with a learning disability but the standards are always so low I can fake it. I'm trying my best to finish school so I can get a good job so you can keep figuring our what make you happy. I'm stressed. I hate my job. And my wife's telling me I'm not meeting her needs from the first week we have been married. Jenna. You have to think hard. I'm not sure what will happen if you push me to a breaking point again before you get home. I love you . . . but I can't handle anymore of this. You said I break you all the time. If you break me . . . I will snap.*

Me: *Okay well . . . time is all I can give right now. Time and silence. I'm at a loss. I'm not sure how I'm to blame for all of this, babe. But I don't want you to not want me, so I'm just going to take another step back. That's all I can do at this point. You're the love of my life. And I just want you happy.*

You know what? We, as in the reader and myself, need a break. I need a break from your bullshit. So let's take a moment to reflect on the awesome things I did while dealing with your crappy attitude. While reflecting on my trip fills me with a shameful grudge against you, I also remember the fantastic things I experienced: eating macaroons in France with a favorite client, going to a sex-themed Christmas market in Germany, getting my ear pierced by an eighty-year-old woman in Poland. On Thanksgiving, I spent the whole day on a fabulous tour of Champagne, France, drinking myself silly. Each wonderful experience filled me with more determination to make us work. How could life be so wonderful and *so goddamn hard* at the same time? Despite our fights, I wrote off our struggles as growing pains. I showed your picture to everyone, enjoying the bulging eyes as other women drooled over your edible pectoral muscles and abs. Peer validation helped fuel me through our fights and your petty insults. I knew they had to be my fault; you were too pretty to be as big of a dick as I made you out to be, right?

Finally, the European portion of my trip was winding down, in Amsterdam no less. I arrived on a Saturday, and by the time you woke up that day I was high as a kite and enjoying all the debauchery Amsterdam had to offer. You'd been "sleeping" for twelve hours, which I thought was weird. You had even turned your phone off. I could tell because my texts to you would stick around in text purgatory before being delivered all at once a few hours later, when you turned your phone on again. I was at one of the sex shows that Amsterdam was famous for, but seeing that your phone was finally on, I decided to ask where you'd been for twelve hours.

Me: *You just get up?*

Psychopath Adonis: *Yep.*

Me: *You slept twelve hours?? I'm jealous.*

Psychopath Adonis: *Kinda.*

Me: *Kinda?*

Psychopath Adonis: *What are you doing?*

Me: *What do you mean kinda?*

Psychopath Adonis: *I definitely need to you chill out. I take a break go to the gym then play some golf and you have a mental breakdown. You said you wouldn't even be able to talk to me much this week. I never know what to expect and you want me to always be available. Not fair, sweetheart. I'll talk to you when I get up.*

I dismissed my uneasiness, trying instead to focus on the synchronized humping of the copulating adults in front of me. I decided to not push the subject. To this day, I have no idea what the hell you were doing that night. I don't think I want to know. Ignorance is, and has always been, blissful as hell.

Most of Amsterdam was me getting high, walking around, and eating a lot of noodles from wok restaurants. My childhood dreams came true walking through the Anne Frank house, seeing where this famous little girl lived for a short period. I cried as I saw how small the home really was, trying to picture Anne quietly tiptoeing in the tiny space, getting her first kiss, fearfully hiding from raids. I went to the Van Gogh museum, pissed that my favorite paintings were apparently in New York, wishing I had taken shrooms before going. Then I walked to the Heineken Brewery and quickly left again—why the hell would anyone pay fifty dollars for a beer tasting?

Our fights petered out a bit, making my transition from Amsterdam to Nepal easier. I was *so* excited for my upcoming trek through the Himalayas. You know how much I planned for this—Jesus, I spent a whole month just finding the right shoes! I researched it constantly, imagining the trialing yet rewarding experience that awaited me. A week had passed since that weird Saturday night when you'd disappeared, but I'd pushed it out of my brain, because I was destined to enjoy the Himalayas.

Kathmandu was intense; I don't think I ever told you that. Military in uniform walked around with canes and guns. The men stared at my blonde hair as women walked around, doing their daily chores. It was such a loud city, the air thick with smoke and exhaust. I loved it though, as I thrive in energetic and chaotic countries. I sent you a text when I woke up, our difference in time zones meaning you would still be up. However, you didn't text back. I was slightly concerned but brushed it off.

I walked the city, stopping in some gardens, bartering for a beautiful blanket, buying an adorable friendship bracelet. I had curry again for dinner, talking to a wonderful woman from Florida who was hiking to Everest Base Camp the next day. I told her about you, bragged about how funny you were, laughing as how fast we got married. We shared a delicious beer and gave our farewells. I went back to my room, texting you again, a little worried. It had again been twelve hours, for the second weekend in a row, and I heard a little voice whisper, *he's cheating on you.*

As I write this letter, I am just so utterly furious with you, mainly because I now know what you were doing. I highly doubt you'll ever fully confess your transgressions. Honestly, I doubt you can admit them to yourself. You've wrapped yourself into a world of lies layered atop like blankets, shielding you.

On December 4, we spent a solid hour texting back and forth. You even sent me an article about a husband who had an open relationship with his wife. I read it with a very open mind. We had talked occasionally about a threesome and you even gave me permission to have sex on this trip, although I promised repeatedly I would *never* do it. You set weird stipulations, like "take a photo of him inside you," and "just be honest if you do it!" I always laughed it off because it sounded profane and ridiculous.

The texts on this particular morning were steamy and salacious. I'm not comfortable sharing the whole conversation, mainly because it involved a lot of nasty sex talk. Nothing seemed out of place, especially when you wrote, "I want my big dick inside you," and "I really want to see you with your swimsuit around your knees." When we were done chatting, around 8:30 PM on the fourth, we said goodnight and I went and explored Kathmandu with a bounce in my step. I texted you when I returned, to fill you in on the hike details.

(*Time's are changed to reflect TX standard time, as Nepal time is a bit confusing.*)

December 4, 11:53 PM

Me: *So I met with the trekking guy. Super nice! I meet my guide tomorrow. I'm actually going to take the bus to Pokhara. I figured it can't be any worse than the buses in Morocco and I survived those just fine haha.*

December 5, 3:57 PM

Me: *I bought a blanket. It's a beautiful hand-stitched material with multi-colored elephants.*

Me: *That's my big purchase though. It was less than $100 so don't freak out hahaha.*

5:45 AM

Me: *OMG I cannot wait to tell you the funniest story.*

7:44 AM

Me: *Text me when you're up! Maybe we can FaceTime if you ever wake up. :P*

10:09 AM

Me: *Okay, I have to admit I'm a little worried at this point. I'm pretty much worried about anything and everything actually haha, but I guess I wanted to say hi one more time before my busy day tomorrow.*

11:36 AM

Me: *Okay, I have no idea how to take this. I hope whatever you're doing is fun.*

12:06 PM

Me: *Look, I don't know what's really going on but I'm nervous. You haven't responded in 15 hours but the last I knew you were just going to sleep. Now maybe more happened but I don't know. All I know is that I feel helpless, because I don't know if you're okay. Please please please text or call me. I'm trying to just sleep but I'm struggling.*

12:39 PM

Me: *Baby I love you.*

1:45 PM

Me: *I can't sleep. So many scenarios are going through my head. I just want to hear from you, so you can yell at me for overreacting. Or talk to me about where you've been.*

1:55 PM

Me: *I'm really scared. I can't stop crying. I'm exhausted. I just need to know you're okay.*

3:12 PM

Me: *Are you there?*

3:45 PM

Me: *So. I had a friend stop by the house to see if you were home and you aren't. So now I'm questioning where you are. And why the fuck you're putting me through this.*

Me: *I'm so fucking hurt and angry right now.*

Me: *It's almost 4am. I have cried my fucking eyes out because I was so worried. I feel so dumb and so stupid.*

7:18 PM

Me: *I am simply just scared now Psychopath. Where the hell are you??*

7:31 PM

Me: *I am now having people call the hospitals and jails.*

7:54 PM

Me: *Babe, it's been almost 24 hours. If I haven't heard back from you in the next three hours, I'm booking a ticket home to come find you. No joke, I'm that scared.*

8:29 PM

Me: *Babe, I found airfare. A flight leaves in six hours. PLEASE GET BACK TO ME before I cancel my entire trip.*

8:32 PM

Me: *PSYCHOPATH ADONIS! PLEASE!*

9 PM

Me: *I'm sending the whole island after you! I want to find you safe!*

9:40 PM

Psychopath Adonis: *OMG. Way out of hand. Call you in 15 minutes.*

You sent this text while I was on the phone with my friend Ghost. We had just been trying to figure out what you could have been doing.

"What if he's with a girl?" she asked.

"He wouldn't do that to me. He's too pious, too moral. He's been with like seventy girls, but he said he took his time with them, the Jesus guilt eating at him."

"He slept with you on the first date."

That silenced me. What would I do if you'd cheated? I felt a spark of doubt ignite in my heart, jealously sweeping through me like a tornado. I imagined you then with a busty blonde—your favorite—and I wanted to crush your skull. I knew something was incredibly wrong; I just wanted answers.

It brought me back to a question you texted me only a month before:

Psychopath Adonis: *What would you do if I did cheat on you? I don't think we've talked about that.*

Me: *I would be devastated, honestly.*

Psychopath Adonis: *Ok. I just thought I would ask.*

Me: *I don't know if I could forgive you. I already have so many trust issues.*

Psychopath Adonis: *Would you go fuck some random?*

Me: *I don't know. I have never had someone physically cheat on me. Walrus did a version of cheating but swore he didn't meet them.*

Psychopath Adonis: *Oh . . .*

Me: *Why do you ask? Are you feeling tempted? Too horny? I worry, you know.*

Psychopath Adonis: *No. Just asking. I am horny and miss sex.*

Me: *What would you do if I cheated?*

Psychopath Adonis: *I mean, I would probably never know. I'm not sure.*

Me: *What do you mean you would never know?*

Psychopath Adonis: *I mean, I said you could with rules. You would have to tell me or I would never know. You're in another country.*

Me: *Oh I know I would tell you.*

Psychopath Adonis: *Really?*

Me: *Yeah. I know I would, because I cheated on my first husband. I told him the very next day. The guilt ate me alive.*

Psychopath Adonis: *Oh.*

However, during your disappearance, I didn't recall this conversation. It wasn't the only time you promised me you weren't feeling tempted, so I didn't think I needed to worry. Yet you didn't mention doing anything that weekend, and just the day before we'd had a super positive and happy conversation. So where had you been?

I FaceTimed you immediately. Upon seeing you, my body was racked with hyperventilating sobs, snot pouring down my puffy face. I was so happy, so incredibly *relieved,* to see your annoyed face. I didn't care about anything or anyone at that moment; I just knew I needed to be with you. Envisioning you dead almost broke me in half, and I knew then I needed to go home.

You were remorseful, guilt plain as day on your face, your mouth pulled into a shamed grimace as you realized how worried I'd been. It was almost as if you'd just realized how much I actually cared about you. You made apologies, trying to explain that you had left your phone at the gym that morning and by the time you realized it, you had already started golfing. I didn't care that the story didn't match up to real life (since you loved working out at three AM); I was just so happy you weren't dead. I loved you so intensely that I bought a ticket home that night. I canceled my trek and everything else I'd planned for the next forty-five days. I just wanted to work on our marriage.

I flew home from Kathmandu, enduring twenty-seven hours of travel and four scary flights. I wrote you a beautiful love homage and put it on my blog, announcing the early end of my trip. I don't think you ever read it, so I'm going to put it here. Maybe you'll begin to understand what the fuck you did to me.

Coming Home

Before and during my trip, I was often asked the same question: What inspired you to do this?

Much to my own chagrin, my response was always "a shitty relationship." And honestly, that was true. However, I also wanted to be productive and commit to a true journey to find myself.

I definitely succeeded.

I learned I'm not good at roughing it. I prefer the chaos of Third World countries but I loathe searching for toilet paper. I also learned that I can spend days barely talking to people and be totally fine. Some days, my husband was the only person I spoke to, and usually for only an hour.

I also learned I need my husband.

*Something I deeply struggled with during this trip was that need for him. My whole soul ached to be near him. I was constantly conflicted because of it and it took me a long time to figure out why. I finally realized it was because American women are raised to **be independent**, almost to the detriment of relationships. We are taught to not need a man; that being single is SOOOOO AWESOME. Everyone kept telling me to enjoy myself, to go on this adventure . . . when I actually didn't even want to leave. I felt guilty, like I was letting my friends down. I inspired so many people, so I kept my dirty secret hidden: the trip was planned for all of the wrong reasons and happened at a very inopportune time. I was freshly married and I didn't want to go anywhere.*

The first two months of my trip were HARD. I was so unhappy it isn't even funny. I missed my husband so much that eventually he started getting pissed. He missed me, too! He couldn't understand why I was so miserable on this "amazing" trip. "Go meet people!" he said, not realizing I struggle to connect with people NORMALLY, let alone in a foreign country. I searched for purpose, for a productive way to spend my trip.

Finally, when I became inspired to write my book, I started getting happier. Alas, that is when Psychopath Adonis and I began to have all-out drag-out fights. They were downright awful. Writing my life story dragged up so many awful memories—memories that infuriated me. He began to resent how much I spoke about the book. We even decided to not talk for a few days, to see if that diffused the situation. It didn't. Fighting made me miss him even more. I grew impatient with my trip, counting down the time until I was home again. I wasn't enjoying it at all.

I knew right then I needed to go home. I needed my husband. Sure, a trek to the Himalayas sounds amazing. But being with my husband sounded better. Within an hour, I'd booked the first flight back to Hawaii and packed my bags. After three months of straight travel I was going home.

I think I was sad for about an hour, especially when I had to go and cancel in person with my trekking company. I had this excursion planned for months and months. I realized, though, that my marriage was more important than any cold shower or food poisoning. My husband made sure I was positive, pushing me to try and stay, but my mind was made up. I couldn't mentally take it, being away from him any longer. I tell him all the time that he is my "center," and he really is. He celebrates everything about me, except my dislike for doing the dishes. He stimulates me, motivates me, supports me. He is the love of my life. I would give up everything for him and he doesn't even have to ask.

I write this blog some thousands of meters in the air. Sometimes the turbulence is so bad I'm terrified that all my hopes seeing my husband in twenty-six hours will be dashed. I clutch the seat in silent fear, willing the metal death trap to stay afloat. Today is not the day, Death.

I'll be laying low for the rest of 2015. I'm focusing on being a housewife while recovering from terrible nutrition and jet lag. I'll gleefully make my husband meals, unpack all of my care packages, and revisit my trip with him through thousands of iPhone photos. To me, what we are about to embark on is an even bigger adventure. Don't get me wrong—I'll always be a traveler.

I just hope he joins me on the next trip.

When will I learn my lesson: part three

Dear Psychopath Adonis,

I thought we were the dream team. I thought we could overcome all of our challenges and celebrate our triumphs over margaritas and a mutual love of weird sex. I had a lot of aspirations for the both of us. Sorry about that.

It was so incredibly exciting to see you again upon my arrival back in Hawaii. I felt like instead of walking away from something, I was walking forward, toward a new beginning. I made all kinds of vows and reminders to myself, determined to be the best wife.

Do the dishes after I eat.

Workout every day.

Buy your favorite foods.

Give lots of blow-jobs.

Watch my budget.

Cook.

Help you find a job for after the military.

Just shower you with love.

You weren't able to meet me in immigration, so when I exited the airport, I ran into your arms, causing both of us to almost tumble onto the sidewalk. You showed up with a lei and a sign with my name on it. It was one of the sweetest things you had ever done. That first day together we couldn't stop laughing, touching, being happy in general. I begged you for a burrito for lunch, from the place where we had our first date—only fitting that we eat there again on the very last day we were ever really happy, right?

We went home and I fully expected sex within the first hour of getting there. Naturally, your germaphobic hands wouldn't touch me until a thorough shower and scrub, but I never expected you to deny me sex entirely. But after all that dirty sex talk and enduring three months of draught, you'd only kiss me. When you did finally kiss me, after much cajoling on my part, it felt hesitant, guarded. I was confused. What man wouldn't want to fuck his wife after three months? I tried to talk to you about it, but you begged off, citing exhaustion. "My workouts have been intense and I'm just really tired."

I went to bed feeling hurt, ugly, unwanted. However, I decided to show you how much I loved you in the language you understood best: acts of service. I agreed to switch to your nightshift schedule, so the next day, we both woke at midnight, which made you so happy! While you were at work, I started to clean up the house, making grocery lists, even got in a workout. I jumped into adulting like I hadn't just been in Nepal forty-eight hours prior, like the past three months hadn't even happened. I got so much done those first few hours, my excitement growing as it came time for you to come home. I imagined us cuddling and fucking like rabbits all afternoon. Maybe you were just tired the day before, or maybe the ten pounds I'd lost were for naught. I shaved every inch of myself, plucked my eyebrows, washed my hair. My three months around the world washed away, down the drain, the only proof of my trip the friendship bracelets on my right wrist. I didn't even mourn the cancelation of my trip; I was just so determined to make you happy.

Around nine AM, while you were at the gym, I decided to check my email one more time. That's when I noticed an email from Mileage Plus Dining, my miles program where we registered all of our cards to earn more points for our honeymoon. Frowning, I clicked it, unable to recall where the hell I'd eaten last that would have counted toward this.

Congratulations on your 115 points earned for your breakfast at Cinnamons Restaurant!

My heart stopped. The date . . . it was the day you disappeared. You never mentioned having breakfast with someone. You mentioned lunch with a random guy at golfing, but failed to mention waffles and bacon. I did the only thing possible: I FaceTimed Ghost.

"I think Psychopath Adonis cheated on me."

"What happened?"

I told her about the email and her face went grim at the implications. I knew what it meant—why else would you not mention it? I decided then the best way to approach this was the infamous "Trap That Motherfucker" technique that all women use when they just want to see a man squirm.

You had just worked a long day and then went to the gym, but were due home in about ten minutes—plenty of time to plan an ambush. You walked through the door, not even giving me a kiss but just a passing hello, and started pulling off your shirt to wipe the sweat off your face. *Do not look at his pecs do not look at his pecs do not look at his pecs.*

"Hey, I have a question for you." I was sitting on the couch, cross-legged, eyes innocent.

"What's up?" You smiled at me, breath slightly heavy. I hesitated a moment. You were so beautiful then—how could you possibly have betrayed me?

"We promised that me coming home was a fresh start, right?"

"Yep."

"So is there anything you might want to tell me? Anything at all?"

You paused, pretending to think hard, like maybe you'd overspent on a smoothie or something a couple weeks ago but weren't sure.

"Nope, nothing I can think of. Why?"

"You're positive? Because if you tell me now, it will be okay." You paused again, this time for a little longer. You gave me a nonchalant shoulder shrug and flashed another smile.

"I can think about it if you want me to."

I wanted to rip your fucking face off. I felt heat rise to my face, reality feeling like a dream state—couldn't possibly be real.

"What did you really do on Saturday?"

Your whole body seemed to skip a beat. You nervously rubbed your chest, drawn inward to contemplate the next sentence. My eyes were involuntarily drawn to your pectorals, to your smattering of chest hair. You shaved almost everything, but always left a little chest hair for me to gobble up. I loved that. It's the small things, you know?

"I told you. I went golfing."

Pounce went the lion.

"Who did you have breakfast with then?"

Your face froze. I wonder: What did you feel right then? Panic? Guilt? Fear? I wish I could have crawled into your tiny Neanderthal brain to find out.

"What do you mean?"

"Who. Did. You. Have. Breakfast. With?" I asked again, drawing out each word like punctuation, while simultaneously curling into the couch and wishing someone would hug me.

"A friend." You walked away from me, heading into the kitchen. You were stalling, attempting to disguise it by getting a glass of water.

"What kind of friend?"

You came back into the room and sighed in resignation. I knew what I was about to hear.

"A girl."

"What girl?"

"A girl I was dating."

A girl you were dating?! I wanted to scream. I wanted to leap off the soft, gray couch we'd picked out together and tear your eyeballs from your thick skull. We had been married for five months. FIVE FUCKING MONTHS, YOU PIECE OF SHIT. Instead of screaming profanities and insults, I quietly said, "Tell me *everything*."

"Are you sure you want to do this right now?"

"Of course I want to do this right now!"

You wiped your face in apprehension, as if to clear your brain so the lies could more easily pour forth. You admitted to dating this girl since Halloween, the day you disappeared for fourteen hours. The day you told me I was crazy and that I had no right to ask you to check in. The day you dressed as Caitlyn Jenner.

"How many times? What did you do?"

You wiped your face this time in a mix of frustration and submission—you'd been caught with your hand in the cookie jar, only the jar was pussy. Asshole.

"You really want to know all of this?"

"Duh."

Then you spun a tale of how I had threatened divorce so many times you thought we were over. That I was needy and you thought for sure when I got home we were going to get divorced.

Because all those times I told you I loved you and missed you apparently didn't count for shit.

You claimed you went on three dates with her and had only kissed her. Only two weeks before, you admitted you missed my kisses the most. "We kiss so well together," you'd said. I imagined you making out with some busty blonde while I was most likely missing the fuck out of you that very moment from halfway around the world.

I sat there, stupefied, incapable of forming a coherent thought. I've never actually been an overly dramatic person. Sure, I can get loud and angry fast, but I don't break things, hit people or even make my partners sleep on the couch. I forgive quickly, choosing love over hate every single time. Instead of anger, however, this time I just felt sad. I loved you with every fiber of my being. I canceled a dream trip for you and flew almost thirty hours to come home, to work on our marriage. And this was the welcome I received: an ungrateful shitty husband.

So I did what I felt was right in that particular moment: I decided to stay.

You came over to me, apologetic and heartfelt. "I promise to never do it again. I really thought we were going to get divorced, you mentioned it so many times. After our fight in Poland, I really thought we were over, because you talked about unhappy you were. I love you and I want us to work." You went to kiss me, but I turned my head away. I needed to process all of this, to work through the rejection.

You went to the task of making dinner, trying to force normalcy into the situation, while I sat in stunned silence, staring out the balcony at the sunshine and mist. How could the world keep turning when mine was falling apart? It would be one thing if you had just screwed some random woman. But you dated this woman. You courted her. You texted her all the time—most likely ignoring mine while focusing on hers. All the times you told me that I was distracting you, that you had so much to do, *you found the time to date another woman.* We went three days barely speaking while I was in Poland because you thought space would help us. Did you go on a date with her then?

I decided there and then, as I peered from our apartment toward the mountains, the only choice I had was to stay. Ours was such a young marriage, and the odds were stacked against us from the start. Maybe I *was* too needy. Maybe I pushed you away. I felt culpable, like half of your mistake was my burden to bear.

We ate dinner, keeping the conversation light, preparing to go to bed in the next few hours. When we got into bed, I did something I probably shouldn't have.

I coerced you into sex.

It wasn't my finest hour and now, looking back, I feel nauseous. But in that moment, I just wanted to be close to you, to feel wanted and loved. I felt that if we tried to work on our intimacy, that maybe we could move on from this. I think you hoped that, too. I was a sad fool; we didn't even attempt foreplay past three minutes of awkward kissing. You just pulled my panties down and pumped away for about five minutes. The whole time I felt such a mix of emotions: thoughts of you kissing another woman swirled in my head, mixed with the relief of finally being close to you. However, as usual, you reached climax before I'd even warmed up.

You rolled off me, muttering half-assed apologies for not getting me off. I burst into tears. Subconsciously I knew then that I'd lost my husband—I just wasn't willing to admit it yet. I began to cry quietly, unable to voice my concerns. You did your husbandly duty and asked why I was crying, but I'm not sure you truly cared.

The following week we both seemed to walk on eggshells. I woke up each morning silently mourning my trip, receiving cancellation emails and responding to friends who wanted to know why I'd come home. Sure, I put on a brave face with every curious and concerned message, telling everyone that your bozo move had made me realize what really mattered, but I kept my mouth shut. I just couldn't bring myself to admit that my handsome husband, my seemingly perfect marriage, was fucked. I wavered between elation and rage—furious at what you'd done while still trying to process it all.

I wasn't fooled; I didn't think that we could just move on from this. You had lied to me, day in and day out, for *months*. A man does not do something so horrific and have an actual conscious, which led me to believe that there had to be more than what you were admitting. On the day I refer to as, "the day I found out my ex-husband bought a bitch pancakes," I also demanded access to your phone and email. The time for respect and privacy were over. I went through it while you showered and found it had been more or less wiped clean—no emails photos, or texts from anyone besides Baby Momma and myself. I clicked on her name, curious to see how honest you had been about her. Her texts popped up, with photos of Baby Bamboozled in every text for the past month. You seem disinterested, only responding with requisite replies. I looked at my stepson for the first time and simply felt sad. So much had been lost in your betrayal.

I closed your phone before you could catch me, not finding any proof to satisfy the gnawing feeling in my gut. While I strove to gain your acceptance, I found it almost impossible to come to terms with the idea of you dating someone behind my back. I put my nose to the grindstone though, waking up with you every day at midnight, dedicated to becoming the most dutiful wife. You filled me in on the other activities that had kept you busy while I was gone, including going hiking with friends and going to the beach.

You lamented about how I'd gotten so jealous about Cunty McTwatterson. "You and Cunty would have gotten along so well!" you said. "She isn't even pretty. She has this hump on her chest, some surgery from when she was a child."

"Oh, so she's like a reverse Quasimodo?" I joked and you nodded, laughing. I honestly felt bad about my accusations—I genuinely didn't want to be *that* kind of woman. So I emailed her, saying, "Psychopath Adonis said we could be great friends and now that I'm back in town, I'd love to meet! How does coffee sound?"

The Friday after, "the day I found out my ex-husband bought a bitch pancakes," we decided to resume our ritual of margaritas and weird sex. I kept hoping we could just get back to normal, to move on from your shitty behavior and unpredictable anger. Except you still wouldn't have sex with me. We got drunk and watched porn but didn't even attempt sex. You tried the next day and fell flaccid midway through. We were reaching a boiling point; I think the guilt kept you soft, which challenged your pride. True to form, we found ourselves arguing that Sunday morning over chores. You accused me of not working hard enough, stating that the stress I caused by not doing the dishes is the reason you couldn't stay hard. I was confused. Hadn't I given you enough? I cancelled my dream trip. I willingly became a housewife, but wasn't good at it. You told me that a good housewife would wake up before you did at midnight and have your uniform ready, breakfast done, lunch made. I was desperate to make you happy, so I agreed to try harder. I just wanted you to spontaneously fuck me like you used to, but even after the fight, you would only cuddle. You barely even kissed me.

That little niggle in my brain began to scream like a banshee.

Departing from it all: I finally learn my lesson, once and for all

These letters were first drafted during my divorce vacation in Ecuador, usually involving a bit of booze. Despite the stressful divorce, Ecuador was amazing. I went to the Amazon, explored the small town of Baños (which was incredible), had the best day of my life white water rafting and canyoning, while meeting some fantastic people. One of my favorite parts of the trip, though, was when the entire town of Quito lit dolls on fire for New Year's. It was an Ecuadorian tradition to write past hurts on the dolls and burn them at midnight, as a way of saying "GTFO" to grievances.

I found myself a doll at the last minute — a three-foot-tall Chucky doll, with a creepy smile painted on its face and clutching a bloodied knife. I got it for twelve dollars from a street vendor, excited to find this ironic piece of art.

On this Chucky doll, I wrote the names of all of my exes, as well as the words they called me. I'd planned to burn it at midnight, excited to start 2016 with renewed vigor. Yet as I sat at the picnic table, taking shots of rum and smoking weed, I noticed the extreme interest others had in my doll. I was overprotective of it at first, challenging a British girl when she grabbed it to write words on it. She thought it was a community doll, but I made it clear that it was my doll, my burdens, my fresh start. She walked away looking a bit bewildered at my possessive venom, but also disappointed. That's when something clicked.

Once people heard about why the dolls were burned, many wanted to write on them, to find relief from their own pains. That's when I realized something that changed my life forever: I'm not the only person desperate for a fresh start. Everyone carries burdens, whether it's their own cheating Psychopath Adonis, or their uncles, their parents, a boyfriend, a girlfriend. Not everyone had the money to buy a doll — why the hell should I be the only one promised a fresh start?

Feeling inspired, and a far cry from sober, I grabbed a marker and walked up to each person in the hostel, offering them the opportunity to write on the doll the name of the person or thing that had hurt them the most. I remember a drunk girl looking at me, sobering up for a moment to ask, "Is it okay if I write three names on here?" I gently smiled and said yes; I had put about seven names on the doll, so who was I to judge? People would turn away from the crowd, trying to hide the words and names as they wrote. Their shame was their own — it was none of my business to pry.

By the time midnight rolled around, there were over fifty words/names written on that hideous doll. When the clock struck midnight, we circled around Chucky and I gave an amazing, albeit very drunk, Hollywood-worthy speech before lighting that fucker on fire. People roared in delight, toasting the burning doll, the immolation of their pain. Our traumas were connected, even for a brief moment, by this Chucky doll. It was one of the top-five best moments of my life and a big reason Ecuador will always hold a place in my heart. I was reborn in the land of color and adventure. I felt as if my past was being reduced to ashes and I was the Phoenix, rising above it all.

Dear Psychopath Adonis,

This is my final letter to you. It's been exhausting writing all of this. Often I find myself thinking of the beginning of the end, how I found out about everything you'd done. I teeter between wondering if I should accept more culpability, but then shake my head at the thought. No matter how much we argued, no one deserves being treated in the manner in which you behaved.

After "the day I found out my husband bought a bitch pancakes," I spent six days making a serious effort to please you, and while I struggled with my new self-imposed role of housewife, I believe we were both trying our hardest. The Monday after our weekend of failed and disappointing sex, we got into another fight, this time with me pleading for honesty. I didn't feel like you had been entirely transparent and begged for you to just tell me everything. You were exasperated with my plaintive pleas, rolling your eyes and just responding with,

"When will you believe me? Is this how it's always going to be? With you questioning me?"

You swore repeatedly that afternoon that you had nothing else to hide and that you just wanted to move on. The argument changed to an emotional-abuser's beloved tactic called, "gaslighting." Instead of just accepting that maybe six days wasn't long enough to demand that I move on, you switched the accusations onto me, lamenting how lazy I was as a housewife. "Why weren't my lunches pre-made?" you'd ask, letting me know you expected me to pre-make them every day. "Why aren't my uniforms set out and prepared? If I'm making all the money, you should helping ease my stress." In my mind, I resented you for your expectations. I wasn't your maid, so why did you expect me to be one? But I kept my mouth shut, desperate to avoid another fight.

Instead, we spent two hours discussing a battle plan to get along better. You created a cooking and chore list for me to follow every day, giving me your expectations as to exactly when your laundry should be done (Mondays and Wednesdays) so your life could be easier. I can only imagine the thoughts ping-ponging around in your empty brain. Probably something along the lines of "gotcha, bitch."

Something kept nudging me though, keeping me from completely trusting you. I resolved I would go through your phone while you slept, like I had done so long ago with Walrus. If I found nothing, I could just move on with my life and try to be the best wife possible.

We went to bed that night, around five thirty in the evening. You still steadfastly refused to have sex with me, but curled me into your sexy pectorals, even allowing me a fifteen-second kiss—with tongue (oh, lucky day, y'all!). I craved more of you, but was willing to take whatever affection you were willing to dole out. When your snores became a dull roar, I slipped out of bed with your phone and entered the pass code: your mother and sister's birthdays.

It took some serious sleuthing, since your whole phone had been wiped almost entirely clean. I clicked this and that, hoping to stumble on something to justify or ideally subdue my concerns. Fifteen minutes later I was ready to murder you. My arms were shaking, my teeth chattering with rage. I could feel my skin boiling with heat as I returned to our bedroom. I found incriminating evidence in your Sent folder, all from the last two weeks of November. Which meant there were so many more I was missing.

Hi, 6'3", 210 pounds, 3"*

Hey, looking to fuck a pregnant chick. I want to eat you out. Interested?

I'd like to join you and your girl. Never had a threesome.

Then I saw the emails from the woman you claimed was just a friend. Emails to Cunty McTwatterson, who I had just invited out to lunch because you said we would get along:

You: I'll be perfectly honest: I want to have an affair with you.

Her: You flatter me. If I weren't such a loyal wife to my NAVY CHIEF HUSBAND OF TEN YEARS THAT I HAVE THREE KIDS WITH I would totally jump your bones.

You: I understand. I just find you so sexy and attractive. We can still hang out right?

Her: Yep, just no hanky panky ;)

Her: That massage yesterday was just what I needed.

You: Happy to help. You're so sexy. My wife misses me a lot and I don't care. (I'm absolutely paraphrasing and being a dick about it.)

You: Wear something sexy when we hang out tomorrow.

That dumb bitch.

I wasn't quite thinking about Cunty when I sat down on the bed with you sleeping soundly in the corner. Instead, my mind concocted a game plan: how to escape and survive the next few minutes, days, weeks. The pressure was daunting and I must have made some type of whimper, because you woke up and too groggy to feel my anger and asked what was wrong. I didn't know how to answer. How does one begin this kind of conversation when we just had a similar one a week prior? Your warm, muscled arm snaked around my waist, trying to give me comfort, most likely thinking I'd just had a nightmare.

"I have to ask you a question." I said, my voice stony.

You heard the tone and perked up. "What's wrong? Jenna, what's wrong?"

"What did you do when I was gone?"

"This again? Nothing!"

"Did you have sex with someone else?"

"No! I told you I didn't!"

"I went through your phone."

"So?"

"You forgot to delete your sent emails."

My words were met with silence. You sat up, cross-legged, leaning against the wall.

"Why weren't you honest with me when I asked? I gave you so many opportunities. So many. I knew I was missing something, I even asked you again, today, what I was missing. You could have just been honest! How long did you cheat on me?"

You sat there, still in the darkness, considering your options: Do you be completely honest with me? Or do you finally end this charade of a marriage?

You took a deep breath. "Since the beginning. When you left. When you left, I hated you, Jenna. I hated you."

Option B, then.

I was stunned. How had I become "hateable" when I'd merely done what you had encouraged? "Go on the trip," you'd said, leaving me feeling so blessed to have a supportive and loving husband. I had told you about this trip on our second date. It's not like it was a surprise. I didn't ask for this shit, I didn't ask for this marriage. I just thought you were in it with me, together. I felt myself rip in two. I suddenly needed to know everything.

"Did you have sex with anyone?"

"No. I really suck at it. I tried. I even tried to have a threesome. But it's hard as a guy."

My mouth was dry like a desert, and I croaked as I tried to find an appropriate response. I scooted back on the bed and leaned against the wall, tucking a blanket around me. It was my only defense against the onslaught of verbal blows.

"Do you even love me?"

You stared into nothingness, taking a few moments before answering. "I don't know."

"Why did you marry me?"

"Honestly? Because you said we might have a threesome."

"You married me for kinky sex?"

You nodded. My eyes grew to the size of saucers as understanding dawned on me: you didn't love me. You never loved me. I was married because of my sexual prowess. Something inside me tore a little more. You took my silence as a trust fall, thinking my lack of response meant I would take you back like I did six days prior. The flood gates opened and words rushed out of your mouth.

"I'm just empty," you admitted. "I have been since college, when my cousins betrayed me in a business deal. I don't trust anyone and I don't really feel anything. Everyone I've known has betrayed me."

My hackles were raised. "I would have never betrayed you!"

You looked at me with dead eyes. "I don't believe you. I don't feel anything," you continued. "I don't even care about Baby Bamboozled. I wish he had never been born. And my parents? I don't care about them, either. In fact, I hate them, too. I hate them."

I wanted to crawl into a hole and die. I kept pinching my arm, praying this was just an awful nightmare and I would simply roll over and wake up, hugging the man I'd been so madly in love with only an hour before.

"Why did you do it?"

"You just weren't the person I thought you were. We talked about divorce a couple times and I just gave up."

I started shaking again, shock setting in, a sense of numbness. My brain was like hardened rock—survival mode kicked in.

"All people are evil," you continued, "everyone is evil."

"No!" I wanted to punch a hole in your chest and rip out your heart, as you had just done to me. "People are not evil. You are and you tell yourself that others are to make yourself feel better. I am not like you. I am a better human than you."

You just shrugged, already apathetic to the situation. I knew right then I could never stay. I couldn't continue this. If there wasn't mutual love and respect, our relationship . . . it was nothing. We had nothing.

"I want a divorce," I said, my voice strong and final.

"Me too." You spoke the words as if you had just agreed that a cinnamon roll sounded good for a snack.

I left the bedroom, quietly and determined. You didn't deserve to see me cry. I closed the bedroom door, walked to the couch, and sat down.

Then. I. Lost. My. Shit.

The life with the sexy husband with goals and charisma had instantly evaporated. Everything I wanted in life, with you, up in smoke. I called Ghost and blubbered everywhere, terrified of the inevitable hardships. How would I support myself? I hadn't made any plans to move to Austin after you proposed, so all of the months that could have been spent marketing were lost.

After ten minutes you came stumbling out of the bedroom, grabbed something out of the closet, and then went back inside. I heard commotion, and out of curiosity went to investigate.

You were disassembling your gun.

Ghost was on the phone, listening to me slowly ask, "What the fuck . . . are . . . you . . . doing?"

"I don't want you to shoot me."

I couldn't help but laugh at the absurdity of it all. Shoot you? A better revenge is leaving and making you live with your choices. Your sculpted ass wasn't worth prison. I closed the door and for a second relished the temporary mirth.

Those first eighteen hours after discovering your misdeeds was the worst of my life. Probably even worse than when my mother found out what my father had done. I knew I couldn't be with you anymore. It's one thing to overcome infidelity, especially if there's still love in the mix. But your selfishness was astounding. You were without remorse, without care. I wanted to think you cared about me, but now I know everything was a lie.

I arrived at the courthouse the next morning bright and early, almost six months to the day we agreed to love one another forever. The paperwork was a doozy, and while you filled out some of it at home, they were the wrong files. So I texted you, begging you to just come down and help me get this done. You didn't fight me or beg to discuss things, although later you got so pissed when you realized that you hadn't thought anything through. I asked for alimony, to pay to help me get on my feet and to cover the loss of income; you called it "hush money," claiming that it was a fair trade for not getting you sent to jail for knocking up an Army Officer. Instead, we pretended like we barely knew one another as we filed the paperwork. In fact, eye contact was avoided so staunchly that we might have been strangers. Tears poured down my face in slow rivulets, drops landing on the forms. "Infidelity" was neatly printed under "reasons for divorce."

When you left to file paperwork down the hall, the clerk offered assuaging placations. Then, to top it off, you made me pay for the divorce, claiming I was lucky enough to get even a small amount of alimony, which merely helped pay for the thousands of dollars spent canceling my trip and work with upcoming clients.

I hated you. Every time I looked at you, the words repeated over and over again in my head. I imagined all of the lovely types of revenge I could enact, ruining your life, "hush money" be damned. I could tell your parents what a shitbag you were, that they had a secret daughter-in-law, or I could tell Baby Momma, who was still holding onto hope that maybe you and her could be together, what kind of man you really were. I could tell the military that you had knocked up a Captain when you were but a lowly enlisted peon. I feel bad for Baby Bamboozled, who you sired but to whom you have zero interest in being a dad.

Within forty-eight hours of finding out, truly, with a dickhole you are, I decided to leave Hawaii for good, no matter the cost. There were too many haunting memories and endless hate for me in Hawaii. I needed to start fresh, in a new location. What continued to astound me were the horrendous things you said and did while I made plans to leave the island. It's as if you blamed me for choosing myself over you. You refused to help me leave the island, preferring to throw insults at me whenever you could. Christmas was less than ten days away, which meant I had to escape as soon as possible. The little tree I had bought only twenty-four hours prior sat in the corner of the living room, mocking me with its merriment.

After three days of misery, screaming low blows and insults every chance we got, you suddenly flipped a switch. I had just talked to the chaplain on the phone, telling him I wasn't being forced off the island, that I was leaving you willingly. I didn't share the drama, because I was eager to escape the island and my compliance soothed your anger. You came home with a friendly attitude and pitched the idea of having a drama-free weekend. At this specific moment in time, I was relieved at the offer, the turmoil in my heart being overwhelming enough.

So we spent the remaining time as if nothing had happened. I made meals and cleaned the house; you pretended to be my friend, being the charismatic man I still unfortunately loved. We even attempted "Margaritas and Weird Sex" night one last time, which ended up being a masterpiece of a fiasco. It didn't work, not in the slightest, and afterwards we lay in bed naked, while you cried convulsively, making noises I've never heard a grown man make. You encased me within your arms, quietly whispering, "I'm sorry, I'm sorry, I'm sorry," into my belly. Your keening moans broke my heart.

I think for the first time in your life, you began to realize how much you had failed us both. At least, this is what I'd like to think. Perhaps you were just sorry for being a terrible lay.

The fragile truce ended when I found out that the mail you had consistently delayed picking up at a friend's house contained an overdue bill that turned into a collections notice. I gave you a derisive look, accusing you of choosing strange women over me, but always giving me the excuse that you were so busy. You met my rejection with rage, screaming that I could go fuck myself. You knew I was right. I knew I was right. You just hated being wrong.

My last act was making you a final dinner—stuffed shells with chicken. I also made a sweet pumpkin cinnamon sugar bread. You rejected both, refusing my final peace offering. Why a peace offering? Seriously, who the fuck knows. I think I was just exhausted from the drama, hoping to greet the holidays with a slightly less achy heart.

You went on a date the next day—you know, the day your wife was leaving you for good. You disappeared, coming back three hours later dressed in your typical date clothing. I'd like to say it didn't affect me, but that would be a bald-faced lie. That fucking hurt.

Right before I left for the airport, I took fifteen minutes to write "Bye Felicia" on yellow Post-its, leaving them all over the house—in your food, your shoes, the cleaning supplies. One in the dryer. One in your school books. I used to write you Post-it love notes; this time though, I wanted to piss you the fuck off with every one you found.

I imagine your rage and smile a little. And by a little, I mean a lot.

You continued to send nasty text messages throughout the divorce process, as if the whole situation was my fault. The way you viciously insulted me, I almost felt as if I was the one who'd cheated and lied for months. One of the worst interactions happened when you'd shipped my car, but had to ship the insurance and other paperwork.

Psychopath Adonis: Tell me where you want your car stuff sent.

Me: Do I need to pick up my car? (I had shipped it to California and he dropped it off.)

Psychopath Adonis: idk. You need to figure that out.

Me: You could have asked. Now you can wait a couple days because I'm traveling and have to wait on responses from other people.

Psychopath Adonis: Whatever. I'll just put it in your lockbox.

Me: If I need it, I'll need it to be shipped.

Psychopath Adonis: I'm not here to serve you.

Me: I'll actually need it expedited.

Psychopath Adonis: You can work on my time or I'll just have to get to it when I can.

Me: FYI that's the exact same thing.

Psychopath Adonis: Anything that cost money is coming out of what I "owe" you.

Me: Oh Psychopath, I wouldn't expect you to behave any other way.

Me: I will have an address to have it shipped in less than 12 hours. I just have to wait for my friend to wake up so he can give it to me.

Psychopath Adonis: I'm sure he will give it to you.

Psychopath Adonis: I hope you get used over and over again.

Me: Nah, you don't really mean that but I appreciate the sentiment anyway.

Psychopath Adonis: Oh no I really do! I hope you enjoy tons of guys!

Me: Me too. Please send me tracking info when you have it. Thanks!

Psychopath Adonis: Let me know and I'll do the same!

Me: Do what?

Psychopath Adonis: When you start sleeping around. I don't want to and you get me in trouble because we are still "married."

Me: hahahahahahhahahahahahahaahahhahahahahahahahah aahhahahahahahahahahahahahahahahahahhahahahaha hahahahahah

Me: Psycho, what I do from now on isn't your business. You're my husband in name only. You've already been dating a few months now. What the hell would sex add?

Psychopath Adonis: So your little friends aren't going to say shit if they see me out?

Me: LOL My friends trust me to take care of things.

Me: Just tell them we were in an open relationship like usual.

Psychopath Adonis: ::thumbs up emoticon::

Me: Just remember to wrap it before you tap it.

Psychopath Adonis: Ha! It will be finally nice to cum during sex again!

Me: I hope you can get it hard!

Psychopath Adonis: Oh it works! Just when I'm attracted to the other person.

Me: That's probably why you masturbate so much.

Me: This is fun!

Me: Just stop, Psycho. You're only making yourself more mad.

Finally, in February 2016, I had to block your phone. You wouldn't leave me alone, always finding small ways to talk to me. Most of our remaining texts were about shipping my belongings, which was a hot shit sandwich, but an impulsive message one night gave me some hope that maybe you would realize how nasty you were being. See, I left you the book How to Win Friends and Influence People, hoping it would help you make your way through this world that disliked you more than I did. You took my advice and started the book before I had even left the island.

Today I did things from the book ... and people noticed ... said I was a better person. It hurt. Knowing people like me not being me ... I guess I'm sorry that I was a bad person. I hate not being me and not expressing what I think ...

In the time since our divorce, multiple people who have known you, including one of your most recent girlfriends whom you also shattered, have reached out to me. I've become a beacon of support to the people you destroy. Imagine my shock when a high school friend, who learned about me from your college girlfriend, reached out and told me I left just in time, that you've been a dick since high school. She worked in domestic abuse cases and is confident, as am I, that you would have eventually started to beat me. The cheating would never have ended, and I would never have been perfect enough. Your above text is nothing more than a weak moment of lucidity.

You've learned zilch.

◆

Psychopath Adonis Epilogue:

If we're being honest (and we normally are), I recognize how some of my behaviors and expectations must have frustrated Psychopath. I am very guilty of creating unachievable expectations for my partners. While this doesn't excuse his reactions, his anger, his lies...I recognize that I am culpable.

A couple months after writing this letter, I was also able to recognize the blessings that Psychopath Adonis bestowed upon me. I want to send the man chocolates and maybe some garlic, which he's allergic to. I not only went to Ecuador and had an incredible time (which you've probably gathered by now), I moved to an amazing city where I was able to live alone for the first time in years, adopted a cat (he was allergic to them, so it was the first thing I got, even before I got a bed frame), and my wedding photography business flourished in ways I couldn't have even imagined.

We finally stopped speaking in August 2016, when he was due to leave Hawaii after getting out of the military. Continuing on the path of being a fucking awful human, he completely trashed the apartment, robbing me of the majority of the $1,900 deposit I had paid on it when we moved in. I took the little amount I had gotten back and bought myself a puppy.

I don't think I'll ever forgive him for ruining my trip and betraying me in such a massive way. My hatred towards him is hard won, a complete 180 change from the absolute adoration I felt a year ago. My comfort is that his good looks, which are his only saving grace, will eventually fail. His bones and muscles will degrade and he will be a lonely old man with nothing and no one. I can't imagine a more fitting ending to a despicable life.

* *Deets changed to hide the identity of this psychopath. I'd like to think that giving him a small dick will piss him off more than these letters ever could.*

A letter to a fellow traveler

Upon arriving in Ecuador, the divorce gift/trip I gave myself after leaving Psychopath Adonis, I was a broken woman. Almost hourly I had to silently chant words of affirmation.

I am grateful.
I am worthy of the love I deserve.
I do all things with grace.
I am fearless.

I doubted myself deeply, unwilling to trust my instincts. I tried so hard to not hate men as a whole and asked the Universe to send me something—anything—that might help me heal from the deep scars covering my heart. Guy after guy, year after year, life had begun to wear on me. I was exhausted from it all, wishing I could just give up. Then I met Mountaineer.

Dear Mountaineer,

I hope you never read this, because I'll feel sheepish if you do—especially if you figure out this was intended for you. It's just that . . . that one-hour conversation we had over breakfast in Ecuador was actually incredibly meaningful, and in a multitude of ways.

We met up early that morning, intending to go to the famous swing in Baños, but as we walked outside it began to sprinkle. We kept walking along the colorful streets, chatting, when suddenly I turned to you and said, "I kind of don't want to do this now." You breathed a sigh of relief and smiled. "Thank god, because I don't want to either."

"Breakfast instead?" I suggested. You nodded and we made our way back to our hostel, laughing at how much pressure people put on themselves to cross off the "things to do" in certain locations. I didn't regret skipping the "iconic" swing shot because I got a greater and longer lasting gift instead.

Making our way upstairs to the rooftop restaurant of our hostel, we settled into a worn wooden table and ordered from the waitress. "Un café, por favor," I asked. "Can I have a coffee?" you said in English. I smiled at you and asked whether you were learning Spanish at all. You shook your head, chuckling unabashedly.

My heart was heavy, and despite being a little in love with your beard, I felt no compunction about opening up about my divorce and how much my ex had hurt me. I think you heard me crying in the hallway the night before, telling my sister that I didn't understand what had gone wrong. You didn't bring it up, but seeing as you appeared around the corner as soon as I ended the call, I think you heard more than you let on.

I appreciate that. Dignity is everything in a breakup.

Your slow energy calmed me, and we soon found ourselves in a fascinating conversation about love and communication. See, I'd also overheard heard you talking on the phone to a girl only two nights before. You had clearly and efficiently communicated your emotions, leaving zero room for interpretation. We didn't speak that evening, but I went to bed thanking the Universe for the opportunity to eavesdrop, if only to assure me that emotionally mature men exist. I immediately added to my Dreamy Man Wish list a man that could clearly communicate.

Imagine my delight when I had the opportunity to nosh on pancakes with you—to talk frankly about love with a virtual stranger. You told me stories about the girl you've been fascinated by and in love with for years, lamenting the age gap and life experience that got in the way. I told you about Psychopath Adonis and I remember you asking, "Why were you with him?"

I looked off into the distance. "Honestly . . . I think I just really loved his biceps."

You laughed hard and loudly at my honesty, citing a study you'd read where women admitted that abs and a cute butt were all well and good, but biceps were what we truly loved. Now that I think about it, I almost always check out a man's biceps.

I appreciated the simplicity and honesty of it all. I was attracted to you, and I'm probably not terrible to look at, but ours was a conversation without expectations. There was no voice in the back of our heads whispering, "yes . . . but how do they kiss?"

It's truthful and kind conversations like this that make me love traveling so much.

You taught me that men don't always want me for my boobs or legs. You taught me that some men could articulate their emotions, without prodding. You showed unpretentious friendship, however fleeting it was.

Our breakfast ended and we went to part ways, but found out we were leaving Baños at the same time. I was heading to the rainforest and you . . . elsewhere.

We ended up going to the bus station together to save money on cab fare, separating to our respective buses. I watched you from mine, playing in my head the future of the fork in the road not taken. You smoked a cigarette, seemingly deep in thought as the chaos around you passed by. My bus drove off and I gave you one last look, thanking the Universe for the simple, generous gift of conversation.

Mountaineer, you're probably off in the woods somewhere, but maybe once in a while, you'll think of the purple-haired girl in Ecuador who made you laugh. Maybe think of the road not taken. Or don't. I hope you get the girl in the end, no matter what.

A letter to a womanizer

There have been a few men in my life that I've always returned to when things got tough. I think of them as my bandage for reality. The letter below is to a guy who probably doesn't realize how much of an asshole he really is. Or maybe he does. Either way, he deserves a shout out.

Dear Lone Ranger,

Over the past seven years, you've become a symbol of distraction for me—a siren's call lulling me with the words "let's fuck." I can't imagine the opinion you have of me, since each time we've been naked together I've been in a shitty, man-hating frame of mind. The first was when I was on a break with Army Man, before he and I married. The second was after Psychopath Adonis, and the third unfortunately occurring only a month after the second experience.

Houston, I believe we've found a pattern.

The first few interactions happened at the local country bar in Waikiki, back in 2010. It had a low ceiling coated in dark paint, Christmas lights stapled to the wall, sticky residue coating every possible surface. It wasn't the best bar, but it was a sausage factory, the dream Saturday night vacation for every thirsty woman.

This bar became the normal weekend refuge for Shwasty and I. She was in a miserable marriage and I was hunting for my goldilocks-esque dick, creating the perfect dream team. Our only issue is that we had perfected the Resting Bitch Face before society had recognized it as a health crisis, so we often were left alone at cocktail tables. This didn't bother us too much, as we usually just spent hours downing cranberry vodkas, judging the redneck transplants with too-clean cowboy boots and the girls wearing flannel in ninety-degree summer days.

Only the occasional brave souls approached us, seeing through our RBF façade. I remember noticing you flitting around the bar, familiar with all of the faces, two-stepping the night away with any girl that agreed. On one particular evening, Shwasty had struck up a conversation with your friend Tonto, a surly asshole who conducted all conversations with a detached look in his eye. You sauntered up to our table and introduced yourself, offering to buy everyone a drink.

I asked for a beer, offering a demure smile while I gave you the up and down. I was smitten with your country boy look, the jeans that hugged your ass, the tattoos covering your body. You returned with libations, giving mild conversation on random topics I can't even remember. All I knew is that you had nice wrists and an interesting face.

Week after week, Shwasty and I came to the bar, hoping against hope that you and Tonto were there. Sometimes you weren't, sometimes you were. Sometimes we barely spoke and other nights, we spent hours hanging out and dancing. The anticipation drove me crazy, hoping that you would make the first move.

After a really rough day at work, I showed up at the bar with Shwasty in tow, determined to fuck you. I had tunnel vision, laying on the seduction thicker than cake icing. I wasn't interested in waiting, letting my hand in your crotch do the talking. I nibbled on your ear, and I think at least once sucked on your finger, my brain hazy with lust and booze. One thing led to another and we were in your car, driving to your apartment.

You were a fantastic kisser. My brain had shut down, single-minded on one thing: your dick. While whispering nasty words in your ear, I simultaneously yanked off your shirt and pants.

"Do you have a condom?" I murmured breathlessly.

"No . . . do you?"

Annnnnnd we were done.

As I tell my brother, "Always wrap it before you tap it." I immediately made it clear that you were not going to enjoy my honeypot without a condom.

Instead, after a few hours of foreplay, we simply fell asleep, entangling ourselves in the sheets. You made me feel sexy, and also grieved that there didn't seem to be any prophylactics within a mile radius. It was as if the Universe was mocking my need for you.

I left you that morning, regretting that we never got to enjoy a righteous tumble. I moved on with my life, our tryst spurring Army Man to declare his love to me. We ended up getting married, and eventually you found a girl that you dated for a really long time. Facebook kept us in touch over the years, the texts turning steamy and nasty as fuck when we were both single at the same time.

Six years after that unfulfilling night of almost-debauchery, I found myself in Texas, single and ready to forget Psychopath Adonis. You'd moved to Texas a couple years before and had always offered to hang out if I was in town. For over a month, we messaged back and forth, not only exchanging sizzling photos and sex talk but also talking about real-life things. I told you everything Psychopath Adonis did, my pain obvious and plain as day. I felt as if I could trust you, and by the time we met up in San Antonio I was so sure we were going to have transcendent sex.

On my way to the bar, I called Shwasty and told her my plans. She was excited for me, exclaiming, "It's been six years?!" I told her how empathetic and yet salaciously supportive you had been for the past month, bragging about how good the rebound sex was going to be.

I showed up to the bar and ordered a large beer, hoping to quell some of my nerves. You were running late, but you arrived with delectable tacos, which made up for making me sit at the bar and chat with old men.

Your energy felt off. The easy chemistry we had years ago wasn't there; the conversation was stilted right off the bat. As booze was consumed, you definitely opened up a little more, but not in an intriguing way. I mentally bucked my apprehension, replaying the chemistry we'd had six years prior. Maybe today was an off day?

Then you pet my face.

"Did you just pet me?"

"Yes, I did. Don't you pet an animal before you ride it?"

I guess it was slightly charming, with a crass sense of humor attached to it all. I laughed because really, I didn't expect anything less than what had happened six years prior. I remembered how you'd whistled at me while I walked around naked and thought, "I could use the self-esteem boost . . . this will be worth it."

After about three beers, the tension began to ease, with us finally connecting over shared stories of travel. We bonded over our love of Italian food and wine, regaling one another with stories of generosity from Italian people. You told me about a wine you'd gotten in Pompeii and invited me back to your place to try it, to which I heartily agreed.

I followed you in my car, perhaps a bit too drunk, tailing you as you weaved in and out of traffic. When we arrived at your house, I stood in the driveway and looked up at the stars while you went around back to open the front door. I grew heartsick, thinking about my experiences in the Sahara and the Amazon, where real stars existed. Not for the first time, I just wanted to flee the moment, this country, this life.

Instead, I just plastered a smile on my face when you opened the front door and invited me in, letting your two massive dogs greet me first. I cooed at them, rubbing their soft ears, enjoying how you commanded them, in my drunken state thinking that it was so alpha of you.

You opened the wine that you'd gotten in Pompeii and we quickly finished both small bottles while you ranted about politics. It wasn't the most seductive topic, especially when we eventually began to argue with one another. I felt like I was back in Hawaii with Psychopath Adonis, the conflict arousing yet off-putting.

My head was swimming after drinking both small bottles of wine from Pompeii but I didn't care. I was distracted when you finally kissed me. Damn. You were still an excellent kisser. However, as we made our way to your bedroom, I could feel it again, that disconnect I'd felt earlier. A week later, I would see on your Facebook page a meme about removing emotions and only drinking through life, but I was still under the impression that you wouldn't treat me like shit.

Upstairs was a man-cave of sorts, an upstairs living room dedicated to video games. Much to my surprise, you turned on your console, almost completely ignoring me, to play a little bit of your game. I sat beside you, trying to wrap my brain around what was happening, when your Great Dane came over and plopped his massive bulk between us. I laughed, attempting to push him aside, my feeble efforts going unnoticed by the beast.

I was a bit schnockered at the time so I pretended everything that just happened didn't bother me in the slightest, my mind's eye on the prize. Eventually, after about thirty minutes, we tumbled into your room, hands flying everywhere. You picked me up and threw me onto the bed, taking off your shirt and my pants in one deft movement. Your body was covered in tattoos, which is always sexy as hell. A man could have a flying spaghetti monster on his bicep and if you're drunk enough, it's still a turn on.

You went to town with your head between my legs, and while I wasn't entirely impressed, it's the thought that counts. I reciprocated, but while going through the motions I felt in my gut an impossible sense of grief, flashes of Psychopath Adonis popping up, taunting me. I shoved the memories aside, trying to focus on the task at hand.

After fewer than ten minutes of foreplay, a condom appeared and was quickly applied. You climbed on top of me and went to town just like any drunken guy. I was into it for a bit, until you did what I call "the Leech." It's an infuriating sex move that men pull, where their arms hook behind the girl's shoulders, locking her into place as they pound away, their face smothered into the pillow and single-minded brains forgetting the girl below them.

I struggled to break from your grasp but you tightened your grip, which sent a bubble of panic through my chest. I became forceful, shaking my shoulders, making noises of protest. You let go, oblivious to my panic and just assuming I was giving a nonverbal cue to change positions.

It was about that time I dried up like a desert. I think it was a mix of dehydration and derision. I stopped us in the middle of things, begging for water and lube. I took the moment to try and mentally collect myself, trying to pretend that everything was okay when it really wasn't. You came back, none the wiser, bringing both forms of liquid.

We finally finished and you rolled off me to go find a towel, already focused on getting ready for bed. You set the bed up for both of us to sleep, since it was close to one in the morning, and patted the mattress, inviting your massive Great Dane to join us. In less than three minutes, you'd passed out and I was left cuddling your dog, wondering where the hell my sense of worth had gone. I slipped in and out of consciousness, finally giving up on sleep around four in the morning, when your dog launched me off the bed with his paws.

So I snuck out.

I tiptoed down the stairs to my car, praying to the gods you were a heavy sleeper. Your dog didn't even notice, probably grateful to have his entire side of the bed back. I drove home, feeling so stupid and filthy.

What the hell was I thinking trying to hook up with someone only weeks after having my heart shattered? While we both knew it was going to be a hookup, I don't think it was crazy to expect more respect from you.

You texted me only a couple hours later, at 6:30 AM, asking where I'd gone. Not one to cause conflict where it wasn't needed, I just joked that your dog had made it clear I wasn't welcome. How could I find the words to describe what an asshole you were? You said, "We had great sex," and I refrained from rolling my eyes, unable to say the same.

The ironic part of it all was that before this failed encounter, I hadn't planned on writing you a letter. You even joked months ago on Facebook, asking if you would be in this book. Back then you were just a man to cross off my Fuck It list. Now, you were the man who taught me I'm past the age of hookups.

Fast forward to a month or so later. I've had time to work on myself and do some deep thinking. I had attempted dating a little bit, which left me feeling disgusted. After three failed dates, I decided to focus on myself and enjoy being alone. We hadn't spoken since that morning in January and I had already written you off as a dick.

Valentine's Day was quickly approaching, the month of February being quite meaningful to my failed relationship with Psychopath Adonis. We had met in February 2015, and had our first date and even made our relationship official all in that month. I basically found myself drinking for hours . . . alone . . . at home . . . every day.

Three days before the hallmark holiday, you randomly messaged me on Facebook. My plans for the "holiday" were to veg at home all day, avoid social media, and drink myself into blissful unconsciousness.

Lone Ranger: What are you doing this weekend I might come visit.

Me: I don't have a ton going on. I finally get my PS4 haha so I had planned on finally buying Dead Island 2 and vegging out.

Lone Ranger: So no clothes wine and Dead Island 2?

Me: Yep hahaha.

Lone Ranger: Sweet when should I come over lol.

Me: hah! When were you planning on coming to Austin? Where are you staying?

Lone Ranger: lol I was coming to hang out with you, dork.

I admit: I was apprehensive. While the idea of getting laid on Valentine's Day was appealing, when I would undoubtedly be miserable, I also didn't want to emotionally damage myself again. However, after careful consideration, I realized we had to discuss our previous hookup. I knew if you treated me like that again, I could never forgive you.

Me: To be frank, there is nothing awesome about being shoved off a bed by a Great Dane. LOL

Lone Ranger: haha he is funny.

Me: You would think it's funny since you had space.

Lone Ranger: lol you could have pushed him off the bed.

Me: I'm a guest! haha I hadn't seen you in six years! For some people that would be like shoving a baby off a couch!

Lone Ranger: lol yeah I wouldn't have treated it like that. I mean what . . . thanks for the awesome sex and blow job Jenna but don't you ever push my dog off the bed.

Me: Some men are weird. I would know, I'm writing a book about the weird men I've met.

Lone Ranger: But am I in it?

Me: Maybe.

Lone Ranger: Well what did you write about me? Did you compare me to a unicorn with the powers of a Jedi master?

Me: hahaha no. Butttttt I did give you the fake name of Lone Ranger. Everyone gets fake names.

Lone Ranger: lol Lone Ranger be interesting to see what you wrote.

Me: haha well, your dog DID shove me off the bed.

Lone Ranger: Well I think I'm safe from the Jenna wrath in your book. I have been pretty awesome to you.

Me: Wellllllllllllllllllll yes and no. More yes than no.

Lone Ranger: What lol I have never been mean to you. Well at least I don't think I have been.

Me: Can I be honest?

Lone Ranger: Sure.

Me: Soooooo I was in a terrible mindset when we met. I think I'm only just now accepting that I have mild PTSD from Psychopath Adonis. It was that rough of a relationship. ANYWAY, so I think between that and building up six years of anticipation wanting to get naked with you, I actually left your house feeling shitty. Because as soon as we were done, a dog was placed between us and you just passed out. I just left feeling like . . . I don't know, like I was just a notch with a name. But we were super duper drunk (or at least I was haha), so I get that. And I'm only telling you this because I do like you as a person. Any other dude I would have ghosted, but you HAVE been a great friend. So I'm sorry if maybe what I'm saying is rude, but it's been bothering me to be honest. And if you don't want to hang out now that's fine.

Lone Ranger: No it's fine and I didn't really didn't know you had left till I woke up that's when I texted you. You should of woke me up I'm a heavy sleeper. Haha you weren't some sexual conquest of mine. But I definitely didn't mean for you to feel that way. And nothing you said was rude. And yes I still want to hang out why wouldn't I?

Your contrite response mollified my concerns, so we began to plan Valentine's Day, but in a non-romantic way. There were no promises of chocolates, although I offered to make us dinner before we went out on Sixth Street to party. I didn't know what this meant; was this a date? Not a date? Naturally, my brain blew everything out of proportion. On one hand, the logical portion of my brain, knew we weren't a good fit. On the other, I had daddy issues.

The dreaded yet anticipated evening arrived, the sun shining and the weather delightful, especially for a day in February. I made us a relatively yummy dinner, which was ready when you showed up around six PM. I greeted you at the door sans pants, my hair and makeup impeccably done, the aroma of stuffed chicken and beer bread permeating the air. You came in with the usual swagger, greeted me with a hello and plunked down on my couch. I watched you with growing disappointment as you whipped out your cell phone and immediately began fiddling with various apps.

I let you sit there for about ten minutes, your silence overpowering my music. What the bloody hell had I gotten myself into?

"So . . . do you think maybe we could converse a little?" I said tentatively, trying really hard to not be a twat about it. It was too early in the evening to pull an attitude.

Caught red-handed, you sheepishly agreed and put your phone away so you could watch me cook.

Pulling information out of you was like pulling teeth. Maybe you're the strong, silent type, but who the hell knows. You would flip-flop between being engaging and detached. It was fascinating for me, as an empath, to feel such a difference.

We stood at my kitchen counter and ate the dinner I made. It wasn't my best meal and the bread was undercooked a little bit, but you complimented the chicken, which made me feel better, We finished eating, almost entirely in silence. I figured you were probably like Psychopath Adonis, requiring libations to relax. My hunch being correct, we eventually found ourselves in my bedroom, canoodling. By canoodling I mean I let you jerk off on my tits, because I was riding the crimson tide and wasn't in the mood for much else.

When all was said and done, we went back to the living room, practically in silence, leaving our shame in the bedroom. That's when Tonto roared in on a motorcycle, clad in leather, looking like he hadn't showered in three days. It was the same Tonto from years ago, this time out of the Army and definitely more relaxed. I found myself having an engaging conversation with him while you continued to sit on the couch, playing with your phone.

The rest of the night was a little crazy, with us going to Sixth Street around eleven and not leaving until four in the morning. It was my first time to the Dirty Six and you both were determined to show me a good time. Tonto and I had a good banter going on, while you walked around, eyeing the crowd and ignoring us for the most part, an unspoken agenda motivating you.

This agenda became apparent by the second bar, when you began to hit on random women. Between Tonto trying to convince me to go home with him and you ignoring me only three hours after we had foreplay, I was befuddled. What the fuck does a girl do in this situation? After each failed attempt with randoms, you would amble back to me, grab my ass, and smile.

By the sixth girl it became apparent that not even my feelings mattered to you. When we reached the fourth (or was it the fifth?) bar, I subtly complained, stating that I felt a little territorial. You grinned, shifting over to grab some of my flesh, and whispered, "Yeah, but who am I going home with?"

Me, unfortunately.

After drinking an entire bottle of wine at home, and then adding beers and whiskey, was plastered; I never felt it when the ground came up to greet me as I tripped. I laughed it off each time, wobbling in my heels, complaining about my feet hurting. The next day, my shins were lined with bruises.

Around four in the morning, the bars in downtown were shutting down, shooing out all of the drunkards. Our bellies ached with hunger, so we went in search of the best food truck we could find in an attempt to appease our drunken appetites. You managed to find one where they served Indian falafels that were so spicy even I, lover of spicy food, begged for water.

We sat with this other couple, and I don't know if it was the way the red wine and whiskey mixed in my belly, but I became instantly entranced with the woman at the table. I was drawn to her like a moth to flame and begged her for a kiss. I eventually had her in my lap, whispering sweet nothings in her ear, still begging.

"I don't do that for show" she cooed, teasing me with her softness and sweet smells.

I never did get that kiss.

You and I took an Uber back to my house and all I remember is rubbing my hand on your crotch, biting your ear while you murmured, "I'm going to fuck you when we get home."

The next morning, proof of our calamity of a hookup was strewn all over my apartment—a bra over there, panties flung onto the arm of my couch, jeans in the middle of the floor. At the end of the day, no matter how selfish you can sometimes be, one thing can be said: you were a delightfully aggressive lover. I woke up sore and on the couch, mainly because you snored so loudly I had to take refuge in the living room.

You woke up and we went for round two, which was undeniably gross as I was still on my period. We finished and you hopped in the shower while I cleaned up. I had gotten up earlier, brewing coffee and putting cinnamon rolls in the oven, but you only drank the coffee, trying to politely engage in forced, cheery conversation.

I sat on the couch as you nonchalantly gathered your belongings, giving me the most awkward kiss on the cheek before walking out the door, leaving me feeling bewildered. But to be fair, what the fuck else did I expect?

You didn't message me for two weeks. During that time, I have to admit I was a bit sad. I felt like if you didn't have such a fortress built around yourself we probably could have connected and had a pretty decent go of it. When you finally broke the silence, it was merely to talk about tacos. It was then I realized that you weren't on some other level—you were just a fucking idiot who deserved nothing from me.

Will we ever hook up again? Hell no. I'll never let another man treat me like that.

A letter to the men that didn't choose me

Dear Men Who Didn't Choose Me,

I write this while drinking bitter black coffee with my cat curled up beside me. The sun hasn't quite risen, but early birds and worms, you know? I've been eager to finish this book, hoping for some serious cathartic epiphany, and I certainly got a few. I've spent my *entire life* punishing myself for my father's crimes. Which reflects, maybe unfairly, the reasons we never stayed together.

Some of you have been good men and we just weren't a fit for various reasons, like my neediness or your inability to keep your dick in your pants. Some of you were so horrifically selfish that I avoid thinking about you. Some of you were weird as fuck and I don't like to be out-weirded.

If this book, these letters, have taught us anything, it's that I have terrible taste in men. I'm an empath, and attracted to the worst kind of narcissist. The more selfish and damaged a man, the sexier he is to me. I've thrived on conflict, on the struggle, based on the idea that *Romeo and Juliet* was a romance, not a tragedy. I've been searching for the man who would commit suicide for me, never realizing how unhealthy that was.

Ladies reading this: find a man who will make you cupcakes on your period. Not one who tells you that a woman is over-emotional because of what's between her legs.

When I was with you, I gave you my best, my all. It's obvious time passing hasn't abated my disdain for what we did to one another. Yet I'm grateful for every single one of you, because I wouldn't be who I am if not for you. There are literally dozens of other men I've met throughout my life, but only twenty or so received letters. Should you feel flattered?

Probably not.

I'm determined to start my thirties with every single bad memory placed firmly behind me. They've sculpted me, changed me, morphed me, but they haven't broken me. They will fuel me, motivate me, and when I'm on the mountain of my empire of happiness, I will stand at the top and flip each and every one of you the finger.

Thank you for not choosing me.

A letter to a man that changed it up

I wish this book was going to end with me being swept up into a happily-ever-after, but as I'm sure you've learned by now, there are two truths about my life: I struggle in relationships and Christmas is a shitty holiday for me.

Hamstring was a life changer. A game changer. An inspiration. He made me feel worthy in a way no other man has. For a while, he was a Prince Charming chapter—until he wasn't anymore. I hope this letter teaches my readers that just because someone is nice doesn't mean you're meant to be together. Someone doesn't have to beat you or cheat on you to be an incorrect life mate.

Dear Hamstring,

I had this letter typed out for months, eager and excited to give it to you as a Christmas gift. I imagined your eyes watering, a soft smile play on your lips, the joy crinkling your big blue eyes.

Then you went behind my back and read this letter before I could have that opportunity.

This is one of many reasons I had to break up with you.

This writing process has, to put it bluntly, really, really sucked. You experienced the writing process with me and witnessed the toll this book has taken on me, watching as I paced in circles in the living room while mentally trudging through Lone Ranger's chapter, or sharing advice when I asked if Walrus' ending was poignant enough. Your patience was one of your greatest attributes.

When I met you, I refused to believe that you would be the one thing I truly needed after Psychopath, trying more than three dozen times to scare you away. I didn't want this. I didn't want any of this. I didn't want a savior, riding in on the proverbial white horse, so soon after Psychopath Adonis and Lone Ranger.

I didn't deserve it.

On February 27, 2016, I woke up in bed, alone with my cat, positive I would be alone for the rest of my life. I felt that while I had a lot to offer, I was also a three-time divorcee recovering from daddy issues.

As was my habit, the first thing I did was check all of my social media and dating apps. I didn't have a lot of profiles up, just on Tinder and Plenty of Fish. My profile has said roughly the same thing for a few years, hell bent on scaring away anyone who might feel motivated to send me unsolicited dick pics.

Minus the cliché things (I'm fun loving, I love my cat, I love to travel! ::giggle::) I'm a travel-wedding photographer, I keep very busy but I would love to add someone to my life that makes it better! I'm currently building my business, being brand new to Austin. I love to cook and eat healthy as well, but don't worry, I love a good steak!

And for the win, what makes me unique: I'm the antithesis to a majority of women. I can cook, I have an appreciation for good beer, I work out, and I am independent to a fault. I've traveled all over the world, with a desire to see more! I'm blunt, I don't suffer fools, and my biggest flaw/asset is my honesty.

I won't make a huge list of what I am and am not looking for, but I will ignore messages from people who send fewer than two to three sentences, are incapable of proper grammar and basic spelling, and have gym selfies all over their profile. I like my man in shape, but seriously, that's laaaaame. Please have normal man attributes, such as a job, car, goals, and the ability to squash bugs.

There you were, your profile photo a selfie taken in a smudged mirror, adorned in blue plaid. You took the time to write a whole paragraph, telling me how fascinating I sounded, as well a little bit about yourself, and lord knows what else . . . I was just intrigued. A private chef? Articulate and educated? I wish I still had those messages, but Plenty of Fish wipes messages after a certain period of time. What we still joke about though, is my response to you. "Not even a hi," you tell people. I laugh, not ashamed of my forward response.

I have three questions: do you want children, are you LGBT friendly, what are your political views?

After Psychopath, I never wanted to date an asshole bigot ever again. I think I wanted children, I know I definitely wanted to keep the option open. I also never wanted to waste another fucking second on a man who wasn't a good fit. If you didn't like my boldness, we would never work.

Instead, you responded, talking about how you wanted kids, you had been in charge of your school's civil right's program, and that you were not a Republican.

All of the right answers.

One thing led to another, with Sunday passing by in a flash, the messages piling up. After about eight hours, I felt comfortable giving you my number, so we could schedule a Skype hangout where we chatted "in person" for another four hours. You lived two hours away, so we decided to make sure everything was kosher, so we didn't waste the drive. I was smitten as fuck, enjoying how easy the conversation was. No longer the girl who minced words, I let you know right off the bat I had been married three times. You shrugged and told me about your own muddied past. After sharing some of our demons, neither of us saw any obvious red flags. We knew it was time to meet and set a date.

March 1, 2016. You drove the two hours to my house, where I settled on the bright idea to cook you a meal. You, a private chef. I even chose one of the most difficult meals: fried chicken. I don't know if others feel the same way, but fried chicken terrifies me; what if I don't cook it properly and then poison everyone that consumes it, and then they die? I always imagine spending twenty years in prison, all because the chicken was raw.

I heard the knock on the door but waited a solid thirty seconds before answering. Instead, I stood there in my kitchen, pounding heart threatening to suffocate me. I clenched my fists, terrified of this . . . this moment and I didn't even know why. I gathered my courage and turned the handle slowly, taking one last deep breath.

You stood there, eyes ablaze with anticipation, holding a box of glasses. I laughed loudly and reached for them. I'd briefly mentioned that we would have to drink the champagne you planned on bringing in mugs. You said you would bring drinking glasses, but I didn't think you were serious! Still laughing, I moved aside so you could come in, hoping that you didn't judge my basically empty apartment. I'd moved to Austin with barely any money; I basically had a cat, some plates, and a couch. I didn't apologize though; in fact, I wasn't even wearing makeup. I didn't brush my hair. I don't think I even had on a bra.

Despite my efforts to show how little I cared if you liked me, our first date was magic. You brought my favorite champagne, ate my burned fried chicken, and then gleefully made out with me for hours. I would often catch you looking at me, stars in your eyes. After everything I'd been through, you were like a long awaited dreg of beer after a long Monday. I wanted to drink in all of you, everything you could offer.

I'd like to say our story after that first date resembled two people riding off into the sunset, the wind in our hair and hands held tightly, but instead it was a hot fucking mess. We made it to our third date before I became overwhelmed by your kindness; there is such a thing as too nice, especially for a woman who thinks she doesn't deserve even a simple card. I called you after our third date, Chinese takeout at your beautifully decorated apartment, and told you I wasn't ready to date someone.

I really truly wasn't.

I had arrived in Austin with one purpose: start a successful business. A man didn't fit into my idea of what life was meant to be anymore. I genuinely believed that the Universe had doled out all of my chances and it was high time to start a cattery. In fact, I had just adopted a cat only a couple weeks earlier and named her Fallon. I thought I had shit figured out, finally. Then you came along.

The day after our third date, I called you and broke the news with a heavy sigh: "I don't think I want to date anyone right now." Silence. I could hear you breathing on the other side, traffic from New Orleans in the background. You were traveling for work and wouldn't be back in Texas for a week.

"Did you hear me?" I asked, hoping I didn't have to repeat myself.

You swore and I envisioned you rubbing your eyes in frustration.

"Please, Jenna, don't do this. I really like you and I know we would be a great fit. I'm willing to give you all the space you need, please just don't do this."

I hedged, standing in my kitchen, drinking my third glass of wine.

"I don't know . . . I just don't think I have the time to date and I certainly don't have the emotional capacity to care for someone. You're so nice and I'm . . . not. I don't want to take advantage of you. I never want you to feel that way. I've treated men like shit in the past and I don't want to be that person anymore."

Our conversation went on like this for a solid hour, with you pleading on the phone and me drinking my fears on my couch. I never wanted to hurt someone again; I never wanted to hurt again. The last six months had been some of the worst in my thirty years on this Earth and I couldn't handle any more crap.

"Look, you need a bookshelf? Right?" You said it as if you were willing to up the bargaining chips.

"Yes . . ." I hedged, not wanting to go down this path.

"Okay, how about I come over next week, when I'm done with my trip. I'll bring you a book case, build it, cook you dinner, and bring you more champagne."

Is this dude for real? I recall thinking, my mind racing.

"Hamstring. . . that's too much. I'm not willing to have sex with you. I want to make this clear. I want boundaries set up, no expectations. I mean it when I say I'm not ready. I can't give anything to you right now. If you want to come over, build and cook . . . I would be a fool to stop you. Just know that it doesn't mean you're getting sex."

You breathed a sigh of relief for the first time in sixty minutes. "DEAL!" you crowed with delight. I hung up and took a moment to reflect on what was happening. It had only been two months since I walked out on Psychopath—how could it possibly be that I had found someone sane and healthy so soon afterwards?

You came over a week later when your trip in NOLA was over. We'd kept in touch during that time, and distance definitely made the heart grow fonder. I loved that you were always within reach, never making me wait more than a couple hours for a response from a text. The phone rarely rang more than three times before you answered. Despite my apprehensions, I was also excited to see you again.

You showed up as promised, making me delicious London Broil, plying me with champagne, and building me not only two bookcases but a desk as well. Your generosity blew me away, and despite my wish to keep all my walls up, I felt a couple crumble that night.

Dating me in the beginning couldn't have been easy. I can visualize saying this to you and waiting for you to roll you eyes, replying with, "Well, if that isn't an understatement . . ." It's true though, mainly because my fear of hurting you was stronger than my fear of being alone. In fact, my fear of being alone had disappeared, replaced with a need for solitude. I would freak out when we spent too much time together, lashing out when I felt like you were being too nice to me. I resented my resentment, mentally beating myself up because I didn't want fifty balloons in my living room after being picked up at the airport. I didn't want a handwritten card for every occasion. I didn't want to be told I was beautiful every day, because I just didn't deserve it. I hated myself for being angry, because what woman wouldn't die over a dozen lilies being hand-delivered with a kiss?

I was an ungrateful little shit.

Your patience was boundless; you never let me treat you like shit but you also let me know it was okay to be afraid. For a whole month, you asked me to be your girlfriend. I think it was almost a dozen times before I acquiesced. On our way back from a wildlife park, you asked me again, this time with an edge to your voice. I would never give you an answer, never replying with a "yes" or "no," always leaving the door open. But this time, you finally broke and said, "JUST SAY YES, JENNA. YOU KNOW YOU WANT TO, SO WHY AREN'T YOU SAYING YES?"

I smiled and still didn't reply. Instead, when we arrived back at my apartment, I set up the perfect way to say yes.

"Hey, babe, could you tell me if I have enough whipping cream for dinner?"

You went into the fridge, pausing for a second, while I busied myself searching for pasta.

"Wait . . . what?" you said, absolutely puzzled as you pulled a sticky note off of the cream on which I'd written "YES!"

I looked at you, my smile reaching ear to ear. Your eyes shined brightly, a little soft at the edges, happiness radiating from you in waves.

"Do you mean it? Does this mean what I think it means?"

I laughed and you came in for a hug, squeezing me tight.

"Yes, Hamstring. I'll be your girlfriend."

Even then, when I knew I wanted to be with you, I still fought the happiness. The last time I was happy, it had been the biggest lie of my life. It didn't help that almost weekly, Psychopath Adonis crept in with emails and phone calls. While the majority of the emails involved shipping my belongings, he eventually threw a fit when I didn't close our joint account quickly enough. He wrote five emails, all going unanswered, basically demanding that I obey him. I was itching for a fight one day in April, and Psychopath, ever the drama queen, was happy to oblige.

After the fifth cry for attention, I turned to my boyfriend and said, "Maybe I should just let him know this behavior will not be tolerated."

And it won't be. Psychopath, I don't want to talk to you. I don't want to hear from you. I don't want to help you with the iPad I stupidly left you. I'm not near our credit union, so you can get rid of the account. I got the money I deserved, money to help me start over after your blatant and still somehow unsurprising selfishness.

I want nothing to do with you, ever again. You're alone now and you deserve that. If it's conversation you crave, know that Austin has been AMAZING for me, personally and professionally. I've cut my hair short, gotten three tattoos, eaten too many tacos, and got a cat. I found an incredible, kind, and talented man as a boyfriend, and professionally I'm soaring. Booked twelve weddings since I got here. You are a blip in my life story, a funny anecdote to fill a chapter. If you want to know more, go to my blog. I wrote you a letter. ;)

I don't even hate you anymore. I'm so apathetic to you as a person that if I heard you drowned in the ocean, I would only stop to think "He didn't have much going on in his soul, but what a waste of a pretty face." Just kidding. I would go eat more tacos and love on my boyfriend, not caring about you at all.

Are you getting how much I don't care? I really hope so. Because if you email me again, at all, I'll call your command and make your life a living hell. Leave me the fuck alone. Go back to the gym and pick up married women, you're good at that.

Bye, Dick Face.

You and I were on the way somewhere and I pressed send, feeling vindicated. I had been so pleasant during the divorce, because I so desperately needed the alimony to start over in a new city. I'd kept my mouth shut, quietly disappearing from his life to make my own future easier. You were uneasy with my vicious email, but I thought for sure it would make him stop. Instead, a few hours later we rolled up into Taco Bell to get a late-night snack and my phone jingled. I knew he'd responded.

Sat, Apr 2, 2016 at 10:01 PM

"Well fuck you and your little dick bf. Call whoever you want, you have nothing cause your a ex wife. I don't want to talk to you. I want you to call navy fed cause I don't want your name on my account. But if you want to be rude about everything good luck. Fine, game on."

Sat, Apr 2, 2016 at 10:04 PM

"Don't write me back just fix things. I don't want to hear from your overweight ass. You think you can start shit . . . Keep it up. I have files of everything . . . So don't start shit."

Sat, Apr 2, 2016 at 10:11 PM

"You better stop threatening me."

The second message threw me into a tailspin. Being called fat by him again hurt me to my core. I mentally shut down, immediately hopping into the shower when we arrived back at my apartment, spending too long in the hot water. When I got out, you were there, full of concern . . . and I didn't care. I had collapsed in on myself, Psychopath Adonis still able to affect me from thousands of miles away, *and I hated that*. Would he do revenge porn like Hockey Freak? We'd had some weird sex and, trusting him at the time, I had let him film things. What if this was 2004 all over again?

I began to cry, unable to speak. I sat in my towel, dripping wet hair, letting you hold me on the bed. You patted my back, slowly stroking it, telling me what a shitfuck he was and how I didn't deserve this.

This is when I started to fall in love with you.

Psychopath Adonis responded once more, after our last email, apparently calming down from yet another rage episode.

Sun, Apr 3, 2016 at 7:35 AM

"You know what. It's all fine. I'm sorry. I'll leave you be. I'm glad you're well and I'll never bother you again. Best wishes."

I didn't respond, choosing to see the truly psychotic behavior behind his words. I decided that night to move on and put Psychopath good and firmly in my past. Every day I reminded myself I was worth more than him. I deserved you; I deserved everything you were offering me.

You also taught me that I deserved the whole goddamn world. You loved me even when I gained ten pounds. You let me rage over ridiculous things, like how badly people park or when assholes talk in the movie theater. When I got too intense,

I liked how you give me a steady gaze, sometimes smiling, asking me, "Are you done?"

Am I ever done?

You loved me when I cried, even if it's over a stupid movie on Netflix. You loved me with purple hair; you loved me with pink hair. You loved me when I was so drunk I became an obnoxious jerk. You even loved me when I worked a solid hundred hours in a week.

And I loved you for all of this and then some. I loved you even when you drove me to the point of insanity, insisting on chattering because the quiet made you nervous. I loved you when you struggled to better your own life, striving for more. I loved how you traveled to Jamaica with me, after only being together for three months, and let me convince you to do some crazy shit like ride horses in the ocean. I loved the fact that you cuddled my cat even though you were seriously allergic. I loved that you got Pride tattoos with me, to show our support for the LGBT community.

What you also don't know is that every letter, every sticky you wrote, I kept. I had big plans for them, hoping to collect all of your love and make them into art. Something to give you if we ever got married. They're still sitting in my desk, organized into a plastic bag. I have no idea what to do with them now. It would feel like throwing away pure love, but I can't keep them for forever.

I'm angry with you, still. Not just because reading the draft of this letter was one of multiple times you betrayed my trust, but also because you've spent the majority of your time with *her* since we broke up. You went to *her* after bawling your eyes out in my apartment. You've stayed with *her* for most of it. How do I know? Because I'm a fucking creeper that was worried about you and looked up your phone GPS. I broke it off with you, scared that you would do something stupid, but I didn't think you were *that* stupid.

In the end, I recognized that we just weren't a good match long term. We didn't really have anything in common other than our love of food. You were religious, I'm not; you wanted kids and I'm leaning toward not wanting any. You sucked at financial planning and I don't. Even those closest to you voiced concerns, and while you brushed off their words, I couldn't. *I just couldn't.* I also couldn't be in a relationship where looking at another man, let alone even talking to a male peer, was met with suspicion. You were desperate enough to keep me that you were willing to let me sleep with other people. You were willing to bend your own morals to keep me around and I couldn't let you do that. You also betrayed my trust a couple times, including reading my diary by "accident." I couldn't be in a relationship like that.

Of course, we had big dreams and the best intentions, but I recognized that after eight months, I needed to work on myself. I never took the time to heal from Psychopath's abuse. I never got a moment to breathe and ask, "How do I find myself after this?" It took a friend who has known me for over ten years to ask, "What happened to the happy girl I knew?" And they were right. The happy, vivacious woman I was before Walrus and Psychopath had disappeared. I have become an insane cynic, and while it amuses me in some ways, it also saddens me. I can't find that optimism when I'm constantly working on another relationship rather than the most important one: the one with myself.

You gave me the gift of self-worth, which is why I'm not blasting your secrets on this letter, in this book. I'll get over how quickly and easily you brushed me off, even after you sobbed in my kitchen claiming you didn't know how you would live without me, but I hope you realize I never intended to hurt you. I also hope you realize this was for the best.

~~To Jupiter~~ Fuck Jupiter.

A Letter to Present-Day Me

Dear Thirty-Year-Old Me,

We made it!

For your thirtieth birthday, you called your mother, suggesting that mayyybe a pair of Tieks ballet flats would be a good gift. Maybe two in fact.

"Jenna, that would cost over $300!"

"Sure, but it's only like $100 for each decade of my life."

"You think you should get $100 for every decade?"

"Duh. Did you think I would make it this far?"

"Fair enough."

There was this one time, when you were around twenty, that you called Mom sobbing around two in the morning her time. Do you remember it? You couldn't help yourself. She answered with a groggy "Hello?" probably thinking something awful had happened.

"MOMMY! I'M GOING TO DIE. I'M GOING TO DIE YOUNG. OH MY GOD, I'M GOING TO DIE YOUNG. I JUST KNOW IT!"

You were so sure of your impending death and it terrified you. She offered some soothing words, but nothing helped the sense of doom settling over you like a storm cloud.

Well, that was a few years ago, and you've done some crazy shit since. One could argue you were trying to expedite the process of death, but it could also be said that you were just embracing the idea of it.

Over the past decade, while you dealt with shitty men, you've also been to twenty-something countries, most of them completely alone. You've jumped out of planes (albeit kicking and screaming); you've gone spelunking in Budapest; you've weaved in and out of shipwrecks a hundred feet below the water's surface, ridden untrained horses in rodeos, gotten your degree, served your country, and you've even been on a French reality television show. You started a successful business, rescued animals, secretly gave to every homeless person you passed, and stayed up for hours with distraught friends.

You confronted your rapist. You've always stood up for the "little man." You have rallied for LGBT rights, insisting that equality has no limitations. You refuse to tolerate injustice in any form.

Girl, you've lived. You are worthy of real love.

From here on out, your life won't be defined by the men that freight-trained through you. Your twenties were defined by struggles, but your thirties will be filled with success, and hopefully, one day, a man who treats you like a goddess. You'll continue to travel the world, finally becoming bilingual—finally achieving the family you've always wanted. You're worthy of every bit of it.

I love who we've become. For years, we were filled with such self-hate, but that time has passed. We're confident in our goodness and that's pretty cool.

I love you, Jenna. Thank you for not breaking.

A letter to my future

This letter was written on a plane, on my way back to the United States after my divorce vacation in Ecuador. I hadn't moved to Austin yet, I hadn't adopted my cat, and I didn't know where life was going to take me. I want this letter to be taken at face value, written by a woman who had just gone through a horrific divorce and thought herself unlovable. I won't know for sure to whom this letter will apply, but I hope to be able to give it to someone special one day.

Dear Future Husband,

The fact that I'm writing you means I haven't given up hope. What can I say—I'm a completely hopeless romantic, which I'm sure you know by now.

I don't know when you're going to wander into my life. Maybe you'll just stumble in, like literally trip on the curb and land on me. Maybe you'll spill a drink on my dress, apologize profusely, and offer to buy me a new one. Maybe we'll meet at a bookstore and you'll buy me that book I've been eyeing. I'm sure whatever it is, however it happens, I'll probably decide within thirty seconds if I want to sleep with you or not.

It's science, after all.

You're the last chapter in this book because I hope that no matter how many men enter my life before you, you're both the epilogue and prelude to everything.

Writing these letters has been phenomenally hard, because despite my best efforts, I couldn't help but think, "Who will judge me once they know what I've done? What has been done to me?" Future Husband, I'm scared. I'm terrified to my bones that I may never find you. What if I'm a fucking idiot, bumbling through all of these men, these hookups . . . for nothing? What if

I spend hours in therapy, work on myself every day, and you never arrive?

What if I'm reading this book to my cat Chicken when I'm sixty-five and eating Beefaroni out of a can because that's all there is? Will Chicken gnaw out my eyes when I die alone, sitting on my old, purple couch, covered in the million blankets I crocheted while watching repeat episodes *How I Met Your Mother*?

When I meet you, Future Husband, I want to be ready for you. I don't mean like wearing the perfect lipstick-ready, or praying to the gods I remembered to put on deodorant. I mean I want my head to be on straight, to be ready to not fuck it all up. When do I tell you I'm Elizabeth Taylor incarnate, with a marriage punch card almost full up? People tell me I shouldn't divulge this to you, but you know me better than that. I could never lie to you—that's not who I am.

By the time we meet, I will have experienced every type of love there is: abusive love, lazy love, desperate love, selfish love, pure love, passionate love, even sad love. I think love is one of the best, most intoxicating gifts humans can give one another. It's also one of the most costly gifts, sometimes tearing out chunks of your soul. I hope that by the time we meet, you've had all kinds of love as well. And I look forward to creating our own brand of love, something for the ages.

Writing these letters has made me melancholy, more often than not. I've been drinking every day, sometimes pausing just to stare off into nothing, to process my words. I've shocked myself at times, finding answers to questions I've pondered for over a decade. I wrote these letters not only to process my life but also to grow as a person. I've cried a lot. Sometimes I've gotten so angry I've wanted to tear down walls and take a knife to a pillow. Because a shower of feathers makes everything better, you know?

I'm sorry that I thought all my other husbands were "the one." I have no real excuse except to say once more that I had some serious daddy issues. To be fair, Psychopath Adonis was a phenomenal liar—and he had great biceps. I don't know if you have nice biceps or not, just know that they're no longer important to me. If I'm with you, it's because you're my safe place; you're my person.

When I meet you, I want to be bored. That won't make sense at first and maybe it seems like an insult, so hear me out: I want to be bored because every one of my past relationships has been drama filled. I have zero knowledge on how to be in a relationship that isn't rife with conflict. I've not gone longer than two months without it. In my whole life. I grew up in a household where communicating anything important required screaming. Ideally at ten PM.

I want to go to bed early with you, speak quietly, spend our Sundays drinking coffee and eating pancakes. I also like the idea of a quiet wind chime and a purring cat. Maybe three dogs. Can we have a horse? I've probably asked that a billion times, if I haven't already bought myself one.

Let's grow old and bored together, all right? We can mix it up by traversing this world, swimming with sharks in Bora Bora or staying at a nudist resort. I just don't want to scream anymore. I'm tired of screaming.

When I meet you, I hope that my past behavior and pain comes as a shock. I hope that it seems like it must have happened to another person, a different enraged, desperate woman. I've already begun to transform myself, to covet forgiveness and gratitude. I have so many wonderful things to be grateful for, your future arrival being one of them.

Sometimes, to comfort myself, I imagine what you're doing at the same moment. I wonder how you feel, if you're safe, if you're hungry. I've gone hungry before and I would never wish that on anyone. Are you in bed with a girl right now? Are you sleeping or studying? When I meet you, I want to know *everything*: the good, the bad, the really freakin' weird. On our first date, I'm going to ask deep, intrusive questions. My favorite is, "What is your deepest, darkest secret?" I've learned there are only three variations of questions to this question and you learn a lot by which variation is chosen.

I hope your family likes me. And if you don't have a family, that's cool too. We'll be family, all right?

If when we meet I seem standoffish or suspicious when you text someone, don't take it personally. At this point I don't think my trust issues will ever disappear. If I'm marrying you, it's because you're a patient motherfucker. It's why I love you.

Thanks for understanding why I'll never change my last name ever again.

I don't know when we'll meet, but I'd like to think it's before my tits reach my knees. In case it isn't, know that I'll never judge you for having to use those little blue pills. Just give me one, too, all right? I just hope that when we meet we're still flexible enough to have sex in weird places and even weirder positions. I'll pop your hip back into place if needed.

You're the love of my life, and these men, these experiences, have only made me stronger and better. I seriously can't wait to meet you, and I promise: no more major fuck ups from here on out. I'm focusing on myself now, on bettering myself, as a woman, as a human, as a soul.

I'm coming for you, so gird your loins.

Epilogue

I was taking a shower on a random Tuesday, contemplating life in all its complexity, and my brain fell upon this book, as it often did during the difficult process of creation. I realized that maybe, just maybe, I needed an epilogue. A final word. Because I haven't spoken about myself nearly enough, I'm sure. So the next day, I sat down and began to type, hoping to be as inspiring as my non-humble brain can be.

See, I live in fear of this book and the power it holds. It holds power over my self-esteem and my life, something that makes me supremely uncomfortable. People might very well judge me so harshly I might end up friendless, broke, and living in a cardboard box with my pets. I could spout day in and day out how much I'm different from the girl who married Skeletor, but that doesn't mean that my cheating won't haunt me for the rest of my life. I regret what I did. And how many of us have even just a few regrets? I think people who say they "live life without regrets" don't do enough internal reflection. I have exactly four regrets thus far in life. I'm not stupid enough to think that I won't have more, but I'm careful about choosing them. You should be, too. Be forgiving of yourself and the choices you've made. There isn't a manual for life, so no one can actually tell you what you're doing is wrong . . . unless you're a serial killer. In that case, I live in Arizona.

I'd like to think that once this book is out there, I can move on from these men, these experiences, but each is tattooed on my soul, whether I like it or not. The best I can do is move forward and hope that I can help even just one person understand their own patterns in their relationships. I'm not perfect. I struggle in normal relationships, questioning them at every turn, sometimes wishing for the Cat Lady Life, but that was my pattern before this book, so instead I continue to stand my ground, refusing to be the same person I've been.

We cannot live our lives in terror of the unknown. As an entrepreneur, fear is a friend I sip coffee with in the morning, but I let it fuel me alongside the caffeine. The contrived saying, "if your dreams don't scare you, they aren't big enough," is true, as much as I loathe to admit it. So seize the fucking moment, rock this life as hard as you can, because these aren't previews to the movie. Grab life by the balls, look it in the eye and say, "I don't take no shit from anyone." Ignore the double negative.

I don't know if this is a good epilogue, seeing as my life isn't exactly over. I'll still write, I'll still photograph people, I'll still have stories to tell. So I consider these last few chapters as a pause in the moment, a way to say thank you to you, my dear reader, for making it this far. Thanks for trusting me, for sticking through the pain and happiness.

Now go kick some ass.

Acknowledgements

First off, thanks to my editor for dealing with my random questions, doubts, and multiple edits. I'm a sensitive creature, as are most creatives, and you were always gentle about your blunt suggestions. Without you, this novel would probably be sitting on my hard drive, like most books in this world.

To my friend Cassie, for working with me to make the cover of this book a possibility. We burned things in a trash can that probably shouldn't have had things on fire inside of it. We held our breath as we tossed red feathers. I appreciate you.

Second, thanks to my beta readers, because some of you thought you were editors and although I secretly resented you at times for making me push myself and think about the delivery of my words, your support helped me create a piece of work I can be proud of. I owe you a drink next time we see one another.

To my niece, your sweet face inspired me to begin fighting against rape culture. I don't want you to grow up in a world where men like Guilter or Lone Ranger get away with treating women like shit. I want you to walk down the street without fear. I may not be the pinnacle of change in this world, but I sure as fuck will try anyway. Sorry I said fuck.

To Hamstring, I know I was insane. I know I was the most mercurial woman you ever met. But I appreciate your hand in the creation of this book. You put up with my random whims, like wanting to plan a trip spur of the moment. Or eat five breakfasts. Or drink an entire bottle of champagne in thirty minutes. Or watch three horror movies in a day. Or crawl into bed and feel sorry for myself. And I appreciate that you supported my whims with the best constrained smile you could muster in the moment. Your dad jokes always lifted me up, even when I was feeling like shit.

To my friends that have stuck with me: you are my true centers. If I didn't think it would look absolutely stupid, I would tattoo all of your names on my body.

To my art therapist all those years ago, I know you say I saved my own life. But thank you for the second chance, for accepting me back into the art program even though I was a viciously angry teenager who hated everyone on the planet. Your generosity is the greatest gift I've ever received in my whole life. I know we aren't allowed to talk anymore, but please know I think of you and Redman often. And I hope somehow you find your way to this book and realize I'm not wearing the red dress anymore. I'm not for sale. And you're a big reason why.

And to anyone else that has given me a kind word, called me during a break up, or helped me plan an adventure, thank you. After the divorce from Psychopath, I have been determined to pay back your kindness and generosity. I want to do for others what my friends have done for me. And for those that never called, you know who you are and you're officially declared a dick.

Finally, if I've forgotten someone, I'm sorry. I'm a mere mortal.

About the Author

Jenna Avery is an expert in breakups, photography and how to waste hours on Facebook. She lives in Austin with her dog Argo and fat-ass cat Fallon, who will probably eat her face if you don't tell others about this amazing book. She's been to twenty-five countries but is such a homebody that her cheap IKEA couch has a permanent indentation from her laziness. You can reach her at www.jennaaverys.life and follow her photography company at www.mybadassphotographer.com

Made in the USA
Lexington, KY
09 January 2017